HEIRS
OF THE GODS

A SPACE AGE INTERPRETATION
OF THE BIBLE

HEIRS

OF THE GODS

A SPACE AGE INTERPRETATION OF THE BIBLE

by Lee Gladden
and Vivianne Cervantes Gladden

RAWSON, WADE PUBLISHERS, INC.
New York

Drawing on page 289 reprinted by permission of
Thomas Y. Crowell Co.
"Path of Arcturus. The sun is considered as fixed."
Figure on page 211 of PICTORIAL ASTRONOMY,
fourth revised edition, by Dinsmore Alter, Clarence H.
Cleminshaw, and John G. Phillips; copyright © 1974
by Clarence H. Cleminshaw, John G. Phillips, and
Ada Alter.

Library of Congress Cataloging in Publication Data

Gladden, Lee.
    Heirs of the gods.
    Includes index.
       1. Bible—Miscellanea. 2. Civilization,
Ancient—Extraterrestrial influences. 3. Life
on other planets. 4. Religion and astronautics.
I. Gladden, Vivianne Cervantes, joint author.
II. Title.
BS534.G56 1979   236   78–53852
ISBN 0–89256–071–1

Designed by A. Christopher Simon

First Edition

To Our Heirs

MARK

SUE

SHARON

PAULA

ELIJAH LEE

in the hope that they and their descendants, as
well as all their contemporaries,
may inherit a better world.

The Spirit itself beareth witness with
our spirit, that we are the children of
God: And if children, then heirs; heirs
of God ...

—Paul, Romans 8:16–17

ACKNOWLEDGMENTS

Our sincerest gratitude goes to our many colleagues, as well as friends in the clergy and scientific establishment, who gave generously of their time in reading part, or all, of the manuscript during its preparation. Their suggestions, criticisms and corrections have been of inestimable value. In particular we wish to thank Professors Keith Bailor, Howard Burton, Robert Dixon and Charles Jackson, all of Riverside City College, for valuable help in the areas of history, astronomy, anthropology and comparative literature.

Special thanks also goes to Professor Robert Kroger, who made the computations for the appendix. Valuable help with biblical scholarship and interpretation was given by Elder G. Nathaniel Banks, former Regional Director for the Seventh Day Adventist Church; the Reverend Mr. Randal E. Denny, Pastor of the First Church of the Nazarene, Los Angeles; the Reverend Mr. Timothy F. Conklin, Pastor of the Community Bible Church of Riverside; Hubert Page, former Chaplain, U.S. Air Force, and Dr. Bernard Zeiger, former Rabbi of Temple Beth El, Riverside. Criticism and scientific data were also generously provided by Raymond Gladden, Project Engineer, Space Shuttle Program, Rockwell International; the staffs of Griffith and Hale Observatories and the Department of Astronomy at the California Institute of Technology. Needless to say, the opinions and any remaining errors in the book are ours and not those of these many helpers.

A most special gratitude goes to our friend, Ingo Preminger, who encouraged us and helped in securing literary representation; to our untiring literary agent, Aaron Priest, and to our patient and persistent editor, Sandi Gelles-Cole. Without their belief and support this work would not have seen the light of day. We also owe a special and heartfelt thanks to Florence

Gardner who typed through endless nights and weekends in preparing and revising the manuscript.

Last, but not least, our thanks goes to Friederike Zimmermann, who helped with copying and correspondence, and the editorial staff of Rawson, Wade, who guided our project to completion.

CONTENTS

HEIRS
OF THE GODS
A SPACE AGE INTERPRETATION
OF THE BIBLE

CHAPTER I
GENESIS

It was one of those enchanted afternoons in late autumn. The warm California sun drenched the white dunes and long ribbon of beach. Scores of small sailing craft and yachts danced on the rippling waters of Newport Harbor. We had driven down from Los Angeles to attend a business meeting, and because we had left early we had missed a call canceling it at the last minute. As we crossed the bridge, overlooking the harbor, I turned to Vivianne and said, "We might as well stay over. I just don't feel like driving back."

Later in the motel I switched on the television and Vivianne picked up "What's Happening in Newport," a weekly calendar. As she did so her eye was attracted by a plainly bound book underneath it. She laid the calendar aside and began to turn the pages of a Gideon Bible.

We had both been reared in conservative Christian homes —I a Nazarene and she a Seventh-Day Adventist—and we had both grown away from our early fundamentalist training and beliefs.

Years of teaching philosophy and an equally long practice as a clinical psychologist had left me with a willingness to believe only what can be rationally proved or supported by scientific evidence. The beliefs of my early childhood seldom crossed my mind. The imminence of Christ's return to set up an earthly kingdom no longer preoccupied me or governed my plans as it did those among whom I had grown up. When I did think of these matters I regarded them at best as useful myths and at worst as childish superstitions. While I still recognized the value of religion as a social institution, I felt the fundamental beliefs of my childhood must be rejected by enlightened men and women in the twentieth century.

Vivianne had outgrown her early faith in a similar manner. A modeling career in her late teens had taken her to the high fashion centers of New York and Paris. A later career in acting carried her from a studio contract in Hollywood to Broadway. However, though she had rejected her childhood beliefs, her life, even with a successful career, was not meeting her deepest needs.

During our life together we had sometimes spoken of religion and our early backgrounds. Several times we had even visited our families' churches on special occasions. But for both of us there was no going back. Our view of things left no place for the mainstays of folk religion—belief in magic, miracles, the supernatural and the idea of a close control over our destinies by an all-knowing and all-powerful personal God.

As Vivianne leafed through the pages of the Bible, she suddenly sat up. It had fallen open to the account, in Revelation 22, of the tree of life which stands in the midst of the city from which Christ is to rule his eventual kingdom.

After looking it over for a moment she turned to me. "Lee, what do you think the tree of life really was?" I was absorbed in an old war movie and reluctant to be interrupted. Without really thinking I started to give the sort of answer I had often given in class when asked about religious matters.

I started to tell her that it was a symbol from Babylonian mythology which the Hebrews had borrowed—a curious bit of folklore which referred to nothing real except, perhaps, man's eternal yearning for his most impossible dream—immortality. But something in her expression stopped me. I said nothing, and she went on. "Suppose von Däniken is right? Suppose God and the angels were actually astronauts from another world? I'm wondering if they had already discovered the way to stop aging and to live forever. Perhaps the tree of life was something that helped them become immortal."

We had both recently read Erich von Däniken's *Chariots of the Gods?*[1] Suppose—just suppose—astronauts from a very advanced civilization had visited us long ago before history began. The idea is not so improbable, since we are planning to visit other worlds in the near future ourselves, and are already exploring the moon and our nearer planets. If their visit had occurred before history began, the only record would be in myths or legends—myths and legends like those in the Bible. And to the writers of the Bible, astronauts from a civilization thousands, or even millions, of years in advance of our own might appear exactly as God and the angels appear in the Bible. They would live according to natural laws, but the use they would make of those laws would seem supernatural. They could doubtless transport whole communities across the reaches of interstellar space as easily as we can take an automobile trip across country. For them, healing "incurable diseases" or extending life would probably be no more difficult than for us to cure a headache or treat a common cold. They could probably resurrect the dead from the smallest samples of their remains or even genetic records made while they were living. By such means they could, perhaps, even restore the dead population of an entire planet as easily as we can turn radio or television sets off an assembly line.

I knew that some of our most serious astronomers are suggesting that this basic idea underlying some science fiction is true. I had read the Rand Corporation's Stephen Dole,[2] who claims there may be as many as 640 million inhabited planets in our own galaxy. Carl Sagan,[3] the famous Cornell astronomer, believes as many as a million of these may have advanced civilizations—some hundreds of thousands, or even millions, of years in our technological future. If such civilizations do exist and did begin space exploration thousands of years ago (as we are planning to do now), is it not possible one of them, at least, did come here? And if they had the capability of traveling the vast reaches of interstellar space to our world, is it not likely they had advanced capabilities in other fields, such as medicine and biology?

As I expressed these thoughts we both experienced a sudden flashback. It was a picture of the DNA helix—that mysterious, intertwining double chain of sugar and phosphate molecules which lies at the center of every cell in our body. We had recently read the thrilling account of how Watson and Crick had won the Nobel Prize for deciphering the meaning of its sequences of bases—the code which contains the blueprint for every organ of every living thing. We had visited Cambridge University, where they had placed a wire-and-plastic model of the DNA helix at the center of their laboratory. As we discussed it now, we visualized its spiraling arms sprouting the twiglike projections of bases. It did, indeed, look like a tree. Could some perfected version of this device be the "tree of life" spoken of in the Bible? Did astronauts from another world place it, as Watson and Crick had at Cambridge, in the center of a laboratory where they had produced an experimental creation including modern man?

A perfected model of this sort might well contain the key to the process of aging and the secret for achieving immortality. We recalled reading that our own gerontologists are already experimenting with feeding, or injecting, nucleic acids (the basis of DNA) into animals to repair their old DNA which has been damaged or has worn out.

We had read a report by Dr. Hans Kugler, at Roosevelt University, who has extended the life span of mice by as much as 200% using nucleic-acid ingestions. We remembered his startling conclusion that we can extend human life indefinitely by preventing cellular malfunctioning and that maybe someday we will even "be able to live forever."[4] We recalled that Dr. John Bjorksten,[5] one of the world's leading authorities on aging, had recently speculated that an 800-year life span for humans is possible—800 years, by curious coincidence, being the approximate average age attributed, in the Bible, to Adam and Eve and their immediate descendants! How did the writers of the Bible, thousands of years ago, arrive at the same approximate life-span limit as Dr. Bjorksten had? We suddenly realized that if serious medical researchers are talking this way now, then there is nothing unreasonable about the idea that an alien civilization, advanced to our level millions of years ago, might have a real "tree of life" and might be able to produce immortality by eating from it. As I explored ideas with Vivianne our excitement mounted. We began to see that our attempts to apply space age science to the interpretation of this age-old mystery in the Bible might work with other puzzling references it contains. In fact, as we continued to talk and explore passages far into the night, we saw, before we finally fell asleep, that we might just have stumbled onto a brand-new approach to the real meaning of the Scriptures—an approach which we now think of as the space age interpretation of the Bible.

The cancelled business meeting and that unexpected holiday launched us on a search which has continued to the present. After five years it is still going on.

In the process we have discovered a new meaning in the Bible—a meaning which could not have been understood before the last half of the twentieth century. It is a meaning and a message for space-age man. To our surprise, though the meaning is different from the one we were taught as children, the message is the same. We have arrived at an outlook astonishingly close to the fundamentalist teaching of our childhood. Through our knowledge of where our own science is heading and careful study of the original Hebrew and Greek texts of the Bible, we have discovered that the age-old doctrines of orthodox Judeo-Christianity are true. Not in some "pie in the sky" or supernatural or mystical way, but literally; here and now and in a completely natural and scientific sense. The evidence of their truth is in the Bible and modern science.

The Bible is a record of the most important event in the history of mankind—the coming of the Celestials and their continuing role in human destiny! It is essentially a historical record which describes these events literally and truthfully. They were actually here, and we are their creation, or rather re-creation. They have monitored and guided our development and intend to return, in the near future, to colonize our planet. Many of us will live to see their return.

In the Bible they have imparted a plan according to which they wish us, their heirs, to live. Those who have done so, throughout the ages, will be re-created (or restored to life) upon their return.

They and the righteous who are alive at that time will receive the inheritance which they have planned for us—full acceptance, as citizens, in a utopian civilization to be established here on earth. With citizenship will go another gift—the most imporant they have to offer. This is the gift of eternal life, which will enable us, their heirs, to enjoy their heritage forever.

Five years ago the statements I have just made would have seemed sheer nonsense to us. The search through which we have gone has now convinced us of their truth. The evidence which has convinced us is in the chapters which follow and in the Scriptures with which they deal.

We have been astonished by what we have discovered upon careful examination of the Hebrew and Greek texts. Dozens of

passages, in almost every book of the Bible, provide overwhelming evidence that its writers had knowledge of a civilization far in advance of our own today.

There are countless references to spacecraft of advanced
design—some recognizably similar to ones now on our drawing
boards at NASA. There are detailed descriptions of nuclear
propulsion and explosions, closed-circuit television, laser
weapons, the artificial synthesis of life and the uses of energy
forms our most advanced scientists are only now beginning to
suspect. More startling still is the result of investigations we
have made into the fossil record, which, combined with clues
given in the Scriptures, support our belief that we are the
result of an experiment in genetic engineering. Man is the
major artifact—the most convincing proof—that they were
here.

We are their re-creation and could not have emerged by
biological evolution alone. We contain the Celestials' imprint,
or signature. As the Bible puts it, we were made in their image.
And it is an unearthly image possessed by no other animal on
this planet. Only within the last quarter-century have natural-
ists and anthropologists begun to appreciate just how unearthly
that image is. In the pages ahead we will examine this evidence
of man's strangeness—the evidence that we are "heirs of
God."

CHAPTER II

INVASION

And then shall appear the sign of the Son of man in heaven: and then shall all the tribes of the earth mourn, and they shall see the Son of man coming in the clouds of heaven with power and great glory. And he shall send his angels with a great sound of a trumpet, and they shall gather together his elect from the four winds, from one end of heaven to the other.

—Matthew 24:30–31

THE DAY THE WORLD ENDED

On October 30, 1938, Orson Welles created a virtual national emergency by broadcasting a radio version of H. G. Wells' novel *War of the Worlds*. The story, presented as a series of news bulletins, interrupted what seemed to be a live broadcast of music by a popular dance band of the period. Its announcements of aliens from another world landing in New Jersey and invading New York were accepted as actual news by a large part of the listening audience.

The most remarkable thing about the near-catastrophe produced by the broadcast is that Americans, almost half a century ago, had no difficulty believing that beings from another world could invade the earth and were actually doing so. This fact raises an interesting question. If similar evidences of extraterrestrial invasion were to suddenly confront us today, what would our reaction be, now that the space age has fully arrived?

Many of us now living will have the chance to answer this question, in the near future, when we live through an actual conquest of our planet by aliens from another world. This conquest, by beings from a civilization far superior to our own, is predicted throughout the Bible. The quotation heading this chapter is one of the most dramatic descriptions the Bible

9

gives of it. And the Bible tells us this invasion will occur during the lifetime of those who see the founding of the reborn state of Israel—an event which occurred in 1948.

A conquest by a civilization millions or even billions of years ahead of us in sophistication would be unlike any conquest the world has ever known. Even the European invasion of the New World in the Renaissance and the experience of South Pacific islanders in World War II offer no real parallels.

The cultural shock of Indians who had never seen a gun or a white man must have been great when the conquistadors first appeared in the ancient Indian empires. The disbelief of New Guinean natives must have been even greater when they first experienced artillery fire and saw aircraft land. But though these invasions were by aliens with godlike powers, there were limitations. The conquistadors were vulnerable to Indian arrows; they could be captured and killed or evaded. Japanese and Allied soldiers were mortal. It was possible to hide from them and even to negotiate by offering aid and assistance.

But what would it be like to find the world completely under alien control before our detection signals could warn us or defenses be activated?

How would we react to otherworldly invaders with technological powers that could not be resisted; who could neutralize energy sources and jam communications throughout the world from the moment they landed, and who could even monitor the actions and thoughts of every person on our planet? Would we rebel at the future shock of suddenly finding ourselves under the rule of a highly moral occupying force that could and would absolutely suppress all wrongdoing, crime and warfare; an occupying force that would use its inconceivable powers in ethical ways to establish a utopian society here on earth, eliminating poverty, disease and even death? Or would we gladly submit to the rule of invading benefactors who could accomplish resurrection of the dead and even confer immortality on the living who qualified for inclusion in their civilization as fellow citizens?

Imagine with us, for a little while, what it will be like to live through this experience as we foresee it from hints given in the Bible. We are told, by its writers, that it will occur when people least expect it and without warning, as invasions usually do. One day you will be watching a favorite television program or rushing to an important meeting or lying asleep in bed.

Suddenly a trumpetlike voice will shatter your quiet. It will seem to come from nowhere and everywhere at once. "I am the Lord God of the Celestials! In their name I hereby take absolute control of the planet Earth!"

The voice will seem to come from far away, yet it will have the power of 10,000 loudspeakers. It will penetrate to the deepest recesses of buildings and to the most remote and isolated areas like a peal of thunder. And like thunder it will seem to come from somewhere in the sky. When you hear it, like millions of others, you will probably rush out of doors, or pull over in your car and get out to see what is happening. Or, if you are one of the fortunate ones qualified for full citizenship in this new civilization, you may suddenly, and in the twinkling of an eye, find yourself in a totally different place from where you were before—with thousands of others like you, assembled on a great plain awaiting some kind of announcement or instructions.

If you are in the first group you will look around as you reach the outdoors or get out of your car. A strange sight will greet you. People will be collecting everywhere as the streets fill up. Others will be peering out of windows or standing in half-open doorways. Cars will be coming to a halt anywhere and everywhere, with occupants leaning out the windows or standing beside them. And everywhere people will be looking toward the sky.

All at once it will light up as though a gigantic flash of lightning had streaked it from east to west. Its brightness will be more dazzling than the noonday sun. And, as you watch, its curvature will take on the opacity of a television screen. There, in staggering dimensions which stretch from horizon to horizon, an image will suddenly appear. It will be a gigantic figure with a human face, and as the trumpetlike voice continues, you will see its lips are moving.

In a quiet, unemotional voice it will continue: "All previously existing governments are now dissolved, and all rights and powers exercised under them are hereby suspended." As you listen, you will take in the glistening spacesuit of the figure and the complicated panels of the control room which seem to surround it. It may even strike you as odd that, though its language sounds foreign, you can understand everything it is saying.

But even as these thoughts cross your mind the import of its ominous message will push them aside and rivet your attention. "Those of you who prepared for our coming have already been teleported to Jerusalem, where our holy space city has landed. From there they will be sent to stations throughout the earth to assist in setting up our new, provisional government."

Of course, if you are one of those who prepared, you will not hear this part of the message—you will be experiencing it. On a vast plain somewhere outside Jerusalem, you will be watching and listening to a different version of the sky broadcast which will later outline the program you, and the others surrounding you, will carry out as you report to your assigned stations all over the earth, to bring about the reforms of the new provisional government. And as you listen you, too, may be momentarily distracted by the wonder of your own body as you suddenly discover for the first time in your life what it feels like to have a perfectly healthy mind functioning in a completely healthy body—a body changed "in the twinkling of an eye" into a re-creation of what it was originally intended to be—no defects, no deterioration, no diseases.

Whichever group you find yourself in, however, and wherever you are, your attention will inevitably be drawn back to the strange figure in the sky, and, like billions of others in London, Moscow, Peking, Calcutta, Capetown and all over the world, you will listen, face upturned, toward the dazzling sky image.

The voice will continue inexorably: "Those who accept our rule will find it peaceful and just, but those who oppose us will be ruled with a rod of iron. All war and evildoing are outlawed, and my commandments will be enforced throughout your world." As these words are spoken the image will fade, and the sky will return to its normal color. The clouds will again be visible. And throughout the world pandemonium will suddenly erupt with the fury of a tornado.

Outside Jerusalem a far different scene will be occurring. Here and there, in the great throng of the chosen, exclamations of surprise and shouts of joy will rise as the formerly deaf realize they are now hearing; the formerly blind suddenly discover that they can see. Ex-amputees will leap on restored limbs, and the resurrected will suddenly grasp that they are living once again. Then a great hush will fall on the endless throng of thousands and tens of thousands. As long moments pass by, an unearthly silence will reign. Then, tentatively at first and here and there, but growing and joined by tens, then hundreds, then thousands, a sound of rejoicing will rise. It will rise, and mount, and swell until it seems to shake the very earth under the feet of those assembled. It will grow until it seems their eardrums must collapse under its impact; yet it will increase still more until, at last, it inundates the very earth and sky and drowns them both in a vast tidal wave of rejoicing and praise that goes on and on, seemingly without end.

Later, as the hours pass, the fate of the two groups will become intertwined. If you are among those not "chosen" you may sit, numbed and unthinking. After hours of wandering through panic-desolated streets, you may suddenly and unaccountably find yourself at home, in front of your TV. Should you decide to turn on your television, you will discover every station is carrying the same program.

The image on the screen will be human but will be wearing a spacesuit similar to the one you saw in the sky broadcast earlier in the day. This speaker is one of the humans chosen to help in setting up the provisional government. Suddenly, and with a shock of recognition, you will realize he was a famous television evangelist who died almost a decade ago.

"In the name of the Lord God of the Celestials I greet you! Praise his name who has power over death. I have come back from the grave to administer the provisional government for the United States Celestial Command. Do not be afraid. Remain in your homes. Tomorrow you will receive instructions by TTC, the worldwide Thought Transference Communications System. Each of you will receive instructions in the form of imposed thought patterns which will tell you where to report for registration and assignment to duties. Do not attempt to evade registration and assignment. Our communications system makes it possible to monitor and process data on the thoughts of every human on this planet. There is no place to hide. . . ."

As your initial shock wears off, you may feel a sense of outrage. You're a person—not some dumb animal! You won't submit to this dictatorship with its rigmarole of registration and assignment, and its monitoring of people's thoughts.

Perhaps you will grab up a few essentials and rush out to your car. Everywhere there will be signs of social breakdown and chaos.

As you near the on-ramp of an outbound freeway your motor will suddenly falter and die. Glancing down at your gas gauge, you may discover it still shows half full. Up ahead people will be getting out of other stalled vehicles, looking toward the center of the city. As you strain to see what has captured their attention, you will discover a strange addition to the landscape. Outlined against the reddening sky of sunset, its head framed by ominous clouds of a gathering storm, a tall metallic object will loom. As a streak of lightning lances the sky, you will catch a clear view of the object's details. In the strobe-light whiteness of the lightning's glare you will see it is a strange manlike figure. Towering above many of the commercial buildings clustered around, it will stand like some gigantic tin woodsman escaped from a movie set. Below it you will see a whirr of flashing amber lights, and realize a cordon of police cars are drawn up around it. Out of their midst a finger of light will stab out and flood the inhuman face of the robot. As the searchlight holds, its head will turn, cameralike, panning the city. Below the head its tubular chest and legs will glisten like polished brass as they reflect back the rays of the powerful arc light. As its gaze sweeps your direction you will see its eyesockets burn like ruby lasers. Suddenly, on its left, a formation of jet fighters will streak in and start to peel off for an attack. As the lead plane approaches, the monster's head will quickly swivel in its direction, and a swordlike ray will leap from its mouth to envelop the entire surface of the approaching plane. The craft will suddenly glow incandescently and vanish without a trace. The other planes will bank steeply and wheel abruptly as they flee back in the direction from which they came. Once more the head will swivel around and, as it scans your direction, you will experience a feeling of warmth pervading your body. An odd tingling sensation will radiate from your spine to the tips of your hands and feet and even to the roots of your hair.. With it will come a sudden sense of drowsiness and an overwhelming desire to get back to the warmth and safety of home.

As you make your way past the long queue of vehicles, stalled by the robot's mysterious powers, you will try to hurry your pace. As in a nightmare your legs will refuse to respond. Like leaden weights they will drag under you and threaten to collapse at any moment. And as you stumble along, and the dampness seeps through to your skin, you will remember, over and over again, the ominous words of the resurrected evangelist, "There is no place to hide."

For those chosen by the Celestials, however, quite another scene will be unfolding. There, on the great plain, a marvelous transformation will have taken place. Over toward Jerusalem and Mount Moriah a vast corona of light will play, seemingly radiating from a foursquare structure settled at the foot of the holy mountain. Like some man-made aurora its glowing crown of shimmering iridescence will play across the whole sky, lighting the vast floor of the valley, where thousands upon thousands are still assembled. Its tall spires will stretch toward the sky, and its domes and arches and splendid roofs will shine in its own reflected radiance, turning night into day. Far surpassing any earthly structure, its monumental vastness will stretch almost a mile in every direction and its soaring walls and architectural embellishments will glisten like a diadem set with the rarest jewels. Its many gates will stand open and endless throngs of those assembled will stream in and out, in unending procession, as the leadership of the redeemed inspect their future headquarters and capital.

From the farthest stretches of the sky, silvery modules will slip across the horizon and, in swift silence, streak toward its lofty spires. Others will rise from its very midst and as swiftly and silently vanish into the star-studded darkness lying beyond its corona of light. And from within its walls a great swell of sound will fill the night, which has ceased to be night, telling of the celebration within. Laughter and cries of joy will ring out, and the happy exclamation of greetings and murmur of conversation as friends and loved ones long parted meet again.

On the great plain without, the thousands upon thousands not visiting the city will be celebrating, too, in splendid structures which have suddenly appeared all over its entire surface, teleported by the incredible technology of the Celestials.

The vaulted ceilings, transparent as glass, will admit the radiance of the holy city, reflected by the force field the Celestials will have thrown up around the entire area. This field, extending almost 1,000 miles from the coast of Palestine to the Persian Gulf, will define the ultimate boundaries of a new political state which will include the ever-expanding community of the redeemed in the years and centuries to come. It will serve to isolate them from the world without while ensuring a perfect climate within. But in this inner city of the plain, the greatly expanded and new Jerusalem, these great mansions, combining sleeping, recreational, celebrational and dining facilities, will provide for the redeemed chosen for headquarters duties. There 144,000 specially selected leaders will live out the ages of a 1,000-year millennium while the vast unredeemed populations of the outside nations are ruled with a rod of iron.

But tonight these vast structures have been instantaneously erected by the magic of teleportation. In the social and recreational halls the newly immortal are laughing and embracing their resurrected loved ones while others dance or sing to the accompaniment of music broadcast from the holy city. Here a Harvard professor of philosophy earnestly talks with a quiet, dignified table partner whom he has just discovered to be the great Chinese sage Lao-tzu. At the other end of the same table a nuclear physicist from Stanford turns to introduce himself to his table partner. And even as the stranger nods his head, surmounted by a magnificent brow, in acknowledgment of the introduction, the physicist is paralyzed by a shock of recognition—Sir Isaac Newton! At the far end of another room a group of listeners are gathered in attitudes of transported rapture or dreamy repose around a concert grand. Seated at the piano, apparently unconscious that there is anything else in existence, sits a man who needs no introduction. The muscles of his face swell and its veins stand out; the eyes close and the mouth quivers as a resurrected Beethoven, hearing miraculously restored, draws tears from the eyes of his listeners with the beauty and originality of his improvisations.

And in the holy city itself, those specially chosen for leadership duties in the Celestial capital continue their festivities. Strains of Celestial music and the pure voices of Celestial choirs provide an unending background for the introductions and reunions, the feasting and dancing, and the pomp and ceremony as humans and Celestials alike celebrate the inauguration of a 1,000-year reign of peace and righteousness in a city where they need no sun.

BLUEPRINT FOR CONQUEST

"Fantastic!" I can hear some readers saying at this point. "What imagination! You should have been science-fiction writers." We'll let you in on a secret. We did not make up the account you have just read. It is taken, almost point for point, from the Bible. This is the Celestials' own plan for their conquest of the world, which they revealed to various humans whom they have taken into their confidence.

In 1925, Adolph Hitler published his famous autobiographical best seller, *Mein Kampf.* In it he not only told his life story but revealed his plans for building a new Germany which would rule the world. Politicians and statesmen throughout Europe and America laughed at his ambitions and regarded his blueprint for world conquest as a crackpot's dream. Even when his predictions began to come true, people continued to sit through newsreels and scoff. After he had successfully invaded Poland and cracked the Maginot Line, people began to laugh on the other side of their faces.

In the Bible the Celestials have given an outline for their plan for the takeover of our world. In its prophetic books they have confided, to human writers, an exact timetable according to which their plan will be fulfilled. Unlike Hitler, they were not thinking wishfully of the future. As we will see later, they have accurate methods for scientifically forecasting it. In addition, they are sure about the actual invasion and takeover because they are going to make them happen. Unlike Hitler's invasions, theirs has no element of uncertainty. They have the necessary technology and power to assure success. And unlike Hitler, they have revealed their plan not because they are power-hungry madmen seeking a following, but because they intend to establish a world of peace and justice and because they wish us, their heirs, to share it.

Right on Schedule

When Hitler revealed his plans, no one would listen. It seemed fantastic that a defeated nation that had gone through bankruptcy and was completely demilitarized could conquer the world. It seemed especially incredible that a half-educated ex-corporal who had failed in everything he had tried could lead them. Then he began to follow his timetable. He re-militarized the Rhineland. He forced the Anschluss of Austria. He annexed Czechoslovakia and the Sudetenland. He declared war on Poland. Finally the world began to believe him, but it was almost too late.

In a similar manner, the Celestials have been following a timetable. They are much further along than Hitler was when people finally took him seriously. At first it may seem odd to compare the bloody course of Hitler's conquests with the peaceful takeover of the world planned by the Celestials. Yet the connection between the two is not a mere matter of comparison. There is a much more intimate and historical connection which made fulfillment of biblical prophecy possible. It was Hitler's homicidal final solution of "the Jewish problem" which set the stage for the last great event on the Celestials' timetable—the return of the Jews to their homeland. It took the savage persecution and final extermination of 6 million of their faith to give Jews from all over Europe the desperate resolve necessary for leaving their adopted homelands, their businesses and what remained of their families. It was the horror of the holocaust, the concentration camps and the years of exile as displaced persons, which convinced many that their own national state was the only safe refuge. And it was the example and success of these European Jews which inspired others from all over the world to return to a reborn Israel.

When Is a Prophet Really a Prophet?

Every community has its share of palmists, fortunetellers, tea-leaf readers and the like. Most of them tell you little more than can be picked up by simply observing you or by phrasing their predictions so vaguely that almost anything that happens can be taken as a fulfillment. Their predictions are like the bits of advice or statements found in fortune cookies—"You will form valuable new friendships"; "It is not too late to mend your ways"; "You will take a trip." Since such statements about the future have no precise date, and describe events which happen to nearly everyone at some time or another, there is hardly any way they can fail to be true.

Occasionally, however, a real prophet comes along who tells you exactly when events will happen—events so unusual and unlikely that almost no one believes them to be possible. When these come true we have good reason for believing we are dealing with a genuine prophet.

The Celestials apparently have this ability. They have evidently perfected powers which parapsychologists call precognition. This is the ability to know the exact nature and time of events before they happen. Laboratory tests at Duke University, UCLA, Cambridge and many other centers have shown that some people can maintain a high percentage of success in calling the order of cards before they are shuffled, or the combinations of dice before they are thrown. Generally, however, their success is only statistically significant. They will succeed more than most people over a large number of tries, but they cannot tell whether a particular try is right or wrong.

The prophets in the Bible had far superior precognitive insights. In prophecy after prophecy they foretold events which have already come to pass—and exactly at the time predicted. Of all the predictions they made, none seemed more unlikely, until the middle of the twentieth century, than the return of the Jews to their homeland. After 1,900 years of dispersion, they were inhabitants of every land in the world. In many they had undergone incredible persecutions. Finally, under Hitler, an effort was made to bring about their complete extermination as a faith and as a race. Yet without a homeland they survived and managed to maintain a cultural identity for 1,900 years. One of the greatest historical miracles of all times! The only other miraculous event which could top it was that at the end of this time they should be gathered again, from throughout the earth, to found a new Israel under conditions of the greatest adversity.

"Gathered Out of Many People"

Almost 2,500 years ago an Old Testament prophet, Ezekiel, predicted that his people, the Jews, would return from dispersion among "the nations" (and they have had only one international dispersion) to rebuild their land. This was to take place just before the Celestials' return to earth. Speaking of this, Ezekiel says, ". . . in the latter years thou shalt come into the land that is brought back from the sword, and is gathered out of many people, against the mountains of Israel, which have always been waste: but it is brought forth out of the nations, and they shall dwell safely all of them" (Ezekiel 38:8).* This event took place in 1948 when modern Israel became a state.

Five hundred years after Ezekiel, Jesus repeated this prophecy in the New Testament. He told his disciples that the generation that witnessed his death would "fall by the edge of the sword, and shall be led away captive into all nations: and Jerusalem shall be trodden down of the Gentiles..." (Luke 21:24).

Less than forty years after Jesus' death this came true when the Roman emperor Titus destroyed Jerusalem and tore its temple down, stone by stone. And, true to the prophecies of Ezekiel and Jesus, the Jews were scattered throughout the nations of the world.

Like Ezekiel, Jesus also foretold that the Jews would return, at the time of the end, to rebuild their nation and that those who saw this event would also witness the return of the Celestials during their lifetime. His disciples came to him and asked, ". . . what shall be the sign of thy coming, and of the end of the world?" (Matthew 24:3). He answered them by using a parable involving the historical symbol of national Israel, the fig tree. He said, "Now learn a parable of the fig tree; When his branch is yet tender, and putteth forth leaves, ye know that summer is nigh: So likewise ye, when ye shall see all these things [predictions he had given them which we will

---

* The biblical quotations used in this book will all be from the King James Version unless we indicate otherwise. As it is the most widely read and distributed of Bible translations, we assume it is the one readers will find easiest to consult.

discuss in the last chapter], know that it is near, even at the doors. Verily I say unto you, This generation [the one witnessing these signs] shall not pass, till all these things be fulfilled" (Matthew 24:32–34).

A number of Bible prophets besides Jesus have spoken of events which would occur after the rebirth of Israel, as a nation, and just before the Celestials' return.

We will discuss these in detail in the last chapter, where we will try to pinpoint the actual time of the Celestials' coming.

More important than the exact time, however, are the events which have already occurred as foretold. How did Bible prophets living 2,500 years ago know that the Jews would be dispersed throughout the world? More incredible still, how did they know that against all odds they would return to their homeland in our own time? All other ancient peoples who were their contemporaries have long since disappeared. Yet the Jews have survived, without a national identity, for almost two millennia.

As we shall see in the final chapter, John the Revelator, a New Testament prophet, actually foretold a number of developments which have taken place in our own time or are predicted for the near future.

If we find such accuracy in the prophecies which have already been fulfilled, can't we expect similar accuracy in the predictions concerning the actual takeover of the world itself?

There are two reasons for thinking this is true. First, the prophecies concerning these end-of-the world events are the most precise and detailed in the entire Bible. Second, they described techniques of conquest which are beyond our present capabilities and could have been known to the Bible writers only if they were in contact with a very advanced civilization— more advanced than our own. Yet our own scientists and futurologists say these techniques are possible and will be achieved by us in the future.

Let's run the Celestials' takeover of the world through again in slow motion and see exactly what the Bible has to say about it and how scientists think the technical problems could be solved.

CHAPTER III

HOW TO
TAKE OVER THE WORLD

And I heard a great voice out of heaven saying, Behold, the tabernacle of God is with men, and he will dwell with them, and they shall be his people, and God himself shall be with them, and be their God.

—John the Revelator, Revelation 21:3

The Element of Surprise

Military strategists tell us that one of the key elements in any successful invasion is surprise. In World War II the Allies concentrated on making the Normandy invasion of Europe a complete surprise to the Germans. This included allowing false invasion plans to fall into German hands and feinting invasion thrusts at other possible landing sites in Western Europe. Such measures will not be necessary for the Celestials, who have the technology to land without warning and to seize worldwide control before resistance can be organized. The Bible stresses the suddenness of their return in many places. In the Gospel of Matthew, Jesus tells his disciples, "But of that day and hour knoweth no man, no, not the angels of heaven, but my Father only" (Matthew 24:36).

Again the Apostle Paul, in his letter to the Thessalonian church, reminds them, "For yourselves know perfectly that the day of the Lord so cometh as a thief in the night. For when they shall say, Peace and safety; then sudden destruction cometh upon them, as travail upon a woman with child; and they shall not escape" (I Thessalonians 5:2-3).

Could a civilization hundreds of thousands, or millions, of years in our technological future make such a sudden conquest of the world?

Landing the Invasion Force

In our attempt to describe the end of the world we pointed out that returning Celestials would come in a space city, which

22

would land, without warning, near the site of present-day Jerusalem. The shape and construction of this space city are given in Revelation and elsewhere in the Bible. John the Revelator tells us of a view he caught of it. He says, "And I John saw the holy city, new Jerusalem, coming down from God out of heaven, prepared as a bride adorned for her husband. And I heard a great voice out of heaven saying, Behold, the tabernacle of God is with men, and he will dwell with them, and they shall be his people, and God himself shall be with them, and be their God" (Revelation 21:2–3). Later he adds, "And the city lieth foursquare, and the length is as large as the breadth ..." (Revelation 21:16). The exact dimensions are given in two places in the Bible—the Old and New Testaments. They are just under a mile square by our units. John goes on to say that the space city has twelve gates and is made of a variety of materials which he took to be precious stones— among these he mentions jasper, sapphire, emerald, topaz and streets of "pure gold." Strangely, he adds that the "pure gold" is like "transparent glass." Obviously, he is not speaking of real gold and probably not of actual gems. These are most likely synthetic materials selected for their structural properties and beauty.

It is curious, too, that John the Revelator, who could not have written this account later than the end of the first century after Christ, should have known about space cities. It is only in this century that space scientists have realized the possibility of city-sized space ships (or what Isaac Asimov calls "spomes") that could transport entire communities between the stars.

Speaking of such space cities, Dr. Asimov, a science writer and futurologist, says, "In place of small ships used for exploration and colonization of our solar system, a huge ship might be built for voyages to the planets of the stars. Actually it would be a small planet in itself. On such a 'star ship' there might be hundreds, or thousands, of men plus room for agriculture and herds of animals. Whole generations of men and women might be born, grow old, and die while the star ship traveled from one star to another."[1]

If we, at our present primitive level of space technology, are already talking of such ships, what might an alien civilization, millions of years ahead of us, have accomplished? Almost certainly they could carry whole populations for hundreds or thousands of years, if need be, while the vast distance between their world and ours was being traveled. Their ship would be capable of storing energy from the stars (and perhaps other sources as yet unknown to us). It could recycle its wastes to provide continuous supplies of atmosphere, water and food. Our space scientists are already planning propulsion systems which could drive a ship to within a fraction of a percent of the speed of light (670,615,000 miles per hour). By manipulation of gravity fields (which many of our futurologists believe is scientifically possible) a craft could have the ultimate propulsion system which would, at the same time, give it inertialess drive. It could reach its ultimate speed and stop within fractions of a second without injuring the occupants. It could also repel or dodge particles and debris in outer space by a "gravity shield" or by hairpin maneuvers at any speed. Speaking of such a drive system, Arthur C. Clarke, the noted science writer and member of British astronautic and astronomical societies, observes, "With such a drive our vehicles could stop and start almost instantaneously. Protected by their artificial gravity fields they could run into each other at hundreds of miles an hour with no damage.... They could make right-angle turns or hairpin bends."[2]

Obviously, such a craft could fulfill the first condition necessary for a sudden takeover of the world without warning. Traveling almost as fast as light itself, or the radar signals which might be echoed from it, it could reach the earth before our detection instruments could warn us. It could brake to an almost instantaneous halt from its incredible speed and land without injury to its occupants or equipment. Its coming would indeed be "as a thief in the night!"

How About the Distance Problem?

One of the objections often raised to the idea of visits to other worlds, or visits from them to us, is the tremendous distances involved. Even at near the total speed of light the nearest neighboring star would require over four years to reach. As we will see, the crucial clues given in the Bible suggest that the Celestials' home base is much farther away.

Scientists today accept the idea, advanced in the theory of relativity, that the speed of light is the highest speed attainable. If this is true, then even within our own galaxy distances might require tens of thousands of years to travel. If the Celestials come from beyond our galaxy it might require millions, or even billions, of years for the journey. Obviously, however, such vast journeys are not likely to have been involved. Their space program, like ours, probably called for a stepwise development. From their home planet they would have branched out in several directions toward the closest other planets meeting their requirements. From these they would jump off again to the next nearest planet, and the next, and the next. And so it would continue until sometime, perhaps millions or billions of years after they began, they would reach a planet near to us.

Perhaps, in the process, they would encounter other space missions from other advanced civilizations. Perhaps they would join forces. Perhaps all the advanced civilizations in the galaxy, or our region of the universe, are federated into a single space-colonization effort. However it came about, a time would arrive when the effort, involving one or many advanced civilizations, would find us the next nearest planet meeting the required conditions for colonization.

The actual journey, at this point, might only be a few light-years' distance. It could be made as easily as we will send probes or journey to our nearest stellar neighbors in the near future—easier, since we will probably not have achieved their speed capabilities at that time.

It would also be the case that, once here, they probably would maintain service bases within, or not far from, our planetary system. As we shall see later, the Bible suggests they withdrew from Earth after completing the first stage in their colonization plan. Wherever their holy city was moved, it, or other bases, remained close enough that they could return to Earth in a matter of minutes, as certain Scriptures we will examine later claim.

Apart from all these considerations, however, there is another factor which far outweighs all of these in explaining how they have overcome the problem of distance. It has to do with the nature of time itself as a factor in covering distances. A journey of a few light-years would obviously not be burdensome to immortals, especially if they were bringing their community with them and could carry on their ordinary life activities as usual. It would, however, be a sizable time span by ordinary standards and might test the patience of colonists eager to get on with the job ahead. In truth, however, measuring this time span by ordinary standards is deceptive if it is measured according to light-years of distance, for we are measuring the time required to cover it by earth years. On a spaceship going nearly the speed of light, the amount of time would have to be measured in relation to the speed of the ship itself, and would be different from the time that passed on earth while the journey was in progress. It was Einstein who first proved mathematically, in his theory of relativity, that time does not flow at the same rate for everyone everywhere. The rate at which it passes depends on the speed of the observer and his clocks as they measure time's passing. On a spaceship going nearly the speed of light the passage of time would be slowed almost to a standstill. This is not just a matter of speculation or theory. Laboratory observations on the life span of subatomic particles going at nearly the speed of light have detected such a slowdown in their rate of decay. In the same way, passengers on a spaceship would have a corresponding slowdown in their own decay rates (or aging), as would everything else on the ship, including clocks. At a few feet per hour less than the absolute speed of light the slowdown would be so great that the passage of 1,000 years on earth would seem, to the ship's passengers, to take only a single day, and the journey of a few light-years from a nearby star might take only a few minutes by the ship's clocks.

When this "time-dilatation" effect is taken into account, it is obvious that great journeys between neighboring stars would be no more troublesome, to immortals, than our own commuting to work or one another's homes here on earth.

"A Thousand Years as One Day"

The particular amount of time dilatation which we used here, as an example, was not selected by chance. It was deliberately chosen because it is given repeatedly in the Bible as a comparison between the Celestials' perception of time and our own. For example, the Psalmist David, in speaking of God, says, "For a thousand years in thy sight are but as yesterday when it is past, and as a watch in the night" (Psalms 90:4). Later, the Apostle Peter, in the New Testament, observes, "But, beloved, be not ignorant of this one thing, that one day is with the Lord as a thousand years, and a thousand years as one day" (II Peter 3:8).

Theologians in the past have shrugged these passages aside as mere figures of speech used to emphasize the fact that even a millennium doesn't matter much to immortals. Today, in the space age, we can see these Scriptures for what they really are —two of the most dramatic proofs we have that the writers of the Bible were in communication with extraterrestrials far in advance of our own twentieth-century civilization. How could David, over a millennium before Christ, and Peter, in the first century after Christ, have known about the time-dilatation effect unless they were told of it by the Celestials?

In his interesting work on exobiology, *The Cosmic Connection*, the Cornell astronomer Carl Sagan raises the question of how ancient records (such as sacred writings or legends) could contain proof that their makers were in touch with advanced extraterrestrials. Speaking of this, he says, "There is only one category of legend that would be convincing: When information is contained in the legend that could not possibly have been generated by the civilization that created the legend— if, for example, a number transmitted from thousands of years ago as holy turns out to be the nuclear fine structure constant. This would be a case worthy of some considerable attention."[3]

Now in David's and Peter's assertions that 1,000 of our years are as a day to the Celestials we have such an exact numerical ratio "transmitted from thousands of years ago" which is precisely derivable from the critical constant in Einstein's formulation of the general theory of relativity—the speed of light!

We have already seen that in order to come as "a thief in the night," the Celestials would have to travel at just under the speed of light—fast enough to keep up with our own detection signals. It is relatively easy, using Einstein's formula and a calculator, to compute the precise speed of a spacecraft at which a day in the craft would equal 1,000 years on Earth. Taking the speed of light to be 186,282 miles per second, the speed at which this ratio would exist would be 186,281.999999302 miles per second, or about 13 feet per hour less than the absolute speed of light. (We are indebted to Professor Robert Kroger of the Department of Mathematics at Riverside City College for performing these calculations and providing us with the results. The table showing his calculations and formula he employed are included in the Appendix.)

The problem of acceleration and overcoming inertia might, at first, make such a velocity seem impossible of attainment. However, remember what we said earlier about the possibility of manipulating gravity fields and creating inertialess drive, it is evident that if the Celestials have mastered such techniques, the attainment of any speed short of the absolute speed of light would be possible. Further, using antigravity as a propulsion system such a speed could probably be attained almost instantaneously, as could deceleration and stopping from it.

In the assertion that "a thousand years is as one day" with the Lord, then, we have one of the most remarkable pieces of evidence possible that incredibly advanced Celestials told humans about the time dilatation effect over 2,000 years before Einstein discovered it in our own century. And, according to Carl Sagan's test, it is about as near to convincing proof that the Bible is a record of extraterrestrial contact as we can come by.

WHY DID THEY PICK US?

When Hitler invaded Czechoslovakia and Austria, people began to realize that he was a power-hungry madman. Germans followed him because their national pride had been destroyed and their country crushed by defeat and a vindictive peace treaty. His almost hypnotic powers of oratory persuaded them he had the solution. His successes convinced them he could bring it about in their time.

In the case of the Celestials, no such explanation seems possible. They are highly advanced and moral beings, if the Bible is to be believed. Why would an advanced civilization of peace and justice wish to invade us even if they could? What do we have they would want? Why not some other planet within the millions that probably exist within our own galaxy or beyond? Why any other world if they are truly moral and god-like in their values and conduct?

While no specific answer is given to these questions in the Bible, it contains a number of statements which suggest clues. Putting these together with what is being planned in our own future space program, we can reach a probable answer.

At present our own space scientists and government planners are looking forward to the exploration and eventual colonization of outer space. Migration to other planets or the planets of other stars may be an eventual necessity. If our population problem, pollution and depletion of our natural environment continue, we may find this an attractive and inexpensive solution. It may be that some of these problems can be solved right here on earth as technology advances. But the challenge of exploration and the promise of new rewards will undoubtedly drive us on. As long as new frontiers are out there, something in our nature will spur us on to conquer them as we are already doing.

Of course, our conquest of outer space is not planned as a violent or destructive one. Even in the history of our own planet more advanced nations have sometimes colonized those which were less advanced by methods that were cooperative and economic rather than violent and warlike.

We can assume, then, that long ago, perhaps millions of years, the Celestials started a program of exploration and colonization of outer space. As we suggested earlier, far from picking us as an isolated instance, we may be only one of many thousands or even millions of planets included in their space program. In the New Testament, Jesus suggests that this is so when, shortly before his death, he tells his disciples he must soon leave them. Peter asks him, "Lord, whither goest thou?" Jesus answers, "Whither I go, thou canst not follow me now..." When Peter objects, Jesus goes on to explain, "In my Father's house are many mansions: if it were not so, I would have told you. I go to prepare a place for you. And if I go and prepare a place for you, I will come again, and receive you unto myself; that where I am, there ye may be also" (John 13:36, 14:2–3). Evidently the "many mansions" to which Jesus refers are communities off this earth, where the

Celestials dwell. And the prepared "place" is evidently the holy city in which they plan to return so that their followers, here on Earth, may be with them.

What motives they would have for selecting Earth as one of their colonies is problematic. Perhaps, being immortal, they too have an overpopulation problem which requires constant territorial expansion. Perhaps, being immortal they eventually are forced to migrate from worlds with dying suns to others whose suns, like our own, are still young. Perhaps, being thousands, or millions, of years advanced beyond us, they have reasons that are beyond our understanding.

In any event, it seems likely that they picked our world specifically because it is like their own and is close enough to make colonization easy. Already our own space scientists are able to detect neighboring stars with planetary systems. Two of these, Barnard's Star and Epsilon Eridani, are likely candidates for early exploration and landings as our space program develops. In a few years we will be able to determine the size and number of planets surrounding these and many other stars in our neighborhood of the Milky Way.

If this is true, at our primitive level, then it is clear that a civilization thousands, or millions, of years more advanced than ours would have methods for studying worlds throughout the universe without leaving their home base. Long before they came to Earth they undoubtedly knew of its existence, its structure and climate, its ability to support life and its resources. It was no doubt carefully chosen because it is suited to their special problems and purposes. By monitoring for artificial energy uses and finding none, they probably also knew we lacked technological civilization and could be colonized without the necessity of violence or warfare. Unlike human colonists, who have often enslaved or destroyed native populations where they colonized, the Celestials domesticated and improved the natives they found here. As we shall see in a later chapter, the Bible teaches that they re-created us, by genetic surgery, in their own image with the intention of eventually including us in their civilization. To them we are not domestic animals or slaves, but children and heirs—heirs of the gods!

"A Great Voice Out of Heaven"

In the opening of Chapter II we described a sequence of events which will follow the actual landing of the Celestials. The first of these is the announcement of their return and takeover. Speaking of this, John the Revelator says, "And I heard a great voice out of heaven saying, Behold, the tabernacle of God is with men, and he will dwell with them, and they shall be his people, and God himself shall be with them, and be their God" (Revelation 21:3). The Apostle Paul is even more dramatic in his description when he says, "For the Lord himself shall descend from heaven with a shout, with the voice of the archangel, and with the trump of God . . ." (I Thessalonians 4:16).

In the past, scientifically oriented critics of the Bible have ridiculed the idea that a localized event could be seen and heard simultaneously all around the world, as Paul and John seem to claim of the Celestials' final return. They have pointed out that even major astronomical events, such as comets and eclipses, can be seen only in certain regions of the earth and at certain times. How then could the swift arrival of anything as small as a spacecraft be seen by everyone all over the world at the same time?

This question might have seemed unanswerable until the last half of this century, when the launching of the Intelsat satellites made worldwide radio and television communication a reality. Launched in an orbit synchronous with the earth's rotation, these signal reflectors hover continuously over the same point on the earth and among themselves can blanket its entire surface, instantaneously, with communications reflected from surface stations. It would be a simple matter for returning Celestials to fire synchronous satellites from their approaching space city into orbits which would cover the earth's surface, once they had landed, with signals reflected from their earthly headquarters.

They could, of course, use our own Intelsat satellites, as well, but the advanced nature of their communications systems might make this unworkable.

The nature of these systems can only be guessed at from clue provided by the Scriptures and developments pending in our own communications technology. We can surmise, for instance, that since "every eye shall see him" (Revelation 1:7), reception will not be on conventional receivers or television sets. Only a sky broadcast, of the sort described in the opening of Chapter II, would make this possible. The Bible implies that such a sudden lighting up of the entire sky with a projected image will be the means of visual communication when it says, "For as the lightning cometh out of the east, and shineth even unto the west; so shall also the coming of the Son of man be" (Matthew 24:27).

Looking at our own projected developments in visual communications, there is a technique currently underway which could make this possible—the holographic image. This image, in three dimensions, rather than the conventional two, can be created by laser beams projected on fine droplets suspended in the air. Current planning in television production foresees the possibility of creating a theater-in-the-round in the center of one's own living room where three-dimensional images, viewed from any angle, will act out their parts like actors on a real stage.

The projection of simultaneous horizon-to-horizon images on suspended atmospheric droplets, homogenized by ultrasound, would produce exactly the effect which the Scriptures describe: "Behold, he cometh with the clouds; and every eye shall see him..." (Revelation 1:7).

Auxiliary satellites suspended nearer the surface of the earth, by antigravity, could also pick up radio signals and convert them into audible sound. A civilization millions, or billons, of years in our technological future would doubtless have no difficulty in powering these suspended loudspeakers with enough energy to produce the "trump-like" voice from the heavens which the Scriptures describe. And such an unconventional lightninglike sky image and trumpetlike voice would provide the one sure effect which could instantaneously capture the attention of every conscious man, woman and child on this planet!

"CAUGHT UP TO MEET THE LORD"

In our account at the opening of Chapter II we saw that another event will take place immediately as the Celestials are touching down. This is catching up and transporting to their headquarters the righteous from all over the earth, including those who have died in the past.

At first glance this statement seems to contain two of the most preposterous assertions possible: that people can be instantaneously transported, through the air, from all over the earth; and that the dead can be resurrected. Either statement, by itself, would strain the common sense and belief of most scientificially trained people. Certainly nothing in our present-day technology would indicate that such things are possible.

Let's look at the matter more closely, however, in terms of the Bible and futurology. What exactly does the Bible say about these matters?

In I Thessalonians, the Apostle Paul speaks of the gathering of the righteous in this fashion: "For the Lord himself shall descend from heaven with a shout, with the voice of the archangel, and with the trump of God: and the dead in Christ shall rise first: Then we which are alive and remain shall be caught up together with them in the clouds to meet the Lord in the air: and so shall we ever be with the Lord" (I Thessalonians 4:16–17). And according to Jesus the suddenness of these events will be such that "Then shall two be in the field; the one shall be taken, the other left. Two women shall be grinding at the mill; the one shall be taken, and the other left" (Matthew 24:40–41).

The order of events, according to Paul, then, is resurrection first, then teleportation of them and the living. What does current technology and the forecasts by futurologists indicate about the possibility of resurrection of the dead?

"THE DEAD IN CHRIST SHALL RISE"

This is a question about which we shall have a great deal to say later. For the present we will start by pointing out that resurrection of the "clinically dead" is already possible. The distinction between "clinical" death and final death is a difficult one to make. In many parts of the world, current medical opinion defines final death as the absence of brain waves when tested with an electroencephalograph (the device which records changes in the electrical activity of the brain). Clinical death is often defined in terms of the absence of a detectable heartbeat and respiration.

There are a variety of techniques—mechanical, chemical and electrical—by which physicians can start an arrested heart beating or force respiration. When these occur, resurrection from a degree of death occurs.

Once the body has begun to decay, however, even if it is only the death of brain cells from lack of oxygen (which begins a few minutes after respiration stops), death rapidly becomes irreversible by presently known techniques.

Is it likely that a civilization millions or billions of years in our future could reverse the later stages of death or even reconstitute a dead person who had totally decayed? This problem is an extremely complex one and can only be adequately discussed after we have reviewed a good deal of present biological research and medical opinion. For the present it is enough to note that the DNA code complete in every cell of our bodies (except for spermatozoa and ova) contains a blueprint for reconstructing the entire body in its most minute details. If any part of the body remains—even bones—it would be theoretically possible to reconstitute the entire individual from such fragments. Similarly, our entire experience and learning is stored, like records on magnetic tape, in other coded changes made in the RNA structure of the brain cells. Studies such as those by Wilder Penfield at the University of Montreal, have shown that the brain retains a minute record of everything that happens to the individual. This even includes things of which he may not be consciously aware at the time they occur. Speaking of the moment-to-moment continuity and sharp detail of the brain's recording mechanism, which he activates by stimulating points on the cerebral cortex with electrodes, Penfield states that it is as if "a strip of cinematographic film with sound track had been set in motion within the brain."[4]

If such records could be read and copied, it would be possible to reconstitute an individual (complete to his most trivial habits and memories) hundreds, or thousands, of years after his death. He could be produced with a physical perfection he never had in real life, since his original genetic blueprint could be followed exactly without the usual flaws which arise from accidents or illnesses. He could be reproduced at any stage and age which he attained during his actual life. And all of this could be done even though every trace of his physical remains had been obliterated or lost and only records of his characteristics remained. The problem would not be greatly different in kind, but only in complexity, from reproducing the voice of a person, long dead, from magnetic tape recordings made while he was living. What would be required in the case of resurrection would be a device which could scan and read the DNA patterns contained in the cells of those to be resurrected while they were still living. The scanner would function much as a microphone functions for the human voice. Later the records produced by scanning could be fed into a replicator, which would then reconstitute the individual from suitable raw materials, much as an amplifier and loudspeaker can reproduce the voice of a dead person from electromagnetic records and available air.

The Bible indicates that the Celestials, in monitoring and guiding the progress of their human creation here on Earth, have kept such records throughout human history. The Psalmist David, in speaking of their monitoring and recordkeeping, exclaims, "I will praise thee; for I am fearfully and wonderfully made: marvellous are thy works . . . My substance was not hid from thee, when I was made in secret . . . Thine eyes did see my substance . . . and in thy book all my members were written, which in continuance were fashioned, when as yet there was none of them" (Psalms 139:14–16). Not only does the Bible claim the Celestials keep continuing records on the members of every person, even when they no longer physically exist, but it also claims this recordkeeping extends to the conduct and behavior of each person. Thus their experience and learning are recorded as well. Speaking of this, John the Revelator says, "And I saw the dead, small and great, stand before God; and the books were opened: and another book was opened, which is the book of life: and the dead were judged out of those things which were written in the books, according to their works" (Revelation 20:12).

Recently the press has had a great deal to say about the problem of invasion of privacy in our age of computer science and automated recordkeeping. Spokesmen for government and business talk of developments in the near future which will make it possible to merge records from the Social Security system, the Bureau of Internal Revenue, the military and the Veterans Administration, credit bureaus, motor vehicle departments and law enforcement agencies all over the country. These consolidated records could be kept in a central computer bank, and anyone could find out virtually anything about anybody by merely dialing a telephone number.

Yet such a countrywide information service would be crude and inefficient compared to what could probably be accomplished by a truly advanced civilization like that of the Celestials. We have already argued that their superior communications technology would enable them to monitor the environments, ecologies and technologies of planets all over the universe from their home base. It seems more incredible that they could monitor, record, store and retrieve personal data on living individuals on these planets. Yet, when we consider what we at our primitive level are already doing in monitoring the earth's surface, the claims of the Bible, in this respect, seem more believable.

Our Earth Resources Technology Satellites are already able to photograph the entire surface of the Earth, from outer space, every few days with such fine resolution that individual features of the terrain, such as ponds and buildings, can be distinguished. Our spy satellites can observe such minute details as the numbers on car license plates and design features of houses and buildings from their lofty orbits. Using a technique of spectrographic analysis called "band ratioing," scientists at the California Institute of Technology have even been able to trace from outer space the progress of crop epidemics and the effects of pesticides.[5] Is it improbable, then, that a technology which has had millions of years to mature beyond our own could read the nucleic-acid patterns of individuals or monitor and record learning patterns stored in their brain cells from space satellites, or even their home base in a distant region of the universe?

If such things are possible, then the resurrection of the dead for an entire planet might be accomplished by them as easily as we can turn manufactured items off an assembly line. With a set of master blueprints recorded in a "book of life," and replicating technology, they could reconstitute the dead of all ages "in the twinkling of an eye," as the Apostle Paul puts it. Speaking of how such a replicating machine might work, Arthur Clarke comments: "The scientists of the future will have far more sophisticated tools that can lay bare all the secrets of any object presented to them and automatically record all of its characteristics. . . . The memory would contain the recorded instructions specifying the manufacture . . . of all the objects within the size, mass and complexity limitations of the machine. Within these limits it could make anything just as a phonograph can play any conceivable piece of music presented to it. It is absurd to suppose that machines cannot eventually create any material made by living cells."[6] This would presumably include the recreation of even a complete human being, if records made during his original lifetime were preserved.

As we will see later it is also possible that mass resurrection could be accomplished by nonmechanical means involving forms of energy and types of records which are only now beginning to be explored in parapsychology. While these would probably be more efficient and swifter than the use of a material replicator, their nature will be taken up when we discuss mass resurrection at the Celestials' final return.

The Bible leaves no doubt that the Celestials do intend mass resurrection, and that the promise of eternal life which goes with it, for the righteous, is the most precious gift they have to offer. In Scripture after Scripture, like a golden thread, this promise occurs again and again in both the Old and New Testaments. "Search the scriptures; for in them ye think ye have eternal life" (John 5:39), John, the Disciple, admonishes us. Long before John, the author of Daniel tells how the Celestials foretold him of their return, saying, "And many of them that sleep in the dust of the earth shall awake, some to everlasting life . . . And they that be wise shall shine as the brightness of the firmament; and they that turn many to righteousness, as the stars for ever and ever" (Daniel 12:2–3). Paul, the apostle, assures us that "the gift of God is eternal life" (Romans 6:23) and declares himself to be "In hope of eternal life, which God, that cannot lie, promised before the world began" (Titus 1:2).

Time after time Jesus, throughout the gospels, utters this
promise until the reiteration of it reverberates through the
mind like a celestial echo chamber—"For God so loved the
world, that he gave his only begotten Son, that whosoever believeth in him should not perish, but have everlasting life"
(John 3:16). "Verily, verily, I say unto you, He that heareth
my word, and believeth on him that sent me, hath everlasting
life" (John 5:24). "My sheep hear my voice, and I know them,
and they follow me: And I give unto them eternal life; and
they shall never perish, neither shall any man pluck them out
of my hand" (John 10:27–28). "... they which shall be accounted worthy to obtain ... resurrection from the dead ...
[cannot] die any more: for they are equal unto the angels; and
are the children of God, being the children of the resurrection"
(Luke 20:35–36). "I am the resurrection, and the life: he
that believeth in me, though he were dead, yet shall he live"
(John 11:25).

Could a race millions of years in our technological future
keep such a promise? Do the Scriptures contain the key to
eternal life? We shall examine the basis for this claim in the
chapters ahead.

"Caught Up"

In Paul's discussion of the general resurrection at the time of
the Celestials' return, he adds that those resurrected, along
with the living righteous, will all be "caught up together with
them in the clouds, to meet the Lord ..." (I Thessalonians
4:17). The Greek word translated "caught up" here is a peculiar one. It is not the ordinary word used throughout the New
Testament where its writers wish to say someone catches somebody or something. It is a word which is only used three times
in the entire New Testament and only in connection with sudden bodily transportation from one place to another by apparently supernatural means. Once it is used in the Acts of the
Apostles to describe a mysterious process by which "the Spirit
of the Lord caught away" Philip and suddenly transported him
to another city (Acts 8:39). Paul uses it when he describes being "caught up to the third heaven" (II Corinthians 12:2),
and he uses it again in the passage just quoted from I Thes-

salonians. The word used is *harpazo*,* which is usually translated "to seize, pluck, pull or take by force."

The fact that this special word is used in these descriptions of apparently supernatural transportation suggests that some very unusual process is involved. In the past, higher critics of the Bible have ridiculed the passage in I Thessalonians which seems to picture the righteous sailing through the air, in defiance of gravity, like medieval witches on their way to the Sabbath. How, they ask, could bodily transportation without flying craft be possible? Even witches had an enchanted broomstick.

A look at futurology makes the meaning of these passages and the word *harpazo*, as it is used in them, clearer. In his already quoted book, *Profiles of the Future*, Arthur C. Clarke raises an interesting question. He says: "...we have learned to send sounds and images round the world at the velocity of light, so why not solid objects—even men?" He then goes on to describe a "matter transmitter" which might, by electronic means, scan a material object, atom by atom, and transmit the information obtained from it by radio waves to a distant receiver. The receiver could then feed the information into a replicator, such as we have already described, and a duplicate of the original object could be assembled, atom by atom, from the information transmitted. In concluding his description of such a device, Clarke ends with this dramatic assertion reminiscent of Paul's statement in I Thessalonians: "I do not know how it will be done.... But I believe the time will come when we can move from pole to pole within the throb of a single heart beat."[7]

If the Celestials have mastered the secret of a material transmitter, as well as that of the material replicator, then the "catching up" of the righteous "into the air" and their teleportation to "meet the Lord" would be no more mysterious, in principle, than our present everyday experience of "catching up" images of people and reassembling them on a television screen

---

* Hebrew and Greek etymologies are taken from James Strong's *Exhaustive Concordance of the Bible*. As it is the most widely used of concordances based on the King James version of the Bible, we assume it is the one readers can consult most readily.

thousands of miles away in the twinkling of an eye.

One important difference between this process and the teleportation of the righteous should be pointed out, however. The image we see on our television set is not the original. It is a duplicate. The person of whom it is an image is still back in the studio from which the broadcast is being sent.

With the teleportation of the righteous, however, the originals themselves are apparently to be disassembled (or disintegrated) and reassembled at the other end. Could a technology far in advance of our own perform such a feat? Arthur C. Clarke apparently believes even our own may accomplish the teleportation of people someday. Paul says the Celestials have already mastered this problem. He goes on to add an even more exciting assertion. In the Celestials' version of teleportation the original is not just reassembled; it is also corrected. Each of us is the outcome of original genetic instructions which have been carried out imperfectly. Developmental failures, accidents, illnesses and aging have left each of us with imperfections which fall short of the original blueprint contained in our cells. Paul implies that when the righteous are reassembled, at their meeting with the Lord of the Celestials, they will be reassembled without the imperfections. Speaking of this he says, "Behold, I shew you a mystery . . . we shall all be changed. In a moment, in the twinkling of an eye, at the last trump: for the trumpet shall sound, and the dead shall be raised incorruptible, and we shall be changed. For this corruptible must put on incorruption, and this mortal must put on immortality" (I Corinthians 15:51–53).

Evidently, then, those who are to share in the civilization the Celestials intend to establish here on earth will be reconstituted with sound health in perfect bodies free of aging and capable of immortality, and this will be accomplished instantaneously upon their return. This age-old dream of orthodox Christians, so often ridiculed by higher critics of the Bible, is not only not preposterous, it is just a little in advance of what our own molecular biologists and medical researchers are already planning for our immediate technological future.

We have already seen that the scriptures assert that the Celestials keep track of every human on this planet and keep records of his parts and deeds in a "book of life." These records are so minute as to contain the exact and unique DNA blueprint for each individual. As Jesus observes in Luke: "But even the very hairs of your head are all numbered" (Luke 12:7).

We might wonder why a civilization with truly advanced capabilities would bother with gathering and recording such trivial data, but the answer evidently lies in the very fact that they are so advanced that it is no bother at all. For a civilization hundreds of thousands, or millions, of years in our future to keep track of the DNA patterns of a few billion humans on a few thousands or millions of planets would probably pose no greater problems than exist for the motor vehicle departments of our own states in keeping track of automobile registrations or the FBI of fingerprints.

And if they do keep track of individuals, then focusing energies on selected ones of them which could teleport them, in an instant, to a predetermined gathering place would probably be no more difficult than for us to select specific people, at widely scattered points, to communicate with by dialing telephone numbers.

Is a Worldwide TTC Possible?

At the opening of the last chapter our attempt to imagine the return of the Celestials suggested that they would communicate with those left behind, when the righteous are caught up by a worldwide Thought Transference Communications System. What does futurology have to say about such an idea?

We take it for granted, in the last half of the twentieth century, that we can communicate with almost anyone in the civilized areas of our world, by telephone, in a matter of minutes, or at most a few hours. Even in areas where there are no telephone lines, or at times when we are away from telephone equipment, it is now becoming possible to reach people at will. The introduction of privately owned short-wave senders and receivers into autos and homes, and the possibility even of carrying portable versions in a briefcase or pocket, is rapidly revolutionizing personal communications. Soon we may be able to communicate with those we care to from moment to moment no matter where they are or what we or they may be doing.

The receiving of messages anywhere in the world without special equipment, however, is another matter. To make this possible some method of energizing brain cells without going through the usual channels of the senses must be employed. Recent theories of learning and memory suggest that sensory experience sets up electrical activity in the brain which persists for a short time. This accounts for short-term memory. As this activity continues it seems to produce changes in the chemical structure of the RNA contained in the brain cells. These fairly permanent changes are the basis of learning and long-term memory. Experiments have shown that electrodes implanted in the brain, or even equipment that generates strong electromagnetic fields placed against the skull, can also set up electrical activity which generates memories. It seems likely, to our own futurologists, that a time may come when electromagnetic signals generated at a distance can impose thought patterns on the brain. If this could be accomplished, then each of us could be linked with a central communications center which could impose thoughts at will. If it contained a computer with a vast memory bank we might even acquire direct and immediate access to the world's knowledge, or receive day-to-day instructions, without having to go through ordinary learning processes or depending on direct contact with instructors. Speaking of this, Robert Prehoda, a well-known consultant in technological forecasting for the aerospace industries, says: "A direct link of human intelligence with electronic systems might permit computer stored information to be fed directly into the brain. Equally important, human knowledge might be quickly transferred to the computer's memory system. A human brain directly linked to an advanced intelligence amplifier would present awesome possibilities. Man might become a 'supercyborg' with instant access to all of civilization's recorded information."[8]

To a civilization that can keep continuous track of each individual on a planet, the monitoring and recording of every person's thoughts and the imposition of knowledge and instructions by "thought transference" would be a rather obvious technological development. The Scriptures seem to suggest that the Celestials' monitoring activity extends not only to individual acts but to thoughts as well. Speaking of this, Jesus reminds his disciples, "But when ye pray, use not vain repetitions, as the heathen do: for they think that they shall be heard for their much speaking. Be not ye therefore like unto them: for your Father knoweth what things ye have need of, before ye ask him" (Matthew 6:7–8).

One of the most interesting applications of such a technological development, as Prehoda discusses, would be in imparting large bodies of knowledge by instant imprinting of the brain. This would take place in much the same way that a pressing machine can record an extended piece of music, which might take thirty or forty minutes of performance, as an instantaneous imprint on the surface of a record disc. In this way a person might instantaneously learn a branch of mathematics or a foreign language.

Such a procedure could even be imposed on a large number of people simultaneously by simply irradiating their brains with suitable electromagnetic or other information-carrying signals. This would make the sky broadcast of our opening scenario a possibility. People all over the world would sense they were hearing a "foreign" language, yet surprisingly would understand it, no matter what their native tongue, if their brains had been programmed by a worldwide instant language course imposed as the Celestials land.

That an advanced civilization could accomplish such a feat in a takeover of the world seems less improbable when we read our own futurologists' predictions about "learning machines" and instant education.

Arthur C. Clarke, for example, says: "The mechanical educator could impress on the brain in a matter of a few minutes, knowledge and skills which might otherwise take a lifetime to acquire. Impressing information directly onto the brain, so that we can know things without ever learning them seems ... impossible today ... Though I have no idea how it would really operate and suggest that it may be a complex of techniques, rather than a piece of mechanical hardware, I feel fairly convinced that the mechanical educator will be invented."[9]

"One Like unto the Son of Man"

The last technological marvel which we discussed in our reconstruction of the Celestials' takeover was the use of humanlike robots to carry out their plans and to enforce their will. Again our description of such a robot was not fanciful. The Scriptures give a number of detailed accounts of these devices which closely support our description.

In Revelation, John tells of an encounter with one in these words: "I was in the Spirit on the Lord's day, and heard behind me a great voice, as of a trumpet. . . . And I turned to see the voice that spake with me. . . . I saw . . . one like unto the Son of man, clothed with a garment down to the foot, and girt about the paps with a golden girdle. His head and his hairs were white like wool, as white as snow, and his eyes were as a flame of fire: And his feet like unto fine brass, as if they burned in a furnace; and his voice as the sound of many waters. . . . and out of his mouth went a sharp two-edged sword: and his countenance was as the sun shineth in his strength" (Revelation 1:10–16).

If John's description is to be believed, what he saw, like our robot in the last chapter, had a human form; had a chest and feet which appeared metallic; had burning, laserlike eyes, and was capable of emitting a swordlike beam from its mouth that could destroy whatever got in its way. Other descriptions given in the Bible also suggest these devices emit some sort of radiation which can produce drowsiness in humans and neutralize their resistance to the robot's control. In an encounter reported in Daniel, in the Old Testament, the writer tells how he saw "a certain man clothed in linen, whose loins were girded with fine gold of Uphaz: His body also was like the beryl, and his face as the appearance of lightning, and his eyes as lamps of fire, and his arms and feet like in colour to polished brass, and the voice of his words like the voice of a multitude. . . . Yet heard I the voice of his words: and when I heard the voice of his words, then was I in a deep sleep on my face, and my face toward the ground" (Daniel 10:5–6, 9).

Apparently the Celestials have a great variety of robots (or "servomechanisms," as futurologists sometimes call them), and they are not always human in form. They are generally referred to, in the Old Testament, by the Hebrew word *keruwb*, which is translated "cherub." And although scholarly tradition has regarded cherubim as a species of angel, it is clear, if one examines the variety of uses to which cherubim were put, that they were mechanical devices and not supernatural beings.

In the first place they are usually described as having a metallic appearance and often have mechanical appendages such as wheels or wings. Not infrequently they emit flamelike rays like a "two-edged sword." Also the uses to which they are put suggest craftwork rather than living beings. Samuel and David state that the Lord "rode upon a cherub" (II Samuel 22:11, Psalms 18:10). It seems very unlikely that these Bible writers meant to say the Lord travels piggy-back on an angel. It is much more logical to suppose they were referring to some sort of flying craft. In Exodus 26:31 the Lord instructs Moses to make the veil of the tabernacle from "fine twined linen of cunning work: with cherubim shall it be made." Evidently the word *keruwb* here refers to one of the oldest servomechanisms of all, the spindle, which substitutes for the twirling action of the fingers in spinning thread. The contention of some modern scholars that this passage means that Moses was to embroider cunningly worked angels on the veil will not stand up under criticism. When the Lord wanted embroidery he said so, as in Exodus 28:39, where he tells Moses to embroider the priests' coats. The word used here is the Hebrew term *tashbets* ("threads in squares" to "embroider" or "set"). The word used in 26:31, in connection with cherubim, is the Hebrew word *asah*, which means "do" or "make." This clearly implies that the cherubim are tools used in the construction of the veil —not ornaments "set" on them.

From all these references it is evident that the Celestials have turned most routine labor in their civilization over to various kinds of servomechanisms operated by computerized, artificial intelligence.

The difficulty which Bible scholars have found in discovering the exact nature of cherubim lies in the fact that they have no exact nature. William Smith states their perplexity in his *Bible Dictionary* when he says, "What this peculiar cherubic form was is perhaps an impenetrable mystery."[10]

We shall try to penetrate this mystery in much greater detail in later chapters, where we analyze the civilization of the Celestials. For the time being, however, it is enough to notice that their servomechanisms can do common labor such as spinning or fetching and carrying; they can protect property and carry out law enforcement as the cherubim "placed at the east of the Garden of Eden" with "a flaming sword which turned every way, to keep the way of the tree of life" (Genesis 3:24) did. These cherubim were evidently either our familiar manlike robots, or fixed barriers that emitted laser beams similar to those used in cutting and drilling in industrial processes today. In addition to performing such lowly tasks, other cherubim in the Bible can also transport people and can fly, and the most advanced of them look and act very much like human beings.

The portrait of the robot in our opening episode is not fanciful; it is biblical and, according to the Scriptures, such devices will play a crucial role in the Celestials' imminent takeover of our planet. They will carry out the drudgery of the occupation government's work; they will suppress resistance to its rule, and they will perform courier and low-level administrative duties.

Equipped with elaborate, long-range sensors, possessing advanced automotive and manipulation systems, armed with death-ray laser beams and programmed with artificial intelligence, such devices will make the Celestials' takeover of our world as swift and irresistible as the Bible claims it will be. And through them the warlike and rebellious of all nations will be brought into submission and ruled "with a rod of iron; as the vessels of a potter shall they be broken to shivers..." (Revelation 2:27).

"To Ever Be with the Lord"

For the righteous, however, who are caught up "to ever be with the Lord," the 1,000-year provisional government, and the permanent acceptance into the Celestial Confederation which will follow, will usher in an era of unparalleled peace, affluence and splendor. The wonders of a millennial age in which the arid lands of the earth are reclaimed to fertile abundance, pollution is eliminated, and war, famine, crime, disease and death are abolished are difficult to imagine. Looking down the long centuries to the glories of this period, the Old Testament Prophet Isaiah rhapsodizes: "The wilderness and the solitary place shall be glad for them; and the desert shall rejoice, and blossom as the rose. It shall blossom abundantly, and rejoice even with joy and singing.... Then the eyes of the blind shall be opened, and the ears of the deaf shall be unstopped. Then shall the lame man leap as an hart, and the tongue of the dumb sing: for in the wilderness shall waters break out, and streams in the desert. . . . And an highway shall be there, and a way, and it shall be called The way of holiness; the unclean shall not pass over it . . . And the ransomed of the Lord shall return, and come to Zion with songs and everlasting joy upon their heads: they shall obtain joy and gladness, and sorrow and sighing shall flee away" (Isaiah 35:1–2, 5–6, 8, 10).

Who are the Celestials who promise such a heritage? Why have they selected us as their heirs? What must we do to claim our inheritance? In the next chapter we will take a closer look at our benefactors.

CHAPTER IV

WHO ARE
THE CELESTIALS?

All flesh is not the same flesh: but there is one kind of flesh
of men, another flesh of beasts, another of fishes, and another
of birds. There are also celestial bodies and bodies terrestrial:
but the glory of the celestial is one, and the glory of the terrestrial is another.

—Paul, I Corinthians 15:39–40

Is Anyone Out There?

In the Renaissance, when Columbus set out on his famous
voyage, most educated Europeans regarded him as a dreamer
and a fool. The Earth round? You could get to the Indies by
sailing west? Didn't the Bible speak of the "four corners of the
earth" (Isaiah 11:12; Revelation 7:1)? How could it be round,
then? And, even if it were, how could there be people on
the other side? They would be hanging heads downward.
Wouldn't they fall off? And wouldn't Columbus and his sailors, too, as they sailed around to the underside? These arguments seemed obvious to most good churchmen, in Columbus'
day, and even to the court astronomers.

The idea that there might be vast continents beyond the
shores of Europe, Asia and Africa seemed as fantastic to them
as the idea of other inhabited worlds seems to many of us today. More fantastic, probably, since they believed the world to
be small, flat and square. Not far beyond the familiar trade
routes lay troubled seas teeming with monsters and dragons.
Daring travelers had seen them rearing out of storm-tossed
waves near the awful edge of the earth where thundering
waters spilled into the void below, like some hellish Niagara.
A few had turned back in time and lived to tell their tall tales
to marveling listeners back home. How, then, could there be
vast lands with millions of inhabitants beyond such horrors?

48

Would a good God have created them there knowing they could never be reached by his true faith and church which had been revealed, once and for all, at the center of the earth in Palestine?

Half a millennium after Columbus, we are in much the same position today. Good churchmen and self-appointed "authorities" are assuring us that the idea of millions of worlds beyond our own, containing thousands, or millions, of advanced civilizations is totally without foundation and even absurd. God created this planet as a one-time special setting for a one-time special creation. Why would he want other creations? Doesn't the Bible say that God put "lights in the firmament of the heaven to divide the day from the night; and let them be for signs, and for seasons, and for days, and years" and "for lights in the firmament of the heaven to give light upon the earth" (Genesis 1:14–15)? Isn't this Scripture just as plain as the ones that say the earth has "four corners"? Obviously the stars and planets are just up there for farmers' almanacs and so country people can get along without street lights.

And the idea that those stars are surrounded by worlds containing magnificent civilizations that surpass our own? How could any civilization excel our own? Haven't we already topped the wildest flights of imagination in creating vacuum cleaners and moon rockets and splendid neutron and hydrogen bombs?

What would a really advanced civilization do that could go beyond these things? Even our best science-fiction writers, for the most part, imagine only bigger and better gadgetry, totally automated economies instead of mere vacuum sweepers; intergalactic rockets instead of moon rockets; stellar explosions instead of hydrogen bombs. But the people themselves—their social systems and laws; their art and recreation; their moral values and religions? Undoubtedly it is much harder for us to imagine a Celestial civilization millions of years ahead of us than it was for American Indians, without the wheel, horse or gun, to imagine European civilization before Columbus came.

Yet a truly advanced civilization has already been here. It was witnessed thousands of years ago by a number of perceptive human scribes. Detailed accounts of their visit can be read in the collection of books called the Bible. In its pages we find a wealth of information about those ancient astronauts whom it calls God and the angels. It gives us descriptions of their physical appearance, their language, their habits, rituals and values. It tells of their architecture, their art, their agriculture, their government and their moral precepts. It describes their spacecraft, their communications systems, their weapons and their use of unknown energy forms which can perform miracles of healing, restoration and even resurrection! Let's take a look at what it has to say about our Celestial forebears.

"MANY MANSIONS"

We have already seen that the New Testament suggests there are other inhabited worlds. Jesus' famous remark that "in my father's house are many mansions" (John 14:2) was made to his disciples just before "he was parted from them, and carried up into heaven" (Luke 24:51). He prefaced it by saying, "I go to prepare a place for you" (John 14:2). The implication is clearly that the "place" he went to and prepared was off this world. It was his father's (the Lord God's) "house." The Greek word used for "house" here is *oikia*, which is usually translated as a "family" or "household." Jesus' statement that God's "family" or "household" contains many "mansions" uses another Greek word, *mone*, which implies specific "abodes" or "staying places." If the "household" of the Celestials is in the heavens and contains many inhabited "abodes" or "staying places," then it seems clear that Jesus' reference was to some sort of family, or confederation, of inhabited worlds to which, according to the gospel writers, he returned after his resurrection. This "family" would presumably consist of the Celestials' home planet and all of the others which they have colonized.

What do modern astronomers and exobiologists (researchers into extraterrestrial life) have to say about the possibility of other inhabited worlds and advanced civilizations?

Since the publication of Erich von Däniken's *Chariots of the Gods?* first made the ancient-astronaut hypothesis popular, there has been a rash of critics who have tried to refute the idea of life on other worlds. Most of them either try to argue that it is impossible or take the gentler position that there is no good reason for thinking it is so. Like Columbus' critics, who argued the impossibility of other inhabited continents on this world, these critics have used everything, from Bible quotations and pseudoscience to sarcasm and appeals to their own "authority," to bolster their contention that the universe is a junkyard of dead matter with the single exception of our own planet, Earth.

A few examples will serve to point up the parallel between Columbus and his medieval-scholastic critics and our present exobiologists and their critics. We read in *Gods in Chariots and Other Fantasies*, by the Australian archaeologist Clifford Wilson, that "amino acids in atmospheric particles from space" do not prove there is life out there because "the fact is . . . that such molecules are dramatically different from any life as we know it."[1]

What do the experts have to say about this? In the first place, amino acids (the building blocks of DNA and the basis of all life as we know it) were not found just in atmospheric particles, as Dr. Wilson states, but also inside meteorites from outer space. Atmospheric particles could be of purely earthly origin; meteorites could not. These amino acids clearly come from somewhere "out there." And current astronomical theory regards these meteorites as being the debris from which other worlds are typically constructed. If they have amino acids inside them, they clearly do prove, contrary to Dr. Wilson, that at least the building blocks of life as we know it exist on other worlds. Again we read in Dr. Wilson's book that "there is not yet any good evidence that there is even a single planet outside our solar system."[2] Yet Gerrit L. Verschuur, expert on radio astronomy and professor of astrogeophysics at the University of Colorado, asserts, in *The Invisible Universe* (published before Dr. Wilson's book): "There is direct evidence for at least two other planetary systems associated with nearby stars. Both Barnard's Star and Epsilon Eridani, in the way they are observed to move across the sky, show indications of one or more companions of Jupiter-like mass. Recently, the proper motions of a number of other stars have been measured with sufficient accuracy to suggest that they, too, have planets that orbit about them."[3]

Summarizing this whole issue, Carl Sagan, one of the world's foremost exobiologists and professor of astronomy at Cornell

University, says: "Both theory and observation now suggest
that planets are a common, if not invariable, accompaniment
of stars ..." And he elsewhere states, "We now know that the
building blocks for the origin of life are in the cards of physics
and chemistry; whenever standard primitive atmospheres are
exposed to common energy sources, the building blocks of life
on Earth drop out of the atmosphere in times of days or weeks.
Organic compounds have been found in meteorites and interstellar space."[4]

From these expert opinions, then, we can see that the idea
of life on other worlds is far more believable, in our own day,
than the idea of transoceanic life was in Columbus' time and
has far more evidence to support it.

Yet, as any elementary-school child knows, Columbus was
right. And the elementary-school children of tomorrow will
know that myriads of inhabited worlds lie beyond the reach of
our present-day rockets. Unlike Dr. Wilson, many Bible scholars and churchmen, as well as scientists, are now recognizing
this near certainty of life on other worlds. In a news release,
the evangelist Billy Graham stated: "I firmly believe there is
intelligent life in outer space ... beings who probably look like
the average American ... They're probably at least as advanced
as us, and possibly more advanced—which means they may
have found answers to many of the problems we face on Earth.
Disease, war, environmental pollution may be nonexistent on
these other living planets."[5]

"In Our Image"

When it comes to the question of what these other worldly
beings are like, we are not confined to guesswork. One race of
them, at least, has visited us, and the Bible writers who tell of
it assert that we were made in their image. We, mankind, are
the mirror in which their likeness is revealed. The best in our
minds and culture faintly suggests the sublime range of their
civilization and the loftiness of their moral purposes. But the
resemblance is not just mental or cultural. If we were remodeled by genetic engineering, in the likeness of an alien race,
then Billy Graham's suggestion that there is life in outer space
which resembles the average American (or European or Asian
or African, for that matter) merely affirms what was stated

long ago in the Bible. We are in their physical image, as well.

In the first chapter of Genesis we read that God said, "Let us make man in our image, after our likeness," and "So God created man in his own image; in the image of God created he him; male and female created he them" (Genesis 1:26–27).

There are some who would argue that this passage simply means that man is like God in some immaterial way—his mind, his moral nature or his soul. They would insist that God is an immaterial, spiritual being, and therefore man could not resemble him in a physical way. Those who believe this are the victims of a misunderstanding which arose after the Bible was written.

As we will show in the next chapter, the term "God" is used in the Bible to refer to two different creators. One is the unseen ultimate Creative Power of the universe which creates and sustains everything. It is often referred to as a "spirit," as when John says, "God is a Spirit" (John 4:24). But the Greek and Hebrew words used in the Bible for "spirit" simply mean a "breath" or "wind." What they imply is that a spirit, like the wind, is an unseen power. And when John says, "God is a Spirit," he means that the Creator of the universe is an unseen power.

The idea that a spirit is a kind of immaterial, ghostly person was foreign to the Bible writers and crept into Christianity in the early centuries after the Bible was written. Plato, the Greek philosopher, had taught that the material world is just a shadow of a higher, immaterial world. His follower, Plotinus, taught that God, as the highest reality, must be wholly immaterial. Early church fathers, such as Augustine, wanted to harmonize Christian doctrine with this Greek thinking which dominated their world. As a result, and over the centuries, the idea developed that God and the angels, as the highest realities, are immaterial and "spiritual"; the everyday world, as the lowest reality, is mere matter, and man is somewhere in between—a godlike soul in a material body.

So when John said, "God is a Spirit," he did not mean that the Creative Power that brought the universe into being is a ghostly person. And he was not speaking of the same creator who made man in his image. That creator is also referred to as "God" in the Bible (or the "Lord God" at times), but he is clearly not an "unseen power." He is quite personal, material and humanlike (or rather, humans are like him), as we will presently show.

The confusion of these two creators—one an unseen power, the other a flesh-and-blood astronaut from another world— has arisen because the first two chapters of the Bible, which tell about the creation of the world and man, are the result of a succession of editorial efforts. Using several sources of oral tradition, early editors, such as Moses, tried to weld them into a consistent account. Later, priestly editors, who found discrepancies in this early work, made even further changes and corrections. Because of this it seems that these two chapters tell the creation story twice over: once in very general terms, in the first chapter, and again, in much greater detail, with the emphasis on the creation of man, in the second chapter.

A careful study of these two narratives shows, however, that they are not two descriptions of the same creation. Even a casual inspection of their order in telling the events of creation suggests that this is so. The first account, in the first chapter, says that "God" created vegetation, marine life, fowls of the air, land animals and man—male and female (Genesis 1:11–26)—in that order. The second, in the second chapter, says the "Lord God" formed man, put him in the Garden, made vegetation to grow, formed land animals and birds and brought them to Adam for naming, and, last of all, caused a deep sleep to fall on Adam and took out one of his ribs, from which he formed woman (Genesis 2:7–22).

In the first account life is created in the same order evolutionary biology claims—vegetation, sea animals, land animals and last of all, man—male and female. In the second, man comes first, then the plants and lower animals and, last of all, woman.

And just as these two accounts describe two separate creations—one a general evolutionary creation and the other a special, experimental creation in the Garden of Eden—so there are two creators. And it is the second of these that interests us here, for it is in his image that we were made. Though editorial lifting and rearranging have made it seem that the statement "Let us make man in our image, after our likeness..." refers to the evolutionary creator (since it occurs in the first narrative), we will show that it could only refer to the Lord God of the second narrative, a flesh-and-blood astronaut from another world.

This creator and his companions, the angels, are the ancient astronauts who visited us so long ago and are soon returning to complete their colonization of the earth. They are the gods (*elohim*) whose image we mirror, for they are our ancestors and we their heirs. And it is from an examination of ourselves and clues given in the Scriptures that we can find the answer to that all-important question, "Who are the Celestials?"

In the early centuries of Christianity, after the doctrine that God and the angels are immaterial had become established, church fathers discouraged interpretations which made them too human. They reasoned that a "spiritual" being could not have a physical form. Later, anthropologists called the tendency of primitive peoples to worship manlike gods "anthropomorphism" (from two Greek words meaning "humanform"). Modern theologians have followed the early church fathers in viewing anthropomorphism as naive and ignorant.

If, however, the Celestials are flesh and blood, then they must have a physical form, and if they made man in their image there is nothing naive in assuming that form would be human.

In the end, then, we come back to the simple scriptural statement that "God created man in his own image" (Genesis 1:27). And that the resemblance is physical, as well as mental and spiritual, there can be no doubt, for the Lord God himself states that he is a physical flesh-and-blood being in a direct quote given a little later in Genesis. Deploring the depravity into which man has fallen, after his original sin and expulsion from the Garden, the Lord says: "My Spirit shall not always strive with man for that he also is flesh" (Genesis 6:3). Now the question this raises is "also" in addition to whom? It is clear, from the preceding passage, that the "also" refers to the Lord himself. The implication is that if the Lord and his angels are flesh and can live up to the difficult standards the Lord sets, then it is not unreasonable to ask man to do so too. The Lord, being flesh, knows what flesh is capable of and will not settle for less than man's best. Therefore, his spirit will not always strive with men's wrongdoing.

If further proof is needed on this point, there is much of it throughout the entire Bible. The Lord walks in the Garden in the cool of the day and calls out to Adam and Eve (Genesis 3:8)—he is sensitive to heat and cold and produces sound waves in the air. He confronts Cain and Abel and receives offerings of food (which he presumably eats) and converses with them (Genesis 4:3–15). Moses talks "face to face" with the Lord "as a man speaketh unto his friend" (Exodus 33:11) and on one occasion actually catches a view of his "back parts" (Exodus 33:23).

When it comes to angels, both the Old and New Testaments tell constantly of how men encounter angels and mistake them for ordinary human beings. In Genesis, Abraham and Lot both entertain angels with food and drink, mistaking them, at first, for mere human travelers. Lot's degenerate neighbors even try to get him to turn over his guests to them so that they can force them into acts of sexual perversion— again failing to recognize that they are not ordinary humans (Genesis 19:4–5). Jacob is surprised by an angel, while asleep and waiting for his brother, and mistaking him for a human intruder, wrestles with him all night before discovering his mistake (Genesis 32:24–30). This is especially interesting since it implies the angel was solid enough to wrestle with and was closely matched in strength by an ordinary human. And it is evident the angel did not just take on a human form for this special occasion. The circumstances show he was taken by surprise and anxious to get on about his business, which was clearly not with Jacob. Evidently he was going about in his ordinary, everyday manner and appearance.

Speaking of such episodes the writer of Hebrews, in the New Testament, admonishes early Christians, "Be not forgetful to entertain strangers: for thereby some have entertained angels unawares" (Hebrews 13:2). Evidently then, in spite of medieval theology and contrary to medieval paintings, God and the angels are not transparent bits of ectoplasm decked out with wings. Such ideas are figments of the theologians' and artists' imaginations. The Lord God and angels of the Bible are living, flesh-and-blood beings who so closely resemble humans as to be indistinguishable from them except for their behavior and skills.

The differences between us and them lie in their achievements and civilization rather than in their nature or form. They, coming from worlds perhaps millions or billions of years older than ours, have had untold ages to perfect their natures and endowments in a civilization advanced beyond our wildest flights of imagination. As the Apostle Paul says of it: "Eye hath not seen, nor ear heard, neither have entered into the heart of man, the things which God hath prepared for them that love him" (I Corinthians 2:9).

How Advanced Is Advanced?

As we said earlier, our futurologists and writers of science fiction and fantasy have shown limited capacity for imagining our own future advancement or that of life on other worlds. More often than not their attempts have been confined to describing various technological wonders which they imagine these civilizations might produce. And undoubtedly truly advanced civilizations must greatly surpass us in technological capabilities. As Carl Sagan observes, some of them could probably "rework the cosmos." He even goes so far as to suggest we cannot absolutely rule out the possibility that quasars and high-intensity gravitational waves coming from the center of the universe might be evidences of "extra-terrestrial intelligences."[6]

The fact that very advanced civilizations could doubtless do these things does not mean that they would spend most of their time and energy accomplishing them, however. There are other kinds of advancement that might seem more important to highly civilized Celestials. Even in our own history there are moderately advanced civilizations, such as those of China and India, that did not choose the path of technological advancement taken by the West.

Other Kinds of Advancement

When we ask what other sorts of advancement civilizations millions or billions of years in our future might prefer, the problem offers a wide field for speculation. The best guidelines we have come from our own advanced nontechnological civilizations and the hints given about the Celestials in the Scriptures.

Obviously, one high-priority option would be the understanding and control of their own natures. The reason for this is apparent if we reflect on our own situation for a moment.

We have, for example, much of the scientific know-how needed to solve our most pressing human problems, such as pollution, disease, war, crime and mental illness. Our problem is not so much lack of technology as it is lack of willingness to use our technology in a humane way when it conflicts with the short-range interests of power groups.

We could, for instance, easily eliminate pollution if we could get the auto industry, manufacturers, the government and consumers to do the things environmental scientists tell us are necessary. But these groups will not because it would slow business, hurt profits, take extra effort and require a more austere life style.

Similarly, we could prevent wars if we would give up our narrow national loyalties and support a worldwide system of law and disarmament. And if we stopped wars we could save half of most national budgets and apply these funds to solving other problems such as famine, disease, mental illness and crime.

In all these ways we are a civilization that is technologically too advanced for its moral capabilities. We have more technology than we can wisely use for human good. As a result much of our technology is used to serve our basest and most animalistic desires and to exploit and destroy one another. When we reflect on these problems that plague us at a moderately advanced level of development, it is obvious that our greatest need is not more technology but to catch up with what we already have, in the moral and social spheres.

It seems logical, then, that a truly advanced civilization would reach a point where technology would not be pursued as an end in itself, but would be limited to what could be used for truly human purposes. And at this point it would then concentrate its major energies on developing a social order in which private morality and social justice are universal.

After developing enough gadgetry to make life reasonably secure and comfortable, it would turn its attention to more important goals—eradicating the selfishness, perversion and evil in its members which nullifies the value of so much of our technology. And in their place it would try to create, probably by a combination of genetic engineering and education, a general condition of brotherhood and love for fellow creatures.

The Bible makes it clear that this is one of the highest priorities in the civilization of the Celestials. And this is doubtless why their concern in training us to share it with them is that we develop along similar lines.

REQUIREMENTS FOR CELESTIAL CITIZENSHIP

This is why the Bible does not suggest that the humans chosen as their heirs will necessarily be the rich of the earth, or those with advanced degrees or powerful positions in society.

Jesus said, "Verily I say unto you, Whosoever shall not receive the kingdom of God as a little child shall in no wise enter therein" (Luke 18:17). His point was not that one must be naive, or ignorant, or simpleminded, but rather that candidates must be guileless and possess the loving, trustful nature of children.

Again, he said, "Blessed are the poor in spirit" (Matthew 5:3), "the meek" (5:5), "they which do hunger and thirst after righteousness" (5:6), "the merciful" (5:7), "the pure in heart" (5:8), "the peacemakers" (5:9). Once more his point was not that there is a premium on being a loser—it was rather that people who are genuinely humble, gentle, good and peaceful fit into an advanced society which prizes virtue and justice more than people who are opportunistic, greedy, ruthless and evil. In short, what Jesus was saying was that the Celestials want fellow citizens who are (to use a quaint and rather old-fashioned term) righteous.

MIND OVER MATTER

We can further assume that truly advanced civilizations might develop other powers we are just beginning to understand. Some of these would undoubtedly lie in the area we call "psychic" or "paranormal." If it were possible to achieve many of the technical feats we now perform, with machines, by purely mental means—by what parapsychologists call "telekinesis" and "telepathy" and "clairvoyance"—then this would be preferable to the clumsy and expensive hardware we presently use for these purposes. Our own researchers are beginning to suspect there are forms of power, or energy, which link mind and matter. If this is so, then it may be possible, through purely mental efforts and without gadgetry of any kind, to perform "miracles" of communication, diagnosis, healing and perhaps even the neutralizing of physical laws such as those manifested in death or gravitation. Recent studies indicate that exceptional humans are sometimes able to insert their hands through living tissues without making incisions or leaving wounds. Others can bend metal objects or influence sealed scientific instruments by what appear to be purely mental efforts.

The Bible indicates, in many places, that this is a line of advancement taken by the Celestials and that they often use it in preference to ordinary mechanical technology. Thus Jesus speaks of such a power, which he calls "faith." In describing its awesome potentialities he tells his disciples, ". . . verily I say unto you, If ye have faith as a grain of mustard seed, ye shall say unto this mountain, Remove hence to yonder place; and it shall remove: and nothing shall be impossible unto you" (Matthew 17:20). In another passage, the gospel writer John tells how Jesus performed a feat similar to that of psychic surgeons in passing into a closed room without opening the door and apparently without leaving a hole. Of this he says: "Then the same day at evening, being the first day of the week, when the doors were shut where the disciples were assembled for fear of the Jews, came Jesus and stood in the midst, and saith unto them, Peace be unto you" (John 20:19). Other accounts by the gospel writers also tell of other feats in which Jesus apparently neutralized laws of nature, as when he walked on water (Matthew 14:25–26) or levitated into the heavens at his final ascension (Mark 16:19, Luke 24:51).

AND HIGHER THINGS

Apart from moral, social and technical advancement we can also surmise that a greatly advanced civilization would devote much of its energies to what we call the "higher" things in life— the arts, pure scientific and philosophical inquiry, religion and social enjoyment.

In the Bible there are occasional glimpses into the heavenly life of the Celestials which suggest that this is so. Evidently poetry and music play a rather large part in their activities, for there are many accounts of choral groups singing hymns or songs of praise—angels sang when Jesus was born (Luke 2:13), the redeemed sing around the throne of God (Revelation 5:9). Perhaps this is where the idea got started that people in heaven spend their time singing and playing on harps. Evidently, too, they prize great vocal art. Satan, the alleged choirmaster of heaven, before his fall, is discussed by God, in Ezekiel 28, and in listing his perfections God says, "the workmanship of thy tablets and of thy pipes was prepared in thee in the day thou wast created" (Ezekiel 28:13).

The elaborate ornamentation of Eden, with its jewellike materials and streets of "transparent gold"; and its garden with "every tree that is pleasant to the sight" (Genesis 2:9), suggests a highly developed concern for the visual arts such as architecture and landscape gardening.

In a similar way there are many suggestions throughout the Bible of the Celestials' concern for pure scientific research and philosophical inquiry. Nowhere else is the extent of their accomplishments in science, or the profundity of their wisdom, so dazzlingly presented as in the Book of Job. Here, the Lord, in reproving Job for his audacity in questioning God's purposes, says, "Hast thou entered into the springs of the sea? or hast thou walked in search of the depth? Have the gates of death been opened unto thee? or hast thou seen the doors of the shadow of death? Hast thou perceived the breadth of the earth? declare if thou knowest it all. Where is the way where light dwelleth? and as for darkness, where is the place thereof. . . . Canst thou bind the sweet influences of Pleiades, or loose the bands of Orion? Canst thou bring forth Mazzaroth in his season? or canst thou guide Arcturus with his sons? Knowest thou the ordinances of heaven? canst thou set the dominion thereof in the earth? . . . Who hath put wisdom in the inward parts? or who hath given understanding to the heart?" (Job 38:16–19, 31–33, 36). In what is perhaps the most famous reproof in all of literature the Lord belittles Job's presumption in questioning him with a catalogue of the Celestials' accomplishments which is overwhelming. Over the course of almost four chapters the list continues with references to physics, astronomy, geology, meteorology, physiology, psychology, medicine, agriculture, botany and zoology. And these references do not just indicate a nodding acquaintance with these subjects but a mastery which makes human achievements seem pitiful by comparison. Without boasting or false modesty the Lord simply asserts that the Celestials can control weather, manipulate the phenomena of life and death, create worlds and, as Carl Sagan suggests, even "rework the cosmos" by "binding the sweet influences of Pleiades" or "loosing the bands of Orion."

Again, there are numerous references which suggest that religious ceremony and social intercourse are major preoccupations for the Celestials. At the very beginning of the Bible we are told that the Lord God instituted and observes the sabbath himself, for when he had finished the creation "he rested on the seventh day from all his work which he had made. And God blessed the seventh day, and sanctified it: because that in it he had rested from all his work which God created and made" (Genesis 2:2–3). And again, in the last book of the Bible, we have a description of an actual worship service taking place in the Celestials' holy city. John the Revelator tells how, after being taken up into what appears to be one of the Celestials' spacecraft, he saw a televised ceremony which combined the features of a religious and patriotic celebration. Speaking of it, he says, "And I beheld, and I heard the voice of many angels round about the throne, and the beasts, and the elders: and the number of them was ten thousand times ten thousand, and thousands of thousands; Saying with a loud voice, Worthy is the Lamb that was slain to receive power, and riches, and wisdom, and strength, and honour, and glory, and blessing. . . . And the four beasts said, Amen. And the four and twenty elders fell down and worshipped him that liveth for ever and ever" (Revelation 5:11–12, 14).

And even though John's report is phrased in the language and imagery of a first-century Christian, steeped in Near Eastern religious symbolism, the grandeur and importance of this kind of celebration comes through to a twentieth-century reader. It matters little whether the "throne" was a literal throne or a command center in a control room, as we will later try to show; it only adds to the credibility of the account to discover that the "beasts" are really robots with artificial intelligence and the "elders" senior administrators in an intergalactic confederation of advanced civilizations. It also helps to know that the "ten thousand times ten thousand" and "thousands of thousands" of persons taking part in this renewal of allegiance to the confederation's chief were not physically present in the Celestials' holy city. Their participation in the ceremony described was made possible by an intergalactic communications system similar to ones now being planned by our own communications engineers. While these would be limited to our own planet and would operate through a system of space satellites, they would make possible the linking of every person on this earth to an event being televised anywhere on its surface, and a similar two-way viewing of the audience by those sending the broadcast. Of course, the problems involved in a simultaneous two-way viewing of actors and audience separated by galaxies would require a vastly different technology, and we will speculate on how this might be possible in a later chapter in this book. But John's description, better perhaps than any other in the entire Bible, reveals the scope and the magnificence of the Celestials' religious and civic life.

To "Bring Forth Mazzaroth in His Season"

One of the most remarkable discoveries to come out of our space-age interpretation of the Bible is that heaven, populated by God, his angels and the redeemed, is not some never-never land in a remote corner of the sky. Nor does it exist on a supernatural, rather than a natural, plane as we were taught in our childhoods. The "heaven" of the Bible is literally the heavens of our natural universe. Its inhabitants (John's "ten thousand times ten thousand" and "thousands of thousands") are the populations of the "advanced civilizations" which Carl Sagan believes to exist on a million worlds throughout our own Milky Way and on other unimaginable millions beyond. In short, heaven is not a place, nor a city; it is an inconceivably vast empire of worlds which embraces all of the more advanced civilizations in the universe and will one day, in the near future, embrace us. Heaven is wherever the Celestials have extended their colonization efforts and will soon, therefore, include our own planet as well. Its capital is the home base of the Celestials, a planet which they call "Mazzaroth" and whose inhabitants are called "Nazarites." From this head-quarters issue the decisions and policies which direct the fortunes of a far-flung intergalactic confederation of advanced civilizations—a confederation which makes our own United Nations seem like a child's toy by comparison.

The Bible gives only slender clues as to the exact location of this headquarters. This is not surprising, since its writers had only the most rudimentary knowledge of astronomy and could only use the few stars and constellations with which they were acquainted as guidelines. Such evidence as it does give, however, indicates that their capital is in our own galaxy. The key passage occurs in the Book of Job in a verse already quoted from the thirty-eighth chapter. "Canst thou bring forth Mazzaroth in his season? Or canst thou guide Arcturus with his sons?" (Job 38:32). Bible scholars have generally regarded this reference to Mazzaroth as one of the more obscure and puzzling references in the Bible. The Hebrew word *Mazzârâh* used here is commonly regarded as being derived from *nâzîr*, a root meaning "set apart for sacred purposes." As we shall presently see, it is also linked with "Nazarite," a term used throughout the Bible to refer to particular humans set apart for the Lord's purposes as his special servants. These Nazarites are specifically instructed by the Lord, throughout the Bible, to act and groom themselves in ways which are at variance with the customs of the Hebrews from which they came. No razor may touch their heads or faces, and they may not drink wine or strong drink. Those who voluntarily take the vows of a Nazarite, and are not set aside from birth, are also forbidden to have any contact with dead bodies, including even their closest relatives (Numbers 6:2–21). Among the outstanding Nazarites of the Bible were Samuel, Samson and John the Baptist.

Now this raises an interesting question. What connection is there between a term used to designate the Lord's special human servants and another designating, apparently, some sort of astronomical or heavenly sign, or body?

Traditional scholars have assumed the connection is astrological. The Hebrews had learned astrology from the Babylonians during their long captivity, and the writer of Job was probably familiar with astrological lore. Since "Mazzaroth" is mentioned in connection with heavenly bodies and constellations, they argue it was probably a constellation "set apart" (therefore the connection with "Nazir") by the Hebrews, because they believed it had some special influence on the earth. While no one has been able to identify this constellation the theory has persisted for lack of a better one.

On the surface the theory seems plausible. As so often happens with puzzling and obscure passages, however, our space-age interpretation suggests quite another meaning for "bring forth Mazzaroth in his season"—a meaning which seems much more specifically and amply supported by the Hebrew and by what we already know about the Celestials.

The clue to the correct interpretation of this passage lies in the custom of designating certain humans as "Nazarites." The root *nazir*, from which the term comes, means much more than just "set apart." It implies setting apart for special sacred, or holy, purposes—a consecration. This word was used of the unpruned vines set apart during the sacred sabbath and Jubilee years of the Hebrews (Leviticus 25:5). It was used in the variant form of *nezer* for the gold plate on the front of the high priest's turban which was engraved with the words "holiness belongs to Jehovah." In the same way the official headpiece, or diadem, worn by Israel's anointed kings was called a *nezer*. All of these uses of *nazir* and *nezer* suggest, then, that "Mazzaroth" was not just "set apart" by humans for astrological purposes, but was rather "set apart" by the Celestials for sacred purposes.

Some inkling of what these special purposes might be can be gathered from considering the derivation of the Hebrew word used here. Ancient Jewish sources, such as the Aramaic Targum, equate "Mazzaroth" with the "Mazzaloth" of II Kings 23:5 which speaks of the "hosts of heaven," an expression later translators of the Bible have rendered as the "constellations of the Zodiac" or the "twelve signs, or constellations."

"Mazzaloth," however, is plural, and "Mazzaroth" is singular, as is shown by the use of the Hebrew personal pronoun immediately following it—"in his season." Used in this singular form it is much closer to "Mezzalah" than "Mezzaloth."

And one of the meanings of *mezzalah* is "a planet." Accepting this derivation, we arrive, then, at the idea that "Mazzaroth" is a planet "set apart," or "consecrated," to the special use of the Celestials.

If this view is taken, the link with "Nazarites" becomes clear. If "Mazzaroth" is a planet set apart for the Celestials' special, sacred use and "Nazarite" (derived from the same root, *nazir*) is used to describe people "set apart" for special sacred purposes, then the implication emerges that the Celestials are headquartered on "Mazzaroth" and that they refer to their race as "Nazarites."

The use of this term for certain humans who become their special servants underscores our likeness to them. Like human missionaries, who ask their native converts to call themselves "Christians" and assume Western garb and customs when working for them, the Celestials ask their special human servants to adopt their customs of grooming and diet and to call themselves "Nazarites"—the term by which they designate the race that inhabits their home planet.

The strange grooming and life style required, by the Celestials, of human Nazarites suddenly makes sense if it is an imitation of their own racial culture and life style. They make no sense regarded as an outgrowth of Hebrew culture and custom, for the taboos against cutting of the hair, use of strong drink, and wine and handling of the dead were not part of the ancient Hebrew culture.

And if Mazzaroth was selected by the Celestials as the headquarters of the intergalactic confederation, then it would indeed be "set apart" for sacred, or holy, purposes in the way that its root *nazir* implies. If it were merely "set aside" by human observers for astrological purposes it would not.

Both linguistic analysis and what we have found out about the Celestials, then, support the idea that the Celestials call their race "Nazarites" (just as we call ours "human") and that "Mazzaroth" is their planetary headquarters. And if this is so, then Job 38:32 gives an obvious indication of where Mazzaroth is located. The complete question "Canst thou bring forth Mazzaroth in his season? or canst thou guide Arcturus with his sons?" links Mazzaroth with the brightest star in the constellation of Bootes—Arcturus, a star only 38 light-years from our own planet.

WHERE IS THE CELESTIALS' HEADQUARTERS?

The phrase "Arcturus with his sons" has been variously rendered by different translators of the Bible. The Hebrew word *ben*, used here, can mean a literal son, or descendant, or can be used figuratively to mean a relationship in which one thing is subject to another. The Revised Version of the Bible renders the passage the "Bear with her train" because the name "Arcturus" comes from a Greek word meaning "bear." The New Oxford Annotated Bible gives the passage as "Can you guide the Bear with its children" and the Jerusalem Bible as "show the Bear and its cubs which way to go." All translators seem to agree that *ben* refers to astronomical bodies dependent on Arcturus or a part of some system which it controls. Logically this could mean only one of two things. Either Arcturus has other stars which with it revolve about a common center (i.e., it is what astronomers call a "binary" star) or else it has a system of planets. Modern observation is sufficiently accurate to have ruled out the first possibility. Present-day astronomers agree that Arcturus is a single—not a binary—star. The only other possible meaning of *ben* here, then, is that Arcturus, like our own sun, has a system of "sons," or planets, that orbit it and constitute its "train" or "cubs." While contemporary observation is not precise enough to verify or disprove this, it is certainly a possibility in view of Carl Sagan's statement that "both theory and observation now suggest that planets are a common, if not invariable, accompaniment of stars."[7] And although modern astronomy is not advanced enough to verify it, it could have been known to humans who originated the traditions from which our present Bible comes if it were told to them by Celestials who lived on one of Arcturus's "cubs."

An added support for this view is found in the fact that the writer of Job knew that Arcturus has a real motion through the sky—it is "guided." This fact, not visible to the naked eye, is a cornerstone of modern astronomy. Just as our own family of planets moves around our sun in different orbits and at varying speeds, so the stars in our own galaxy, the Milky Way, move around its center in different orbits and at varying speeds. And because of this, like our own planets, they, at various times, approach toward or recede from each other.

To the naked eye these motions are not apparent. Even the nearest stars are much too far away for these motions, incredibly rapid though they are, to be noticed. Only sequences of observations, or photographs, taken over long periods of time can reveal even the slightest displacement of the stars relative to one another. Arcturus, nevertheless, has for many hundreds of thousands of years been approaching our own sun at a high rate of speed which, at present, amounts to about 3 miles per second. When we consider this fact, God's challenge to Job, "canst thou guide Arcturus with his sons," becomes logical and clear. And the fact that the real motion of Arcturus was known to the writer of Job is one more startling evidence, like David's and Peter's knowledge of the time-dilation effect, that the writers of the Bible had access to information which must have come from extraterrestrials.

And if our reasoning about this evidence from linguistic analysis and modern astronomy is correct, then that information includes the fact that the Celestials' home base, and the headquarters of the intergalactic confederation, is on a planet orbiting the star Arcturus.

COSMIC ARCHITECTS

If this is so, the phrase "Canst thou bring forth Mazzaroth in his season?" requires some further explanation. How can a planet be "brought forth" and why would it have a "season"? Of all the facts we have so far considered about the Celestials' civilization, none, perhaps, testifies so eloquently to their scientific advancement as this question from the Book of Job. The Hebrew word translated "bring forth" here is *yatsa*. One of its primary meanings is "bring forth," in the sense of making or creating. It is the same Hebrew word used to describe the creation in Genesis where God commands, "Let the earth bring forth the living creature after his kind, cattle, and creeping thing, and beast of the earth after his kind" (Genesis 1:24). Its use in Job 38:32 suggests that the planet Mazzaroth is not a natural phenomenon but something the Lord God and his Celestials created. Such an idea is reminiscent of Carl Sagan's remark that civilizations millions, or billions, of years in our technological future might be able "to rework the cosmos"—in short, that their citizens might be cosmic architects! What do our own futurologists have to say about the possibility of creating a planet?

The growing recognition that our own planet is a plundered one—overpopulated and with nearly exhausted resources—has stimulated space scientists and futurologists to consider the possibility of migration to bases off the earth. Recently Gerald K. O'Neill, a Princeton physicist, has suggested that if population and pollution problems continue, by 2074 a large part of the human population could be living in "space colonies" on cities shaped like "giant cylinders twenty miles long and five miles wide."[8] K. A. Ericke, another physicist, suggests that "with their giant factories and food producing facilities [these] cities will maintain their own raw material mining centers on other celestial bodies and be politically independent city states."[9]

If we are already considering such possibilities, what may truly advanced Celestials have already done? Would manufacturing, or creating, a planet outright be a likely venture? If they are truly capable of "reworking the cosmos," as Carl Sagan suggests, why not? Humans, when they have the wealth and means, prefer to build homes to their own specifications and needs rather than accepting ready-built ones already on the market. Might not Celestials, capable of cosmic architecture, choose to create a planet meeting their exact specifications as to size, atmosphere, climate, distance from its sun, etc.? Would this not be even more likely if it were "set apart" as the dazzling capital of an intergalactic federation—a showplace to eclipse into insignificance our own earthly capitals which have been so carefully and lavishly built and ornamented by earthly rulers?

How would they go about such a task? The science writer and futurologist Isaac Asimov has already been quoted in his discussion of the possibility of artificial planets, or "spomes," which could travel among the stars. In the same book he advances the provocative idea that natural spomes might be created by shearing moons or asteroids of our natural planets out of orbit by using nuclear propulsion.[10]

Taken together, these two proposals by Isaac Asimov suggest alternative methods by which a very advanced civilization might construct an artificial planet. The first would be to assemble it from raw materials mined and transported from other planets. A mathematician, Freeman Dyson, at the Institute for Advanced Study, has recently suggested a scheme by which our own neighbor planet, Jupiter, might, in the future millennia, be broken down, piece by piece, and reassembled as a spherical shell near the earth to capture and radiate solar energy to the earth as a means of greatly increasing our energy supply. If we can envision such a procedure and discuss its engineering feasibilities it would surely not have been difficult for the Celestials to have constructed an artificial planet by methods analogous to those proposed for the Dyson Sphere. A second possible method for "bringing forth Mazzaroth" would be to shear a planet or asteroid out of its natural orbit and guide it to a preselected orbit around Arcturus. The suggestion that the bringing forth was done at an appropriate season, or time, might be taken to favor this theory. Wherever it would have been, before being "brought forth," it would have been in some type of orbit which would bring it at times closer and at other times farther from Arcturus. Shearing it out of orbit at the right time, or "season," when it was at its closest approach to Arcturus would accomplish this piece of cosmic engineering with the least cost in energy and resources. The word used for "season" in Job 38:32 is the Hebrew *eth*, meaning "time." It derives from a root *'ad*, meaning a terminus in some sort of advance or enduring progression. Linguistic analysis here clearly suggests that the planet Mazzaroth was shot forth (to take another meaning of *yatsa*) from its natural orbit at the terminus, or point in time, when it made its closest approach to Arcturus, or when, as our own space scientists put it, a "launch window" opened. So it was "brought forth" and captured as one of Arcturus's "sons."

It is difficult to imagine the splendors with which the Celestials have undoubtedly surrounded a headquarters planet, "set apart" at such expense and effort, to be the capital of their intergalactic confederation. As the Apostle Paul reminds us, in another connection, "Eye hath not seen, nor ear heard, neither have entered into the heart of man, the things which God hath prepared..." (I Corinthians 2:9). But as the ancient Romans imitated the glories of their capital city in the principal cities of their far-flung colonies, so we may surmise that the Celestials have employed the architectural styles, the landscaping techniques and the jewellike synthetic materials of construction which grace their home planet, Mazzaroth. And in the millions upon millions of other planets which make up their far-flung confederation we could doubtless find a unity of style and grace which is the mark of their civilizational influence. We have already had a faint glimpse of the glories this implies in our description of the "New Jerusalem," the space city in which they visit their vast empire of civilizations and explore new worlds to be civilized, like our own. This "home away from home" is evidently made to resemble their celestial headquarters, and, though it is only a portable copy of the original, its foundation and walls of gemlike materials such as jasper, sapphire, emerald, topaz and amethyst; its streets of transparent "gold"; its gates like pearl; its pure river of water of life, clear as crystal; its glory of inner light which requires no sun and forever banishes night—all of this suggests that the world it copies is heaven, indeed! And when their holy city has once again come "down from God out of heaven" to signal their official annexation of the planet Earth as one of their colonies, the glories of Mazzaroth will be extended to this planet, too. Like Mazzaroth we, too, will become a part of heaven—the heaven of truly civilized, intergalactic space!

CHAPTER V

IN THE BEGINNING

In the beginning God created the heaven and the earth. And the earth was without form, and void; and darkness was upon the face of the deep.

—Genesis 1:1–2

With this simple statement the opening book in the Bible begins the creation story. And though this story is much like the creation stories of other Near Eastern peoples, it is very different from ones found in other parts of the world. The Sumerians, Babylonians, Assyrians and Egyptians all had similar accounts of the creation. And they all lived in, or around, the area where the Bible says the Celestials first landed and where it claims they created and taught mankind.

These Near Eastern creation stories all agree that the heavens and earth started as a chaos, while creation stories from other parts of the world usually begin with mythic animals or persons who gave birth to the earth or hatched it.

Why are the Near Eastern stories so close to the actual scientific facts while the others are so fanciful and fantastic?

Why, for instance, does the Genesis account say that "the earth was without form and void"? Many present-day astronomers also believe the universe started with a chaos of undifferentiated matter which erupted in a gigantic nuclear explosion. They teach that it was this "big bang" which started the expansion of the universe, hurled the stars and planets into space and is still giving rise to new suns and new worlds.

Why again does the Bible say God brought forth vegetation, followed by sea life, followed by birds, followed by land animals and finally man (Genesis 1:11–26)? This is the same order that is given for the evolution of life by modern biology. How did the Hebrews of five or six millennia ago know these things? Why do other creation stories throughout the world

fail to reflect the scientific facts as the Bible does? Is it because the Celestials, who knew the facts, told them to Adam
and Eve—to the patriarchs—to Moses?

And did they know them because they made them happen?
Godlike as their powers are, it is difficult to believe they
triggered the original cosmic explosion, or had a hand in the
processes that spawned the galaxies or personally directed the
millions and billions of variations and selections which have
caused the evolution of life through the ages.

Even though their civilization may be millions, or billions,
of years in our future it is not credible that they called the
universe into being, for they too are flesh. Like us they are
within nature—they are not its creators.

Yet the first verse in Genesis says, "In the beginning God
created the heaven and the earth," and in the second chapter
we read that "the Lord God made the earth and the heavens,
And every plant of the field before it was in the earth, and
every herb of the field before it grew . . . And the Lord God
formed man of the dust of the ground . . ." (Genesis 2:4-5, 7).

If God and his angels were actually flesh-and-blood astronauts from another world, is it possible to square these statements in Genesis with common sense? Either God and his
angels are creators or they are creatures. How can they be
both?

The answer to this question is found in a critical study of
the Genesis accounts themselves. As we pointed out earlier,
most scholars are convinced that the two accounts of creation
in Genesis 1 and 2 are taken from different sources. Yet these
have become so interwoven in the Bible that has come down
to us that we can no longer tell where one story leaves off and
the other begins, or whether parts of each have been transferred over into the other. Only by comparing these accounts
with what we know about science and textual criticism can we
discover how the creation really happened.

Two Separate Creations

To begin with, it is obvious that the two chapters contain
accounts of two different creations, not of one told twice over.
Of course, some of what is said about the first creation is repeated in the second chapter, but this tells us nothing, since

chapter divisions are a modern invention and did not exist in the earliest written accounts.

The first account states that "God" created vegetation, sea life, birds of the air, land animals and man—male and female (Genesis 1:11–26)—in that order. The second says the "Lord God" (the name is changed from Chapter 1) formed man, put him in the Garden, made vegetation to grow, formed land animals and birds and brought them to Adam for naming, and last of all, caused a deep sleep to fall on Adam and took out one of his ribs from which the Lord formed woman (Genesis 2:7–22).

It has been claimed, by some Bible commentators, that the first account tells of the general creation and that the second retells a special part of the same creation in greater detail. This might make sense, if we assume the writers of Genesis were just careless in keeping the order straight in the two accounts, except for one important problem. If we read on for the next two chapters we find statements which flatly contradict the idea that there was only one creation. For example, in Genesis 4:16–17 we read that Cain, Adam's and Eve's first son, went into the "land of Nod, on the east of Eden. And Cain knew his wife; and she conceived, and bare Enoch."

WHERE DID CAIN GET HIS WIFE?

Now if we accept that both creation stories are accounts of the same creation, there had been only four humans on earth at that time—Adam, Eve and their two sons, Cain and Abel. Then where did Cain's wife come from? The Bible tells of Cain's and Abel's births at the beginning of Chapter 4 but makes no mention of any daughters being born until after Cain "knew his wife." Only in Chapter 5, after Cain had already married and fathered Enoch, and Eve had given birth to a third son, Seth, is any mention made of the birth of daughters. There we find that ". . . Adam lived a hundred and thirty years, and begat a son in his own likeness, after his image; and called his name Seth: And the days of Adam after he had begotten Seth were eight hundred years: and he begat sons and daughters" (Genesis 5:3–4).

The argument of some Bible scholars that Cain must have married his sister is clearly contrary to the plain scriptural record. If a sister had been born before the birth of Seth, it would have been mentioned as those following his birth were. There could be no logical reason for mentioning the births of later daughters, but failing to mention the birth of a first one.

Some Bible students may object that the statement of Genesis 3:20 that Eve was "the mother of all living" and Paul's statement, in I Corinthians 15:45, that Adam was the "first man" refute the theory advanced here. This is not so. The Hebrew text for "all living" makes it clear that the reference in this Scripture is confined to the experimental creation—which Adam and Eve were given guardianship of. So, too, though it is true that Adam was the first "modern" man, *Homo sapiens sapiens*, this does not rule out anthropologists' finds of earlier human types.

If this is so, the conclusion is inescapable that when Genesis 4 speaks of Cain having a wife in the land of Nod, it implies that there were other humans on the earth, at that time, besides Adam and Eve and their children. And if there were other humans, then it is obvious that they were the result of a different creation from the one that produced Adam and Eve. And, if this is so, then the creation stories in Genesis 1 and 2 are not discussing the same creation.

A careful study of the early chapters in Genesis makes it clear, then, that the creation of mankind occurred in two separate stages—one resulting in the natural emergence of mankind, male and female; the other an artificial and experimental creation resulting in the production of a special pair, Adam and Eve.

Upon critical analysis we discover the first five chapters of Genesis clearly imply that mankind originally appeared on earth as the result of a process of creation, by "God," which involved the same stages described in the theory of evolution. But they also go on to imply that after mankind, male and female, had first appeared, another pair, Adam and Eve, were specially created by the "Lord God" in the Garden of Eden. And this happened after descendants of the first creation had already spread to other areas of the earth, such as the land of Nod.

If this is not the meaning of the early chapters in Genesis, then why are there two creation stories that disagree in telling the order of creation, and why is the creator in one account called by a different name from the creator in the other? In the first account "God" is simply designated by the Hebrew word *Elohim* which is ordinarily used to indicate the supreme God, or power. But in Chapter 2 the same word is prefaced by another, *Yehôväh*, which is often translated "Lord" or "Jehovah" and means, specifically, the Hebrew national God. Could the "God" of the first account be the supreme power that produced the world and everything in it, including the Celestials? And could the "Lord God" of the second account be a flesh-and-blood astronaut, "Jehovah," who re-"created" Adam and Eve by modifying a pair of naturally evolved humans through genetic surgery?

SCIENCE VS. RELIGION

Taken literally, the Bible account seems to contradict much of what science has found out. For instance, it says that God completed the creation—from the heaven and earth to man—in six days. Modern astrophysics sets the timetable for the same events at 13 billion or more years. Genesis says man was created outright, male and female; modern biology says he evolved from lower forms of life over millions of years.

In the nineteenth century, higher critics of the Bible suggested that the creation story should be taken as "symbolic," rather than literal, fact. In this way it could be regarded as having some kind of truth and value even if it is not scientifically true. Protestant denominations, called "modernist," accepted this as a way of reconciling religious faith and an educated scientific outlook. Other sects, known as "fundamentalist," insisted that "all Scripture is given by inspiration of God" (II Timothy 3:16) and that the Genesis account must be literally and scientifically true. Therefore, biologists must be mistaken in thinking man has evolved, and both they and geologists must be wrong when they say man and the world are millions, or billions, of years old.

In fact, in 1650, an Irish archbishop, James Ussher, added up the genealogies in the Bible and, tracing them back from the birth of Christ, concluded the world was created in 4004 B.C. He even generously added the time and day—precisely at 9:00 in the morning, October 23 (he failed to add whether it was Greenwich or Eden time, however).

The conflicts between fundamentalists and modernists became so intense, in America, that many people described it as a war between science and religion. In the southern United States, where fundamentalism was stronger, legislatures passed laws forbidding the teaching of evolution in public schools. The famous Scopes (or "monkey") trial occurred in 1925, in Tennessee, when a young high school teacher, John T. Scopes, violated Tennessee's law in his biology class. The courtroom became a showcase for the issue of the Bible against the theory of evolution and science. While Scopes was convicted, the consensus of public opinion was that science and modernism had won a moral victory because of the brilliant arguments of Clarence Darrow, the defense attorney.

Since that time the prevailing situation, in both America and Europe, has been that a majority of people (even those who are religious) accept the evolution of man over millions of years and the fact that our world is billions of years old.

HAVING OUR CAKE AND EATING IT TOO

Our interpretation of the two Genesis accounts revives the issue of modernism vs. fundamentalism and curiously supports both sides. On the one hand, like the modernists early in this century, we feel the first account should be taken for what it is—a poetic myth written by prescientific men of genius. In spite of its mythic form, however, it contains a symbolic account of the creation of the universe which implies the general facts modern science has established. On the other hand, like earlier fundamentalists, we believe there are good reasons for thinking the second account is essentially literal truth. Of course, it exhibits the confusion of prescientific writers trying to describe technical achievements far beyond their understanding. It also has been intermingled with mythic material and pious rephrasings later editors and copyists have added. But, in spite of this, it contains a nearly pure descriptive account of how modern man was created and how he acquired the rudiments of his present civilization. Further, like our fundamentalist forebears, we believe the Celestial beings who carried out this second creation set up an experimental training program for Adam and Eve intended to qualify them for shar-

ing, as citizens, in the colony they intend to establish here
on Earth; that because of temptation by Satan (a fallen Celestial) they sinned and lost their opportunity, and that an alternative plan of salvation (or citizenship) has been opened up
to their descendants generally.

This attempt to take what is generally regarded as folklore
and to treat it as serious scientific history and theological doctrine may appear naive and unenlightened to many who have
been trained in traditional views. It may seem like the pro-
verbial impossibility of "having one's cake and eating it, too,"
but we believe the scientific record (which we will review in
the rest of this chapter) supports our position. We are further
convinced that this position holds fast to the fundamental beliefs of traditional, orthodox Judeo-Christianity.

"In the Beginning"

As we have already pointed out, the first account in Genesis
1 is not a scientific one. It is poetic and mythic. For a more
factual description of the origins of the universe and life, we
must turn to evidence outside the Bible.

This is found in the science called cosmology—a field of
knowledge that cuts across astronomy, physics, chemistry and
biology.

Cosmologists attempt to discover where the universe is heading at present. From this they backtrack and try to discover
where it has been in the past and how it got to where it is
today.

The evidence as to what the universe is doing, at present, is
rather uncertain. According to the most recent evidence (including information received from radio telescopes and instruments on satellites above our atmosphere), the observable uni-
verse is about 25 billion light-years across ($25,000,000,000 \times 588,000,000,000$ miles). This is the observable universe. Since
it shows no sign of ending at these limits it is probably larger,
but there is no way of knowing how much larger.

And since we are at the center of the observable universe
(observation is equally good in all directions), this means our
most distant neighbors are over 12 billion light-years away.
Since light (or other radiation) from them has taken over 12
billion years to reach us, this number gives us a measure not

only of the size of the universe but of its age, as well. The observable universe's outer limits are at least 12 billion years old.

Numbers like these are, of course, so far beyond our powers of imagination that they are virtually meaningless by themselves. Some idea of the enormous spans of space and time they measure can be grasped better if we compare them with shorter spans we can understand. Carl Sagan has made one such comparison between the age of the earth (less than half that of the universe) and the time life has been on the earth. He says: "If the eons that comprise the lifetime of the earth were compressed into the span of a single year, the origin of life would have occurred at the end of January; the colonization of land in November; the flourishing of dinosaurs on December 15; the evolution of mammals on Christmas Day; the development of the first primates near dawn on December 31; and the origin of man at 8 P.M. on New Year's Eve. Recorded history would occupy the last 30 seconds of the last day of such a year."[1]

And yet, vast as the age of the earth is, and vaster still that of the observable universe, there is no good reason for thinking the entire universe may not be of far greater age and expanse than those parts we have measured. In fact, as the evidence continues to pour in, the debate it has generated seems to be heading toward an agreement that the cosmos may be eternal and infinite.

"'THE ALPHA AND OMEGA"

The Bible quotes God, the ultimate Creative Power, as saying, "I am Alpha and Omega, the beginning and the ending, saith the Lord, which is, and which was, and which is to come, the Almighty" (Revelation 1:8). Theologians have generally taken this to mean that God is eternal but that the material universe had a beginning. Cosmologists, confining themselves to more concrete, scientific evidence, have been unable to agree about whether our observable universe, like the Creative Power it manifests, is eternal or had a definite beginning. Some think it has always existed in its present state of density, and that, though it is continuously expanding, new matter is constantly being created to fill in spaces left as existing objects recede from one another. Others believe it may have begun with all of its matter concentrated at one place in a super-dense "cosmic egg."

Under its own gravitational pressure, the cosmic egg then exploded in a "big bang" which started the expansion of the universe and hurled the galaxies, their billions of stars, and the planetary systems which sometimes surround them into space.

At first it might seem that this second view rules out an eternal cosmos, yet some "big bang" theorists are convinced that the "big bang" which began our observable universe was not the real beginning of things. They believe it was only the most recent in a series of "big bangs" which go back into the past infinitely and that the universe contracts and expands, like some cosmic accordion, throughout eternity.

In either view, then, the cosmos, if not our observable universe, would seem to go back into the past eternally and, by the same reasoning, must go forward into the future eternally. Even those who believe in a single "big bang" tend to assume the cosmic egg, or something from which it came, had an eternal existence before the explosion.

"WORLD WITHOUT END"

When it comes to the question of the extent of the material universe, scientific opinion is again divided. Some astronomers believe space has limits and, therefore, the matter within it must be limited, too. Others believe it extends infinitely and that our observable universe, or, perhaps, a cosmos of island universes, may extend in all directions without end. That part of the theory of relativity which implies that space is curved would seem to suggest that ultimately, if it extends far enough, it would meet itself and thus be limited. Yet even so, another consequence of the theory of relativity implies that even a limited space might hold an infinite number of galaxies. For observations show that as our own universe expands the rate of expansion accelerates so that stellar objects near the observable limits are receding at nearly the speed of light. If they were to attain that speed at the actual limit, their size would be foreshortened to zero (the Fitzgerald contraction required by the theory of relativity). Galaxies approaching the edge would then become paper-thin and ultimately an infinite number of them could be accommodated at the actual edge. In either case, then, whether space is limited or unlimited, it would seem that the universe, or universes, within it may be infinite and without end. This newly emerging concept of a material cosmos without limit, in duration or extent, is supported by much that twentieth-century science has revealed and recalls that striking phrase of the Apostle Paul who speaks of the realm of Christ's church as a "world without end" (Ephesians 3:21).

BUT WHERE DOES CREATION COME IN?

At this point some readers may be wondering where creation comes in. If the universe is eternal and infinite, where does this leave room for creation?

The answer to this question is not really scientific at all—it is philosophical. It depends on what we can conceive and how we wish to use language—not on what can be observed.

If we ask how everything started, there are only three possible answers: (1) everything has always existed in some form, (2) it was created by something outside itself, (3) it created itself. If we analyze these, the last two reduce to restatements of the first, and they all present a single possibility. Let's see why this is so.

Consider (2), everything was created by something outside itself. As it stands, this is really nonsense. Nothing is outside of everything—"everything" is all-inclusive. If this "outside" creator is thought of as "God," then God either is a part of everything or is identical with it. If the statement means that God created everything else, then this raises the inevitable question "What created God?" And the only possible answer is that God has always existed. But if God is really everything, or a part of it, then this is the same as saying that everything has always existed in some form, and we are back to (1).

Now consider (3), everything created itself. If this means everything was there before it was, it states an absurdity. If it means the present form of everything came from some previous form, then the question again arises, "What created the previous form?" And the only answer possible is a previous form. But this gets us into an infinite regress—a previous form was created by a previous form, which was created by a previous form, which was created by a previous form, and so on back infinitely. In either case we are just saying what we said in (1) in a different way. We are really saying that everything has always existed in some form, because these "previous forms" are still part of "everything."

The only possible conclusion, then, is that something has always existed from which everything else comes. If we talk of the "something" we deal with "eternal existence." If we talk of what comes from it we focus on "creation." These are not two rival explanations of the universe. They are just different faces of the same coin. There is no real problem of choosing between them. It is a pseudo-problem created by misunderstanding of language.

Reason compels us to believe the observable universe comes from something which has always existed. What we prefer to call this "something" depends on our point of view. The Bible calls it "God" and calls the process by which it produced the heavens and earth "creation."

If science ultimately proves it did this through the explosion of a "cosmic egg," this does not rule out God as the creative power that made it happen. If science proves it has always existed, as we now know it, this still does not make the term "God" inappropriate. To think, as the Jewish philosopher Spinoza did, that "the world of matter is the body of God" is not irreverent, for it is, at the very least, a figurative truth. The only problem is whether the creative power manifest in the universe measures up to all that the word "God" implies.

What Is God?

Does the creative power which produces our observable universe show evidence of eternality, infinity, power, meaning, value? Is it the sort of thing which inspires the attitudes of reverence and awe so essential to the religious outlook?

We have already seen that there is good reason for thinking it is eternal and infinite—reason supported by scientific evidence. Obviously it involves power—inconceivable power, for the universe it produces and sustains is inconceivable in its duration and extent. The only part of the question that remains unanswered is whether it has meaning and value. Does the power that created and sustains the universe show evidence of intelligence and purpose, or is the cosmos a blind and meaningless jumble of events completely indifferent and irrelevant to human needs and hopes? What does science have to say about this question?

Sir James Jeans, one of the greatest astronomers of this century, had this to say on the matter: "The universe begins to look more like a great thought than a great machine. Mind no longer appears as an accidental intruder into the realm of matter; we are beginning to suspect that we ought rather to hail it as the creator and governor of the realm of matter—not of course our individual minds but the mind in which the atoms out of which our individual minds have grown exist as thoughts.... We discover the universe shows evidence of a designing or controlling power that has something in common with our own individual minds—not, so far as we have discovered, emotion, morality or aesthetic appreciation, but the tendency to think in a way which, for want of a better word, we describe as mathematical."[2]

If the power behind the universe is the sort of being Sir James Jeans believes, then it would seem appropriate to describe it as "God." Its relation to the universe is that of Creator, and it compels an attitude of reverence and awe.

The Bible says, "In the beginning God created the heaven and the earth" (Genesis 1:1). If we are right this is the religious way of saying what the scientist means when he says "the universe has existed eternally" and "man has evolved through natural processes." Whether the ultimate power that produced the universe is called "God" or "nature" does not affect what it is or the real relation we have to it.

"Your God Is Too Small"

But isn't this confusing God with his creation? God made nature. Isn't it blasphemous to speak of him as being the same as nature?

J. B. Phillips, the modern Bible translator, has written a provocative little book called *Your God Is Too Small*.[3] In it he argues that if your notion of God allows you to conceive of him, to describe him or to name his attributes—then your God is too small, for God transcends human understanding. Finite man cannot grasp the infinite and eternal. But this does not mean that God is outside of nature. No one who has grasped the findings of modern cosmology could believe this, for cosmology is revealing nature as infinite and eternal. It is destroying the idea of the supernatural, for nature, itself, is "supernatural" (in the sense past ages attached to that term). Because it includes the "first cause," the "prime mover," "ultimate reality," the "ground of being" and the source of all that is real, including what we regard as wondrous and miraculous, it is just another name for what religionists call "God," the ultimate Creative Power.

If this is the nature revealed by modern cosmology, there can be no conflict between science and religion. Science deals with the creation and religion deals with the creator. One cannot be understood without the other. They are different aspects of one infinite, eternal, all-inclusive process.

And if this one infinite, eternal process is the "mind in which the atoms, from which our minds have grown, exist as thoughts" then it is, at the very least, a person. And if it is the mind which has thought the atoms from which Celestials have grown—beings we would regard as gods—then it is at the very least a god. In fact, it is what the ancient Hindus called the "Tat"—the God beyond all gods!

And the world of matter is indeed, as Spinoza believed, the body of God. But this world of matter, as seen through the eyes of twentieth-century cosmologists, is far different from the inert and lifeless machine scientists of past ages believed it to be. The point of view which allowed Bertrand Russell, half a century ago, to describe it as "alien and inhuman" and "blind to good and evil, reckless of destruction," rolling on its "relentless way,"[4] has become as obsolete as the dodo. Modern physics has killed it and given birth to a new viewpoint which sees the world as both mental and material at the same time. As the astronomer V. A. Firsoff puts it, "the quantum physicist is beginning to suspect that 'mind stuff' can be equated with 'other entities of the physical world.'"[5] Sir James Jeans sounded the keynote for this new outlook when he stated, "Mind no longer appears as an accidental intruder into the realm of matter."[6]

If this is true, then God is the very essence of nature and all natural things are a part of God. God is in nature and God is nature. As the Catholic scientist and mystic Teilhard de Chardin wrote: "God, at his most vitally active and most incarnate, is not remote from us, wholly apart from the sphere of the tangibles; on the contrary, at every moment he awaits us in the activity, the work to be done, which every moment brings. He is, in a sense, in the point of my pen, my pick, my paint brush, my needle—and my heart and my thought."[7] Elizabeth Barrett Browning put it even more aptly and poetically when she wrote, "Earth's crammed with heaven and every common bush afire with God; but only he who sees takes off his shoes."

This organizing force is the Creator described in Genesis 1. It is the "Spirit" that moved upon the face of the "deep." But it is also the creation—the natural universe which is, in Spinoza's vivid phrasing, the "body of God." In its limitless power and meaning and value it embraces all that deserves the name of "reality." In its depths and inexhaustible mystery, it fully justifies the reverence and awe which the religious reserve for the Deity. In the Bible it goes by many names: God, the Spirit, the Spirit of the Lord, the Holy Spirit, the Alpha and the Omega—the beginning and the end.

It is the God of the Celestials, and, as we shall see, they taught its worship and laws to patriarchal man.

Throughout the Bible it is the ultimate and central fact of existence—power, spirit, intelligence, purpose—more than a person; more, even, than a god in the conventional sense, though it is called God. Yet it is something with which we can have a personal relation; something which planned and informs our life and the life of the universe; something which gives meaning and direction to all existence.

This is the Creative Power which is revealed in Genesis 1 and is manifest in nature. And though it is, at the very least, a person and a god, yet it is not the familiar, anthropomorphic God of traditional Judeo-Christianity.

We cannot easily imagine it resting after the labors of the creation, on the seventh day, or saying to its heavenly court, "Let us make man in our image." Yet the first chapter of Genesis says the God of the original creation did these things.

How can we reconcile the God of nature, revealed by modern science, and the God of ultimate reality, deduced by philosophy and theology, with the very personal and almost human creator revealed in Genesis1? The answer to this age-old perplexity lies in recognizing, as early modernists did, that

Genesis 1 is a symbolic telling of the scientific facts.

God, the Creator, the ground of all being, is indeed a transcendant, mysterious, eternal and omnipresent power, as enlightened philosophers and theologians in all ages have believed. It called forth the universes of galaxies with their billions of billions of suns and their worlds without end. It jelled the elements in the crucible of the big bang and programmed the mutations and natural selections which led to the emergence of life and man, here on earth, and to godlike Celestials, elsewhere. Modern science has, within the last century, unraveled many of the secrets of cosmic and biological evolution by which this took place. The great creation account in the first chapter of Genesis tells the same story in a more poetic and mythic way. It personalizes and dramatizes the ultimate Creative Power. He surveys his works and pronounces them good; he discusses and consults with his heavenly court; he rests from his labors on the seventh day. The account agrees with the scientific record, but it is couched in the language of myth rather than science. The eons of cosmic evolution are reduced to six days. The big bang is a response to a direct command—"Let there be light!" The painful emergence of man, through the millions of years of struggle upward of prehuman ancestors, is reduced to a single day and he is simply "made"— male and female—in God's image.

If this is so, however, a problem remains. How about Genesis 2? Is the God who walked in the Garden of Eden, in the cool of the day, and called out to Adam and Eve, also the ultimate Creative Power—the God of nature? And is it this God who later speaks to Moses, face to face, as a man does to his friend? Or have we somewhere crossed an invisible line between Genesis 1 and 2—a line that divides the first creation from the second? Is the God who forms Adam from the "dust" of the ground simply nature clothed in the imagery of oriental myth? Or is he a real, flesh-and-blood being who acted and spoke as Genesis 2 reports? Could he have been an astronaut from another world who modified the work of the original creator in a second, experimental creation?

In the next two chapters we will examine the evidence in the Bible and modern anthropology which proves this is so. The discovery of this evidence is the most important result to come out of our space-age approach to the Bible. It proves we are not only children of nature but heirs of the gods and, through them, of a priceless heritage they have wrested from nature— eternal life in a utopian civilization they will soon establish here on Earth!

CHAPTER VI

COLONY EARTH

Thus saith the Lord, The heaven is my throne, and the earth is my footstool...

—Isaiah 66:1

THE COMING OF THE CELESTIALS

We do not know when the Celestials first came to earth. We can only surmise why they came. The facts are lost in the mists of prehistory.

Having overcome death, they left no bone-filled graves. Since their bases here on earth were portable spacecraft, they took their architecture and equipment with them when they left. The only records that remain were written by humans who knew them, and we find some of the earliest of these in the Bible.

Yet, though the Bible gives no clue as to when the Celestials came and only vague hints as to why, it does tell us exactly how they came and where they first landed.

HOW THEY CAME

The Bible says the Celestials first came in the same way and to the same place they will use when they return. We have seen, in our discussion of that final return, that they will come in a spacecraft and will land at the foot of Mount Moriah where present-day Jerusalem stands. In the final book of the Bible their holy space city is called the "New Jerusalem." In the first book it is called "Eden."

At this point I can imagine readers who are students of the Bible saying, "But Eden was a garden. How could it be a spacecraft?" The confusion of their holy city with the Garden arose through careless reading of the Genesis account. Genesis 2:10 says a "river went out of Eden to water the garden," and Genesis 2:8 states the Garden was "eastward in Eden." From the two passages it is clear that "Eden" is used in two different senses. In the narrower sense of Genesis 2:10 it means a center of some sort that was separate from the Garden. In the wider sense of Genesis 2:8 it included the Garden.

From this we can draw an obvious conclusion. Originally "Eden" referred to the headquarters of the Celestials when they first came to earth. As we will show, it was, in fact, their holy space city—a self-sufficient spome in which they were secure from the dangers of an alien world. As our own future astronauts will do, in visits to other worlds, they remained within this secure and sterile environment until they had sealed off and prepared a larger natural area outside. This area, to its east, became the "Garden of Eden." It, too, was probably isolated from its surrounding environment by a force field which kept out the hazards of alien bacteria and predators. From its safe confines the Celestials could direct the first phase of their colonization program while ensuring a totally controlled environment for the Garden experiment.

We know the Garden area was sealed off, because Genesis 2:5 says that no rain fell. In its place the Celestials sent up a "mist from the earth and watered the whole face of the ground" (Genesis 2:6). Those who live in arid parts of the world have seen long perforated pipes lying beside the furrows of farms and vineyards sending up their spray of "mist." For them there is no mystery in this passage. The Celestials irrigated their sealed Garden, ensuring, as good scientists, that no outside pollutants would contaminate their experiment.

That Eden was a sealed spome and not an ordinary land base, or city, is proved by its features. These tally identically with the holy city, the "New Jerusalem" that John the Revelator says he saw "coming down from God out of heaven" (Revelation 21:2) and that they will use upon their final return. Although Genesis 2 describes only a few of its features it is pictured more elaborately elsewhere.

Genesis simply mentions that a "river went out of Eden to water the garden," the Garden being "eastward in Eden," and that the Garden it watered had a "tree of knowledge of good and evil" and a "tree of life" (Genesis 2:9–10). In the book of Ezekiel, however, this description is greatly expanded. And this expanded one matches that given by John in the New Testament. Like John's "New Jerusalem," and the "Eden" in Genesis, it has a river flowing out of it eastward and a "tree of life." And like John's holy city it is constructed of materials resembling precious stones. Further, Ezekiel's and John's lists match closely—jasper, sapphire, emerald, topaz, amethyst, etc. (Ezekiel 28:13, Revelation 21:19–20). A careful study of all these descriptions given in Genesis, Ezekiel and Revelation makes it clear they all refer to the same thing, whether it is called "Eden" or the "New Jerusalem." And John's statement that it is a "city" which comes down "out of heaven" leaves no doubt that it is a spome—a city-sized spacecraft. As such it is self-sufficient and is capable of recycling its own air, water and food supplies and of transporting a community of Celestials across the reaches of galactic space from their world to ours.

WHERE THEY CAME

It is also the Book of Ezekiel which gives our only firm clue as to where the Celestials first established their headquarters. This Old Testament prophet states that its site was "the holy mountain of God" (Ezekiel 28:14). Now though there are various "holy mountains" mentioned in the Bible, the entire phrase "the holy mountain of God" or "God's holy mountain" is used for only one, Mount Moriah, which is also called Mount Zion (Isaiah 66:20; Daniel 9:16; Joel 3:17; Zechariah 8:3, for example). It is immediately east of Jerusalem and was later the site of Solomon's Temple, as well. Interestingly, directions and closely resembled Eden, which had by then been removed from the earth.

The selection of this site was a logical one. Lying within Solomon's sanctuary was constructed according to the Lord's the Fertile Crescent, it was one of the most favorable areas on earth for the Garden experiment. Traditional Bible scholars have generally agreed, from the Genesis description, that the Fertile Crescent was the site of the Garden, though they have usually placed it at the extreme eastern end near the Persian Gulf.

At first this might seem in disagreement with our location of the Celestials' headquarters at Jerusalem. Once more, careful study of the text reveals that this discrepancy again arises from a failure to distinguish between Eden, as a headquarters, and the Garden of Eden as the site of the experiment. From the coast of Palestine to the Persian Gulf is a stretch of about 1,000 miles, and to scholars living before the space age, an organized project covering such an area was not easily imaginable. Even by our own twentieth-century engineering standards it would hardly be feasible. But to advanced Celestials, millions of years in our future, it would have presented few problems. To throw up a force field blanketing and sealing such an area would be child's play for a civilization that could "rework the cosmos." Its mode of production and operation might not be greatly different from natural force fields, such as the Van Allen Belt which surrounds the earth and shields it from dangerous radiations and particles reaching us from space. And to commute, as they must have done, from their headquarters at Jerusalem to a garden near the Persian Gulf would have required little more than an hour's journey by present-day aircraft. With their own shuttles it probably took only a matter of minutes.

A part of the confusion about the location of Eden and the Garden is also due to the fact that the few clues given in Genesis pinpoint the Fertile Crescent, yet fit no exact geographical location within it. For example, Genesis 2:10 says that "a river went out of Eden to water the garden; and from thence it was parted, and became into four heads." It goes on to name these four branch rivers—Pison, Gihon, Hiddekel and Euphrates. Only the last is still identified by its biblical name. Scholars have identified Hiddekel as the Tigris. The others remain unidentified, as do the lands they water. Scripture says the second one watered the whole of "Ethiopia," but no present river from this area does so for modern Ethiopia. Besides, there are no major rivers having their source near Jerusalem.

Again, though the eastern end of the Fertile Crescent is watered by the Tigris and Euphrates rivers, their source is in present-day Armenia. It has no river watering Ethiopia and is nowhere near Jerusalem.

How then can these vague and geographically unsupported statements be reconciled with the Bible's claim that the Celestials' first headquarters was at Jerusalem?

Obviously the Genesis description could be factual only if there have been great changes in the elevation around Jerusalem, and if the term "Ethiopia" once described other lands. Is there any evidence that this is so?

The answer is yes. Jerusalem lies near the termination of the largest rift valley on earth, the East African—a major cause of earth upheavals. Studies of the Dead Sea, near Jerusalem, show that it was once at least 1,500 feet higher than at present. And a river flowing south, from an elevated watershed on this location, could have watered the land of Yemen on the southern Arabian Peninsula. Interestingly, Ethiopian tradition says a large part of Ethiopia's population came from this area. That rivers did indeed once flow through the Arabian Peninsula is well established. H. St. J. B. Philby, an authority on the natural history of the area, asserts it is "certainly beyond challenge that when the ice cap of the last glacial period covered a large part of the northern hemisphere at least three great rivers flowed from west to east across the whole width of the Arabian Peninsula."[1] And that the land they watered was indeed called "Ethiopia" in the time when the earliest Bible books were composed is supported by Scripture itself. For this area, now called Yemen, is identical with the land called "Midian" in the Old Testament. It is from this land that Moses' wife, Zipporah, came. The Bible states that she was the daughter of the priest of Midian (Exodus 2:16 and 21) and refers to her as "Ethiopian." Thus we read in Numbers, "And Miriam and Aaron spake against Moses because of the Ethiopian woman whom he had married: for he had married an Ethiopian woman" (Numbers 12:1). Clearly, then, the authors of the earliest books in the Bible regarded the area south of Jerusalem, on the Arabian Peninsula, as "Ethiopia," and it could have been watered by rivers flowing southward from Jerusalem.

In view of this there seems to be good reason for accepting the biblical location of the Celestials' first earth base. Their headquarters could have been at Jerusalem and still fit the clues Genesis gives about its river systems. Similarly the Garden could have extended from Jerusalem to the Persian Gulf and still have been under daily supervision.

WHY THEY CAME

As we said earlier, the Bible gives no definitive answer as to why Celestials came to our world. The best we can do is to

make educated guesses based on our own experience. Possibly
the Celestials' world, like our own, once suffered a population
explosion and dwindling resources, though, with their advanced technology, it would seem they could have solved such
a problem without migrating. Perhaps their world was facing
the sort of disaster predicted for our own, in time—a runaway
greenhouse effect from an accumulation of chemicals in the
upper atmosphere, a barrier which traps in heat. This sort of
barrier has already heated our neighbor planet, Venus, to
temperatures ranging toward 800°–900° Fahrenheit. Perhaps,
as we've said, being immortal they had outlived their own dying sun and were forced to seek a younger and more hospitable
solar system.

Orthodox theology suggests still another answer: In the
catechism many of us learned as children it says that "God
created man to serve and enjoy him forever."

Actually this last motive is the one which fits best with the
biblical claim that we were made in their image, for it implies
that, like us, they are colonizers. In this case it was simply the
thirst for knowledge and the challenge of new worlds to conquer that urged them on, as it is now urging our own astronauts and space scientists.

We have already seen that their choosing our world was in
no way remarkable, since they are probably following a plan
of expanding colonization in all directions—much as we will
do in our future space explorations. If this is true we were just
the next steppingstone in their line of advance, and the visit
recounted in Genesis 2 is simply the first phase of a program
which is applied to any planet they select.

When their coming is viewed in this light it avoids one of
the common objections to the idea that we have been visited
by advanced civilizations.

This objection is put, in statistical terms, by Carl Sagan
in his previously cited book, *The Cosmic Connection.* He
argues that since we are only one of billions of alternative
worlds in relation to the few advanced civilizations that could
visit them, we may well wonder whether it is statistically likely
we are among the chosen. He goes on to say that probability
theory indicates it would require launching 10,000 expeditions
each year from every one of his estimated advanced civilizations

for us to have been visted at least once. These would be rather discouraging statistics if they really applied.

What this line of reasoning overlooks, however, is that truly advanced civilizations would not go about space exploration in the way we would be compelled to do. As often happens, when writers and futurologists try to imagine what greatly advanced civilizations would be like, Carl Sagan has made assumptions based on our own limited achievements. These assumptions are almost certainly unrealistic when applied to a civilization like the Celestials'.

He is assuming that extraterrestrials would launch expeditions as blindly as we would, at this point, if we were reaching out toward other solar systems. Yet it is likely such civilizations would almost certainly have methods of information gathering that would permit them to select the most suitable worlds before they attempted any launches. Rather than sending expeditions toward any world that might exist, as we would have to do, they could pick only the very few that met their specific requirements. From neighboring solar systems they had already reached or, perhaps, even from their home base they would survey the world they were considering. They would determine its position and orbit in relation to its sun, its physical and chemical properties, its life-supporting capabilities and its technological development.

In the case of our own world they probably did this thousands of years before we were actually visited. And, because they were colonizing innumerable other worlds at the same time, it would probably be further thousands of years, after their initial visit, before they would return to carry out the final stages of their plan.

Carl Sagan's argument from probability theory fails, then, because he applies it to a situation that almost certainly involved choice and planning rather than chance. We were not visited because our number finally came up on the wheel of fortune but because their line of advance made us next on their list.

As we have already seen, clues in the Bible suggest their home base is only about 38 light-years away—a distance not quite ten times that of our nearest stellar neighbor. And since their technological advancements suggest they have been colonizing space for millions, or even billions, of years it is likely that their explorations have been extensive. When we combine this with the fact that ours is a world capable of supporting life and technology we can see that our eventually being selected was not only probable—it was virtually inevitable!

THE CELESTIALS' SPACE PROGRAM

On earth our own first steps into space have required vast bureaucracies and gigantic industrial projects. In these the organization and funding of government are linked with industrial facilities and human resources to create programs of awesome dimensions. Anyone who has lived through the last two decades can hardly fail to associate space exploration with the administrative colossus, NASA, Cape Canaveral and the major aerospace industries. To many the most significant symbols of our civilization are astronauts, moon rockets and project names such as "Apollo" and "Gemini."

Yet impressive as these achievements are, overshadowing even the construction of the Great Pyramid in antiquity, they doubtless seem crude and primitive to a civilization like the Celestials'. For in spite of the fantastic expenditures of money and energy these projects carried only a handful of men and equipment to a satellite barely a quarter of a million miles away—a distance light travels in less than two seconds!

When compared with the problem of bringing a space city one mile square and containing a community of Celestials over vast distances of many light-years, the Apollo Project pales into insignificance. And when we discover the Celestials' journey from Mazzaroth to Earth was probably only a neighborhood jaunt compared with many they have made to far more distant worlds, we begin to appreciate the real meaning of the term "space exploration." Indeed, if we believe the Scriptures, the space mission recounted in Genesis was only the first phase of a single colonization effort to a small planet which is one among thousands that make up their larger space program. What sort of administration, specialists and resources would be necessary to organize and sustain space efforts of this magnitude?

Though we have only hints, here and there, it is possible to piece together some overall conception of the Celestials' equivalent to NASA. "Equivalent," however, hardly applies to an organization that embraces "worlds without end" and organizes the highest levels of natural and artificial intelligence in projects that extend over millions of years.

As might be expected, like its earthly counterpart, the Celestials' space administration is organized into many levels. Its highest decision-making is carried out, on the home planet, by a general staff of senior administrators who serve as aides to their empire's chief, Jehovah.

Several passages in the Bible picture this general staff in action. Typically they are shown grouped around Jehovah in the command center and surrounded by the communications equipment and computers needed to monitor and direct their far-flung space empire. The most detailed of these descriptions comes from the pen of John the Revelator, who, as we saw earlier, was granted a televised view of their headquarters. Speaking of it he says: "... and behold, a throne was set in heaven, and one sat on the throne. ... And round about the throne were four and twenty seats: and upon the seats I saw four and twenty elders sitting, clothed in white raiment; and they had on their heads crowns of gold. And out of the throne proceeded lightnings and thunderings and voices ... And before the throne there was a sea of glass like unto crystal: and in the midst of the throne, and round about the throne, were four beasts full of eyes before and behind" (Revelation 4:2-6).

Traditional Bible scholars have been puzzled by this and similar passages. The reference to a throne suggests command, but the surrounding "sea of glass" and "beasts" with "eyes before and behind" combine seeming metaphors in a strange mixture which has proved impenetrable to conventional textual analysis.

Now, in our own space age, the passage can be seen for what it is. Without Bible dictionaries or commentaries, its descriptions immediately call to mind video images, like John's, which are familiar to anyone who watches daily television. How many times, in newscasts from Cape Canaveral or science-fiction movies, have we all viewed space centers like the one John is describing? Filled with white-suited "elders" and technicians, their walls a "sea" of glassed television panels, they bustle with the pandemonium of flashing lights and "thundering" loud-speakers.

Like John's four "beasts," with "eyes before and behind," they are studded with the consoles of data-processing equipment and computers. Their lighted dials and instrument panels do indeed resemble "eyes" in grotesque mechanical monsters.

To a first-century Christian the term "beast" would be a proper one to apply to something which is inhuman yet "alive" with intelligent function. Its whirring activity, as questions were addressed to it, and its thunderous voice, as it responded, would suggest animal vitality. It could hardly be called a person, since it lacked human form and dignity. Yet to a person who had never seen a computer or heard of artificial intelligence, it would be undeniably "living." The Greek word John used for "beast" is *zoon*, which simply means "something alive." It was not the more common *therion*, which he would have chosen had he really meant an ordinary wild, or dangerous, animal. Now, though our own computers are not yet equipped to give replies in spoken language, experimental models have been designed which can make limited verbal responses. Others are on the drawing boards which will one day give all responses in spoken form and be able to understand inquiries put to them in the same form. Recently, script writers have assigned leading roles to "beasts" that are given pet names like "Hal" and take on benevolent or diabolical character as they direct human affairs or scheme to overthrow their inventors.

How About Long-Distance Calls?

It might at first seem doubtful that a central headquarters could coordinate the interests of an intergalactic empire. How could information be conveyed over vast distances, measured in light-years, quickly enough to be of use? How could responses be sent to far-off worlds in time to serve the purposes which had prompted them?

Yet, even in human history, there are parallels that suggest the problem is not insurmountable. The Roman Empire was one of the largest and most enduring the earth has known. In its time communications traveled slowly. Often many months were required to send messages from its remote borders to Rome. Directives and commands returned even more slowly. Yet it functioned with an efficiency which has hardly been surpassed in modern times. In a similar manner it would seem that an empire of galaxies might function efficiently, in spite of the distance problem, provided its colonies had sufficient autonomy and flexibility.

There is reason to believe, however, that the Celestials may not find delays in communication a problem at all. Modern physics teaches us that the speed of light is an absolute limit for all forms of energy that could carry messages. Information transmitted by radio or television cannot exceed a velocity of 186,202 miles per second. At this rate dialogue between galaxies might require millions or even billions of years for completion. How could an efficient exchange of information take place among societies separated by such distances? The answer may lie in the science of parapsychology. In recent years experiments in this field have produced impressive evidence for the existence of nonphysical energies which can transmit information. Unlike electromagnetic signals they do not diminish with distance and can apparently span great reaches of space instantaneously.

Numerous experiments, both here and abroad, have shown telepathy and clairvoyance can be as effective over hundreds, or even thousands, of miles as when operating within the confines of a single room. Such studies point clearly to some as yet unexplained energy form which transcends the conventional laws of space and time. Commenting on this, J. B. Rhine, a pioneer and leader in ESP research, says: "...there is now a large body of experimental fact that requires the inference of an effective principle which does not display space-time-mass properties and does not affect the sense organs... The case for psi ["paraphysical energy"] is logically a refutation of the mechanistic philosophy of nature..."[2]

More recently our own Apollo space missions, as well as those of the Soviets, have been used to study the effectiveness of telepathy for communicating in outer space. Initial results have been reported as encouraging.

Experimental studies on extrasensory perception indicate that psi energies, as yet unharnessed by humans, provide a means by which an advanced civilization might carry on running dialogues or maintain instantaneous surveillance across the vast distances of interstellar space.

Apart from the scientific evidence there are numerous passages in the Bible that imply the Celestials do maintain interplanetary dialogues and surveillance. Others even give detailed descriptions of the equipment they use for this purpose. We shall examine some of these in chapters which follow.

For the time being, however, it is enough to notice that the science of parapsychology provides adequate evidence to lend plausibility to John's description of a command headquarters from which Celestials control a vast space empire.

COLONIAL ADMINISTRATION

Fragmentary clues in the Scriptures give further details concerning the Celestials' interstellar space program. In addition to Jehovah, as chief, and the "four and twenty" regional directors, the headquarters staff also includes archangels who perform command and liaison functions. While the Bible names only Gabriel, who acts as emissary and deputy for Jehovah, Lucifer, who directed the Garden experiment, and Michael, who led the victorious forces against Lucifer's rebellion, the roster is filled out in the apocryphal literature. In the first Book of Enoch five others are added: Raphael, Uriel, Raguel, Saraquel, and Remiel. Though Lucifer is not specifically mentioned as an archangel before his fall, his description as "perfect" in the day he was "created" (Ezekiel 28:15), his position as director of the Garden experiment (Ezekiel 28:14) and the reference to him as the "prince of this world" (John 12:31) would all indicate that he belonged to the highest rank of Celestials.

At a lower level there are other orders of Celestials who perform intelligence and caretaking functions (Daniel 4:13 and 23, Psalms 91:11 and Matthew 4:6, for example). In addition, they also carry out space exploration and assist in the work of colonization. Aiding them are the seraphim and cherubim. Traditional biblical commentators have assumed these to be orders, or ranks, of angels. As we have already shown for cherubim and will later for seraphim, however, there is good reason to suppose this is not correct. A critical study of the texts describing them indicates they are not even living creatures but rather robots—servomechanisms. Some have been constructed with human form; others resemble animals or are simply automated pieces of machinery. The more complex are programmed with artificial intelligence and can substitute for Celestials in performing the routine work of an advanced civilization. They are variously depicted, throughout the Bible, as flying through the air, transporting Celestials, fetching and carrying, guarding and protecting or attacking and destroying.

Last, and of greatest importance at the planetary level, are the melchisedecs—local administrators in charge of individual colonies, or planets. These again have proved a source of puzzlement to traditional Bible scholars and commentators. The only one mentioned in the Scriptures appears first in Genesis, where he is described as "the priest of the most high God" (Genesis 14:18). Interestingly this is before there was a Hebrew priesthood and even before Abraham had fathered the Hebrew nation. Abraham, however, visited this melchisedec (called simply "Melchizedek" in Genesis) and paid tithes to him, receiving his blessing and acknowledging him as the high priest of the true God.

Now this raises some interesting questions. Abraham was a stranger to the land. How did he know "Melchizedek" was the priest of the most high God? And what God? Certainly not one of those worshiped in the country from which he came. And what was God's priest doing here—in Canaan—long before God had chosen a people, revealed his law or set up a priesthood of human ministers under Moses? Who made him a priest that Abraham would acknowledge?

Some additional light is thrown on these questions by the Book of Hebrews in the New Testament, where "Melchisedec" is mentioned. Here we are told Jesus, too, was made "a priest for ever after the order of Melchisedec" (Hebrews 7:17)—as though the name referred to a class or rank, rather than an individual. Then, speaking of "Melchizedek" in Genesis, the writer of Hebrews informs us that he was "without father, without mother, without descent, having neither beginning of days, nor end of life; but made like unto the Son of God"—one who "abideth a priest continually" (Hebrews 7:3).

Puzzled commentators have suggested that this description

was applied to the Genesis melchisedec because, being a Gentile Canaanite, he was not included in the Hebrew genealogies—hence his lack of recorded parentage and his being without a birth or death date. Unfortunately for this theory it fails to explain why the writer of Hebrews would have gone on to say he was "made like unto the Son of God" and how, being mortal, he could remain a priest "forever." Obviously this condition could be fulfilled only if he were "like unto the Son of God" in the sense of being a Celestial—and hence immortal.

In their eagerness to give "Melchizedek" a human lineage, Jewish commentators, in the Targums of Jerusalem and Jonathan, suggested that he was Noah's son, Shem. This view has been adopted by a number of Christian scholars as well. There is, however, not a shred of scriptural evidence to support it.

The fact of "Melchizedek's" high priestly office, before there was a Hebrew priesthood, and his perpetual tenure in that office ("continually" or "forever"), make it clear that the writer of Hebrews regarded him as Celestial rather than human. Further, the suggestion that there is an "order of Melchizedek" coincides with linguistic analysis of the term itself. The word "melchisedec" comes from two Hebrew roots: *mehlek*, meaning a "king," and *tsedeq*, meaning "right" or "just." In other words, the etymology of the name shows that it is a descriptive title, not a proper name—a "king of righteousness."

One final piece of evidence serves to clinch the argument. "Melchizedek" ruled at "Salem," according to Genesis, and Bible scholars agree that "Salem" was the site which later became Jerusalem.

If this was the Celestials' first headquarters on Earth, as the Book of Ezekiel claims, then it would be logical that upon their withdrawal they would leave one of their number in charge of the new colony. And it would be convenient that he would govern from their former headquarters—Eden, or Jerusalem. He would be the priest, on Earth, of the "most high God" before there was an earthly priesthood. And he, being created immortal, would be "without father, without mother" and "without end of life."

All this makes it clear that the Melchizedek of Genesis and Hebrews was one of an order of "kings of righteousness." Among its members is also included Jesus of Nazareth. Like the first "Melchizedek" he, too, is ultimately destined to rule this world when the Celestials return.

And, by an extension of the same line of reasoning, it is logical that other members of the "Order of Melchisedec" rule other worlds. As we shall see later there is evidence that "Melchizedek" was not even the first ruler here. Lucifer, the director of the Garden experiment, was the first and would have remained so except for his rebellion. In all probability his sucessor was the Celestial who led the loyal forces responsible for his defeat. This was the archangel Michael, who is described as "one of the chief princes" (Daniel 10:13). The Hebrew words used here for "chief" and "prince" mean "ruler" and "high priest."

The Bible identifies no further melchisedecs specifically. The Genesis "Melchizedek" and Jesus are the only ones it clearly identifies. But we do have two references, in the Book of Job, to gatherings of what appear to be other melchisedecs. In these we find "sons of God" attending scheduled staff meetings to receive work assignments. And among them Lucifer appears! Oddly this is after his fall and expulsion from the Garden—apparently his membership among them is still in effect by virtue of his office, a right which has not yet been revoked by the appointment of a successor. And so we read: "Now there was a day when the sons of God came to present themselves before the Lord, and Satan came also among them" (Job 1:6). And again in Chapter 2 we find another meeting which recurs as a regularly scheduled event: "Again there was a day when the sons of God came to present themselves before the Lord, and Satan came also among them to present himself before the Lord" (Job 2:1). The Hebrew word for "present" here is yâtsab, which means to "offer" oneself— presumably for service.

Apparently, then, the administration of particular planets or colonies is the work of melchisedecs. These, with the assistance of watchers and guardian angels, and a work force of cherubim and seraphim, carry out the decisions of the empire's leader and regional directors. In addition they also rule on local matters falling under their jurisdiction.

COLONIZATION—THE PROGRAM BEGINS

The colonization of our own planet began in an uneventful way. It followed a pattern which had been well established over millennia of space exploration. At first, and until Lucifer's rebellion, the administrative machinery functioned smoothly as it had with thousands of worlds before.

Once they had selected our world, the course they followed can be reconstructed with a fair degree of certainty. We can chart its progress by comparing it with the history of human colonizations, our present space program and clues given in the Scriptures.

Their initial visit was the first phase of a long-range plan for permanent settlement. Because of this they had to bring enough supplies to establish a long-term base. It was also necessary to bring a sizable population of Celestials, themselves, who could carry out the preparations. It seems likely they brought plants and animals, or at least genetic blueprints of life forms, from their own world. These were later used to introduce new plants and animals in the same way our own New England colonists did when they settled the New World. Evidently they also brought equipment to remodel and domesticate other native life forms. Probably they included instruments for studying the earth, its resources and its native life with a thoroughness impossible from their home base or other space colonies. They may also have brought equipment to set up forces which could alter the earth's surface, its climate and even its orientation to other heavenly bodies.

How long these preparations took we can only guess. In the next chapter we will try to pinpoint the time when their most critical experiment took place—the remodeling, or re-creation, of man. From the fossil record and clues given in the Scriptures this can be determined with some accuracy. But how many years, or even centuries, may have preceded this crucial experiment is impossible to determine. Similarly, biblical evidence indicates they remained on Earth, or at least visited at frequent intervals, for centuries after the Garden experiment. But the Bible gives no hint as to when their holy space city first arrived and no certain occasion for its withdrawal.

The scriptural evidence that does exist suggests their program of colonization has gone through three stages. Stage I, a period of indeterminable length, was the time when their headquarters was actually located on the Earth. Its site was within the area they had sealed off—the Garden. Within this Garden they created, or remodeled, various forms of life to "seed" the Earth in preparation for their final return. It seems likely they also used this stage to make extensive studies of our world and, perhaps, to reconstruct some of its basic features.

STAGE II—THE PLAN IS REVISED

Stage II began with the withdrawal of Eden and was a period when they monitored their experimental work closely —the more so since their original experimental design had been upset by a rebellion and power struggle within their own ranks. The director of the Garden experiment and chief assistant to the Lord God, Satan, had betrayed his trust and attempted to use created man as a tool in a scheme to overthrow Jehovah and seize command of the colony.

In a society which had renounced evil and injustice for untold millennia, such an act, though possible, could not have been foreseen, and its effect on the colonization project was disastrous. Nevertheless, Satan and the Celestials who sided with him were overthrown and marooned here on Earth along with the created humans they had betrayed. To prevent a total aborting of the colonization plan it became necessary to revise it. The revision was a supplemental program for retraining and salvaging the experimental humans.

As a result this second stage was marked by frequent visits to Earth and the selection of human leaders, or "prophets," through whom the Celestials directed and taught humanity. During this period they also found it necessary, occasionally, to interfere in the course of human events. They did this to preserve the groundwork they had laid and guide their corrupted heirs back to the course they had originally planned.

The third stage was launched to bring about the fulfillment of their revised program. The descendants of their corrupted creation proved to be a "stiffnecked" and intractable lot. The results of genetic tampering by Satan, and their interbreeding with inferior evolved humans, had produced an unstable psychological makeup. The wickedness of man created a problem unique to this planet and required a unique solution.

STAGE III—"FOR GOD SO LOVED THE WORLD"

Drastic measures were called for, and Jehovah made a startling decision. Like human anthropologists who find out about an unknown culture by going to live among its members, Jehovah decided to send one of his own. He would be a Celestial born into the human situation where its enigmas and perversities could be studied from within. By sharing the weaknesses and temptations of men, and triumphing over them, he could demonstrate the possibility and value of the Celestials' way of life. And he would do it in a manner indirect guidance by human leaders and prophets could not. He would demonstrate the redeeming power of total love and its ability to lift men above the woes of the human condition. Through his knowledge and mastery of the Creative Power, or "Holy Spirit," he would show men the way to an inner wholeness of spirit which can regenerate fallen human nature and enable humans to conquer wrongdoing, disease and even death.

And, yes, he could even go through the ultimate experience of death and be resurrected—a final proof of the reality of eternal life and the Celestials' power over man's greatest enemy.

The Bible tells of Jehovah's decision in a single dramatic sentence: "For God so loved the world, that he gave his only begotten Son, that whosoever believeth in him should not perish, but have everlasting life" (John 3:16). At first it might seem that such concern on the part of extraterrestrial strangers is improbable. But we must remember we are their heirs. They had created, nurtured and trained us and ultimately failed to protect us against ruination by one of their own. Their lack, as immortals, of natural offspring, and their sense of unfulfilled responsibility to us—dependent creatures made in their own image—make the extent of their concern and love understandable. And even though it may surpass its human counterparts the circumstances make it believable.

The die was cast. A DNA information print of Jehovah was taken. One of his most trusted aides, Gabriel, was dispatched and supervised the imposition of it on the ovular chromatin of a human virgin, Mary. She and her husband had been selected because of their direct descent from the original created stock and their observance of the Celestially taught religion.

Nine months later an identical twin to Jehovah was born to the human mother, Mary. Jehovah's final step in the salvation of his wayward creation was underway. The clone, Jesus of Nazareth, lived an exemplary life according to high standards set by the Celestials. He taught and manifested the redemptive power of love as a remedy for the ills of the human condition. Finally, in his death and resurrection, he demonstrated the genuineness of the Celestials' offer of eternal life and citizenship to humans who prove themselves worthy.

As a parting gift, before returning to the home base, he initiated a select group of followers into the use of the ultimate Creative Power. He called this his "baptism" and showed them how to use the power (which present-day parapsychologists call "bioplasmic," or "biocosmic") to heal illness, reform character disorders, transcend so-called laws of nature and even resurrect the dead. Most important, he taught that the voluntary opening up of one's life to this power can regenerate fallen human nature and give men a "new birth." By being "born again" humans can not only achieve righteousness in their external conduct but, more important, wholeness (or "holiness") within. Only through such a "rebirth" can fallen mankind become worthy of Celestial citizenship.

With the launching of this third phase a workable solution was at last reached for salvaging a remnant of mankind. The promise of a Redeemer—made to patriarchal man after the fall and carried, by his descendants, into religious legends and myths throughout the world—had at last been fulfilled.

After Jesus' death, resurrection and return to the Celestials' home base his disciples began the work of bringing this solution to the world at large.

"Unto All the World"

At Pentecost they experienced the formation of a new religion, Christianity, which has played a major role in the spread of this final plan throughout the Earth. At Pentecost over 3,000 people, drawn from the farthest reaches of the empire and beyond, experienced the "baptism of the spirit"— the crucial parapsychological and spiritual transformation which suddenly swept humans into a vast evolutionary leap into the future. By setting up the conditions for a mass experience of biocosmic power, and its effects on human nature, ordinary men became, in a significant new sense, "sons of God." Paraphysical manifestations accompanied this outpouring. Some emitted visible auras as they were charged with the "Holy Spirit," or cosmic power. "Tongues of flame" came and rested on their heads, reminiscent of the halos painted around saints in early church art. Parapsychological manifestations— charismatic "gifts of the spirit," such as xenoglossy—broke forth. Men from many nations spoke in "tongues" and understood one another's speech without knowing the languages they heard. Extraordinary psychic healings took place, and a new faith that was to prove the most widespread in the history of mankind sprang into being. The spread of the good news of salvation was underway.

All signs predicted in the Bible proclaim that the third stage of the Celestials' colonization plan is now rapidly drawing to a close. With the rebirth of the nation of Israel their return is, as Jesus dramatically put it, "Even at the doors."

Shortly they will return, in the manner described in the opening chapter of this book, and set up a thousand-year reign of peace and justice. During this time the nations of the world will be molded into a peaceful unity which can be included in the Celestials' intergalactic empire. At the end of that probationary period full citizenship will be conferred on the human remnant that has survived the training and qualified for eternal life. They will begin a new existence, in immortal bodies, as citizens—not just of this world, but of heaven, the confederation of advanced civilizations the Celestials have created.

This, in brief, is the reason why the Celestials came to Earth. It explains why they created us, and the course their plan for us has taken.

It leaves many questions unanswered, however—questions which preoccupy our scientists today as we stand on the threshold of our own space age. What specific techniques were used in our creation? What is the proof that we are not the result of biological evolution alone? Does the fossil record support our claim? How does our space age interpretation modify current scientific views on the origin of man, of races and the beginnings of civilization? We will consider these questions next in the chapter which follows.

CHAPTER VII

THE EXPERIMENTAL CREATION

And the Lord God formed man of the dust of the ground, and breathed into his nostrils the breath of life; and man became a living soul.

—Genesis 2:7

In the last century, higher critics of the Bible ridiculed such passages as the one quoted above. Man created outright from dust—preposterous! Hadn't Darwin proved man evolved over millions of years, and was descended from ape-like ancestors? What did God have to do with it? Obviously the Genesis account is just a curious bit of Hebrew folklore.

Today, at the end of the twentieth century, we are not so sure. Space age anthropology has tried hard to document Darwin's theories, yet curious gaps and puzzles remain. The immediate ancestor of modern man has never been found, though fossils of our more remote ancestors exist in profusion. We are not even exactly sure when or where contemporary mankind arose or how we spread so rapidly throughout the Earth. The origin of races remains an enigma. Most puzzling of all is our miraculous ascent, over five or six millennia, from an animal level of existence to full-blown urban civilization in ancient Sumer. What caused our sudden elevation from the state of a savage, living in caves and using crude stone tools, to that of a sophisticate who lived in grid-pattern cities, constructed monuments we cannot duplicate today, charted the heavens, projected the periods and times of eclipses and comets for thousands of years, philosophized about the mysteries of the universe and created glorious sculptures and literature?

Did the blind, natural selection of chance variations elevate him, or was he assisted in his upward climb? Today, as we stand on the threshold of space exploration, the idea that we

109

have been visited and assisted is not preposterous. The Genesis account of man's creation begins to look more like futurology than folklore.

And yet the fossil record and the proofs of man's evolutionary history remain. How can we disentangle the conflicting lines of evidence that support such opposed views of our beginnings?

"NOT FROM THE APES"

In the time of Darwin, and after, controversy raged hotly over the common misunderstanding of his *Descent of Man.* Many theologians, and some students of natural science, took the theory of evolution to hold that we are descended from the apes. Demonstrating fundamentalists, at the Scopes trial in Tennessee, waved placards proclaiming, "Your grandfather may have been a monkey, but mine was not." University of Helsinki anthropologist Bjorn Kurten confirms their intuition in his recently published and provocative book *Not from the Apes.* In it he observes, "Until quite recently it could be said that man arose from something pretty close to the ancestry of the gorilla just before the beginning of the ice age (3–4 million years ago). In that case early men should be more and more ape-like as we go back in time. Surprisingly, they are not; indeed, the term "ape-man" is quite misleading for these early humans. They point back to a very different sort of ancestor."[1]

In the late nineteenth century, battle lines were drawn sharply between religious fundamentalists and evolutionary scientists and philosophers. Fundamentalists attacked the theory of evolution and evolutionists attacked the Bible. Today the battles are largely forgotten.

Conservative Christians who are scientifically literate recognize that the fossil record cannot be denied. Fossils of earlier humans and prehuman hominids exist in abundance, and their hundreds of thousands and millions of years of age have been irrefutably established by radioactive dating. Such specimens can be seen in almost any local museum of natural history.

On the other hand, archaeologists and textual scholars are increasingly confirming the accuracy of the Bible. Persons, places and events mentioned in it are almost daily being verified by new archaeological finds. Discoveries such as the Dead Sea scrolls prove the accuracy of translations which have come down to us.

Where then does the truth lie? Was man created outright, as the Bible claims, or did he evolve by the stages shown in the fossil record?

MAN A "RE-CREATION"

One of the most important discoveries to come out of our space age interpretation of the Bible is the answer to this question. And, curiously, the answer is both—man evolved and was then re-created by extraterrestrials.

He did evolve, as the fossil record proves, from prehuman ancestors. The fossils are genuine, and their dates are undeniable. They could not have been manufactured and planted by the Devil, as more imaginative early fundamentalists tried to argue. Nor would God have created the world in 4004 B.C., as Bishop Ussher claimed, and then given it an artificial appearance of much vaster age. Apart from the fact that argon-potassium dating methods prove the incredible age of the Earth and its fossil strata, it is contrary to sound theology to suppose God would have deliberately built a lie into the Earth's appearance. The simple truth would have served his purpose better—particularly if the lie was going to mislead men into doubting truths necessary for their salvation.

The fossil record proving human evolution must stand, then. It cannot be denied. Yet modern man also stands. And as he stands he cannot be accounted for by the evidence in the fossil record. In the final stages of his emergence he became too much too fast to be explained by existing concepts of evolution. Some added agency is needed to explain the strangeness and, in particular, the extraordinary overendowments which set him apart from every other animal on this planet.

The Bible tells us this added agency was the activity of Celestials who refashioned him in their own otherworldly image. Unfortunately, it tells us little more. How they refashioned him, their motives in doing so, the techniques they used—all these we must reconstruct from other sources. In this chapter we will attempt this reconstruction from the fragmentary hints given in the Bible and two other sources—our own emerging science of genetic engineering and paleoanthropology. The story that emerges is a truly astounding one, for it proves man is indeed "not from the apes" but is the heir of a "very different sort of ancestor." Let us see, then, how this ancestor went about man's construction.

THE GARDEN EXPERIMENT

When the Celestials first reached Earth they began the preparations necessary for a genetic experiment of much complexity and importance. An area of the alien world was prepared by isolating it and modifying it to resemble their own. Just as our space missions take elaborate precautions to avoid contamination of samples, and quarantine astronauts upon their return, so they guarded against alien microorganisms and pollution. This would be necessary, both for themselves and the plants and animals they created, if they were to achieve predictable results. They did this by marking off a large area and throwing up a force field around it to seal off pollution by air or water and to repel invading predators. The dimensions of this area are not given in Genesis, but they are given for the "New Jerusalem" in Revelation—and we have already seen that it is almost certainly identical with "Eden" in Genesis.

If the two are the same, then the overall length of the Garden was about 500 miles to a side—"twelve thousand furlongs" around the "foursquare" perimeter, as John the Revelator tells us (Revelation 21:16). With its base at Jerusalem, the square would just about cover what geographers call the Fertile Crescent—assuming its diagonal ran from the area of present-day Jerusalem to the tip of the Persian Gulf. This area, in which historians locate the earliest of human civilizations, extends from the eastern seaboard of the Mediterranean, past the foothills of Kurdistan and down to the shores of the Gulf. Within this area there was ample room to create the plants and animals they needed for food and domestic help.

HOW DID THEY "CREATE" PLANTS AND ANIMALS?

In terms of our coming biological revolution we can make likely guesses at the methods they employed. They could, of course, have brought plants and animals with them as our own colonists did in the Renaissance. A more efficient method, however, would be to bring genetic blueprints of their own desirable species or to modify those already here by genetic surgery.

By bringing DNA records of life forms on their own world they could simply replicate them from raw materials, as they were needed, without having to keep and feed them in the meantime. Modifying our own native species would be even better, where possible, since they would already be adapted to the Earth's environment. In the case of their most crucial experiment, man, they almost certainly used the latter method. As we have seen, the Cain story in Genesis tells us there were already humans on earth at the time of their coming. In looking for a native animal to domesticate and leave in charge of their program the selection of one of these manlike hominids, primitive but not unlike themselves, would be a logical choice. With a little improvement and training he could be given the responsibility of the Garden, "to dress it and to keep it" (Genesis 2:15), after they had left. Once the new plants and animals, including man, were established they would spread throughout the earth to make it more hospitable upon the Celestials' return.

Do We Have Look-Alikes on Other Worlds?

This assumes, of course, that beings from another world would resemble our early ancestors closely enough so that they could easily be remade into a reasonable facsimile of the alien beings. Is this likely, and how much remodeling would be required?

We earlier quoted evangelist Billy Graham, who believes there are beings in outer space resembling the "average American." But what do scientists who investigate the question of otherworldly life think? Is it really likely that life here would so nearly duplicate life on an alien world? Science-fiction writers have reveled in imagining bizarre forms which intelligent life might take on distant planets. Scriptwriters have fascinated movie audiences with shots of antlike creatures flying spaceships and balancing relativity equations, of little green men with antennae, of gelatinous blobs that pursue humans like superhuman sleuths. Isn't it extremely unlikely that intel-

ligent life on an alien world would resemble us—especially if
it had had millions, or billions, of years to evolve beyond our
stage of development?

Carl Sagan expresses this skepticism when he points out,
"The evolution of life on earth is a product of random events,
chance mutations, and individually unlikely steps . . . Were we
to start the earth over again and let only random factors operate, I believe we would wind up with nothing at all resembling
human beings. This being the case, how much less likely it is
that organisms evolving . . . in a quite different environment
of another planet of a far-off star, would closely resemble
human beings."[2]

At first glance this argument has a certain common-sense
plausibility. Since life takes such myriad forms here, is it not
reasonable that it would assume even more varied forms elsewhere? Especially if conditions on the alien world were very
different from our own? Why, of all the millions or billions of
forms it could take, would intelligent life elsewhere assume
the one specific form we associate with advanced intelligence
and civilization here?

Unfortunately the argument will not stand up under scientific scrutiny. In the first place, there is no good evidence
that evolution is as blind and random as Sagan supposes. We
have already seen that some astrophysicists, such as James
Jeans, believe cosmic and biological evolution take place in
ways that are meaningful or even mathematical. The adaptive
mechanisms of many forms of higher life so nearly duplicate
machines and electronic devices man has invented it is difficult
to suppose they, too, are not the result of some intelligent purpose that works through nature.

Further, biologists know that many similarities between life
forms here on earth are due to structural properties which
characterize the basic chemicals of life. As has been pointed
out, living organisms are the greatly magnified expression of
molecules that compose them. For example, the fact that
many animals are made in matching right and left halves is
thought to be due to the right-left symmetry of certain molecules that compose them. Similarly, primates (monkeys, apes
and humans) have five-fingered and five-toed extremities because of the pentodal (five-featured) structure of other organic

molecules. Even the location of sense and movement control in the head, rather than the middle or tail, end of some animals is thought to be due to the way cells balance and organize themselves, at a chemical level, in the developing embryo.

Now since meteorites from outer space contain the same chemicals that form building blocks for life here, is it not reasonable to suppose there may be life forms elsewhere which resemble our own? Further, if these chemicals function there as they do here, then it could well be that some of these alien creatures would have bilateral symmetry, five-fingered and five-toed extremities and heads containing sense organs and controls for their bodies.

And if they visited our Earth because they had chosen it for its similarity to their own, it might well be that they would find life forms here that closely resembled themselves. In fact, they might very well discover that the Creative Power that had produced them had duplicated its efforts on this planet. For if our world is similar to theirs, then it would be reasonable to suppose evolution here would parallel the course it had taken there.

Even on earth this parallelism between life forms having completely dissimilar origins is sometimes found. Biologists call this "convergence" of dissimilar types because of a common environment. For example, the cetacea (a group of mammals including porpoises, dolphins, and whales) have the same evolutionary origin as cats, dogs and apes—not to mention ourselves. Yet because of the millions of years they have spent adapting to a watery environment they have come to resemble fish. The parallels are so striking that many people assume they are fish. They have even developed fishlike tails, finlike forelimbs and a hairless surface.

So the idea that Celestials came to Earth and found evolved hominids here who resembled them is not improbable. Nor would their added millions or billions of years of development necessarily have carried them beyond the characteristics we regard as human. For anthropologists point out that even with our own race, the little technology we have developed has so shielded us from natural selection that evolution has virtually stopped for us. In a biological sense we are not detectably different from the cavemen who lived throughout Europe

30,000 to 40,000 years ago. Our evolution has become a primarily cultural and technological one.

In the same way the Celestials would have reached a limit of biological evolution when they achieved our present level of civilization. The added millions or billions of years they have had to develop would have made few changes in their physical natures—except as they artificially improved them by genetic engineering. Their development from that point on, like ours, would lie principally in the mind and spirit.

So they arrived on Earth, closely resembling our human ancestors, and decided to make the resemblance even closer.

How Close Is Close?

Just how closely these hominids resembled the Celestials is open to speculation. If the Bible is correct in saying the remodeled version reflects their image, then we can get an approximate idea by comparing ourselves with our own fossil ancestors.

Such a comparison suggests the differences were minimal. Probably the hominid selected by them would have been more hairy than ourselves. He may have had a smaller brain, and almost certainly it was less efficient. Perhaps there were minor cosmetic differences—a lower or more receding brow, a more protruding jaw, or a less upright posture. Many of the changes the Celestials made might not be evident—even if we could examine a fossil of their re-creation and compare it with the prototype from which it was taken.

Yet the changes they made, subtle as they may have been, revolutionized man's nature and made him a biological improbability—a sapient animal endowed with skills and aspirations no earthly development could give him. How did they accomplish this incredible transformation?

In the Image of God

The operation, itself, would have been a simple one. Tissue samples were taken from a hominid of the selected species. A scanning device could record the DNA pattern of its cells. The record would then be modified. A slight sequence change here, in the code symbols on the information print, would ensure his hairlessness and cause him to resemble them more closely.

Others would provide extra brain cells in critical areas related to memory, abstract thought and creative productivity. One would enlarge the convolution of Broca and make more elaborate and grammatical speech possible. With a few simple substitutions of this sort the genetic "surgery" would be complete.

Now the modified record could be fed into a replicator, along with a quantity of raw chemicals. The result would be man—created from the "dust of the ground" (Genesis 2:7) by the Lord God himself, just as the Bible says. This man, "Adam," would be an improved variety of the hominid from which he was taken—a man recreated in the "image" of God. Not quite as dramatic as Michelangelo's version, perhaps, but fully as effective. The Lord God would then breathe "the breath of life" into him, and he would become "a living soul" (Genesis 2:7). The Hebrew word used here for "breath" is *nshamah*, which means a vital breath or wind—a power. The technique of vivification was probably not different from our own use of electric shocks to restart the heartbeat in cardiac arrest.

A female companion could then have been provided by repeating the procedure. The matching of their genes, however —if they reproduced by the method used on the outside— would introduce an element of unpredictability undesirable in a controlled experiment. Parents who have tried to anticipate characteristics of their own children are aware of this uncertainty. A more satisfactory method would be to clone the man. This could have been done by taking his doctored printout and making one more change—the one determining sex. The Lord, however, chose a more dramatic method. He anesthetized Adam and removed a "rib," so Genesis 2:21 tells us. The cellular material of the rib was then evidently scanned, modified for sex-chromosome pattern, and replicated. The reason for this clumsier method was apparently psychological rather than genetic. The Lord wished Adam to value Eve, the clone, so he made him give up something for her. Thus Adam is moved to remark, "This is now bone of my bones, and flesh of my flesh: she shall be called Woman, because she was taken out of Man" (Genesis 2:23). Adam got the point, and the Lord's object lesson was effective.

As a clone of Adam, Eve was his identical twin (except for

sex). The characteristics of their offspring could be predicted with absolute certainty—a necessity in this sort of experiment where so much was to be entrusted to their care.

The Celestials' First Artifact

Whenever human colonists have migrated to new lands they have generally domesticated plants and animals they found there. In refashioning man to make him more useful the Celestials followed a similar course. Unlike our own colonists, who used slow and inefficient methods such as taming and selective breeding, the Celestials simply remade their domestic life forms to order on the spot.

And in the way they refashioned us they demonstrated their vast civilizational and moral superiority to human colonizers. For while we have usually destroyed, enslaved or at least exploited natives in our colonies the Celestials elevated humans to their own level. In making us near equals they ruled out the possibility that we could become mere "beasts of burden."

They created us not just to serve them but to enjoy them and be enjoyed by them, as the childhood catechism teaches. They designed us as eventual companions and citizens. And in being so designed we were set apart from all other animals on this planet in ways which give irrefutable proof they were here and we are their heirs. Man is one of the most dramatic artifacts they left behind—an artifact of unquestionable extraterrestrial origin!

How to Recognize an Artifact from Another World

The old hymn which says, "This world is not my home; I'm just passing through" expresses a feeling most reflective people recognize and contains at least half a truth. We are indeed, as Christian theology maintains, dual-natured beings—inspired by the divine gifts of a Celestial race, yet linked by ties of evolutionary descent to the beasts of the earth. Thus the Apostle Paul was moved to lament: "O wretched man that I am! who shall deliver me from the body of this death?" (Romans 7:24). This is the very essence of tragedy in the classical sense —man doomed to yearn and strive for more than he can be, yet knowing his ultimate fate is death with the doom of all his dreams. The very gift of reflective thought, which enables him to imagine and long for perfection and immortality, is the fatal power which also reveals his bestiality and his doom. Small wonder modern philosophers have called his insight "existential despair." Like Prometheus, he holds the gift of celestial fire yet is chained to the rock of his animal ancestry.

Perhaps this is why the Celestials have shown such long-suffering patience with their wayward creation—their strange offspring who is half natural son and half bestial stepchild. And perhaps this is why they have gone to such lengths in revising their original plan.

Their motives in creating us were not just those of trainers domesticating beasts, or colonists exploiting savages, or superior beings amusing themselves with pets. They were not even those of missionaries who have sought to elevate "heathen" people by bringing them the gift of a "superior" civilization.

Their real motives include a higher interest so obvious it seems almost human, for we also share it as we reflect their image. Since they do not reproduce sexually they have no children. Being busy with the pursuits of a highly advanced civilization, yet possessing the humanlike need for relaxation and play, they crave the enjoyment children can bring. Like us they have a highly developed need to care for the immature and helpless. Like us they have the need to invest themselves in the growth and development of dependent beings under their care. And like us they enjoy reliving their own development vicariously and taking pride in the achievements of offspring as they fulfill the hopes and expectations of their parents. So they have transferred these needs to those they create and domesticate in their course of space colonization.

Wherever they go they create, or re-create, heirs in their image—heirs whom they can love, instruct, guide and ultimately welcome into their civilization as equals. It is this fact which provides the startling proof that we are not just products of earthly evolution. Unlike any other animal we were remade according to an unearthly pattern. In the process they overendowed us with traits of no earthly use. They could only be of use as their companions.

Because of this we not only have traits necessary for survival (the only kind earthly evolution can give us), but we possess numerous others which are irrelevant to survival. These could not be the product of natural selection, for they distract us from the sordid business of surviving and divert our attention to higher matters. As Jesus points out in the New Testament, "man shall not live by bread alone" (Luke 4:4).

Interestingly, though they do not contribute to survival, these traits are prized as the "highest" qualities of our species, and they single us out from every other earthly kind. They could only have arisen on another kind of world or as a means of sharing with beings from one—and this is precisely where and how we acquired them.

We will presently examine these unearthly traits which set us apart. They include the capacity for philosophical reflection, for religious experience with its yearning for immortality, for disinterested or "pure" scientific investigation and for artistic creation.

Before looking at these, however, it will be helpful to consider the structure in which they are housed—the human body. For even here, at a purely physical level, our nature already shows oddities that give us an unparalleled strangeness among Earth's inhabitants.

THE "FEATHERLESS BIPED"

The peculiarities which set us apart from other animals are typified by the whimsical definition which is sometimes given of the human being as a "featherless biped."

Though our walking on two legs and lacking feathers is indeed a peculiarity it is by no means the strangest or most significant of our oddities.

Among those which have attracted the attention of zoologists, none is harder to explain than our nearly equal lack of hair. Among some 4,000 species of land mammals, including our closest relatives, the monkeys and great apes, man alone is nearly hairless. He is, as Desmond Morris so aptly put it, a "naked ape."[3]

Our loss of a furry pelt defies an evolutionary explanation, for it would be a distinct advantage in most climates and as a protection against a scratching and abrading environment. In fact, we have had to compensate for its loss by the wearing of clothes. Our lack of it is antievolutionary. How then did it come about? Was it engineered by Celestials to make us more like them? Did they remove our pelt, much as we clip, groom and shave our own domestic animals, because they found it more aesthetic?

Again, in curious contrast to our overall hairlessness is our luxuriant mop of head hair. All the great apes—our nearest biological "cousins"—are bald or nearly so. Interestingly, the Lord's special servants, Nazarites, were required to leave hair uncut (Numbers 6:5) and Paul describes it as a woman's "glory" (I Corinthians 11:15). Were these ideas handed down by Celestials who have luxuriant hair and fashioned us in their image?

Another remarkable difference that sets humans apart from the rest of the higher animals is their capacity to engage in sex for expressive and pleasurable purposes, rather than as an exclusively reproductive act. The human female is alone in lacking the estrus (or "heat") cycle which confines female lower animals to mating only when they are ovulating and can reproduce. A woman can enjoy love and sex even when reproduction is not the goal. Similarly the human male alone, among higher mammals, lacks a penis bone. Because of this, sex for him must be preceded by arousal and cannot be quickly completed as a starkly reproductive act—as it so often is for animals in the wild. And both men and women are peculiar, among higher mammals, in forming pair bonding—the tendency to make lifelong, monogamous unions. Are these differences gifts of the Celestials who gave them to us, because they wished to train us in the responsibilities of nurturance, fidelity, sympathy and love so important in their civilization?

THE BRAINY BIPED

Of all the characteristics that set humans apart from other animals none is more baffling or utterly inexplicable than the brain and its remarkable capacities. By itself it is an overwhelming evidence of Celestials' interference in our development.

As a functional instrument it is unrivaled by anything we know—not only in the animal kingdom but in the entire universe. It contains over 10 billion cells—nearly one for every light-year that separates us from our most distant observable stellar neighbors. Neurologists have estimated single ones of these cells may have more than 10,000 connections to other parts of the brain.

It contains natural forms of almost every electronic device known to man. It has conductors, resistors, capacitors, transformers, relays, filters, memory-storage units and retrieval systems.

Unlike the best computer designed by man it can create superb poetry, compose immortal symphonies, envision overpowering paintings, play unbeatable chess and make jokes.

Yet it is so miniaturized it is usually housed in a cavity of only about 1,300 cubic centimeters and weighs barely 3 pounds. How did the naked ape come by such a tool?

To suppose that such a device could have "evolved" by a purely mechanical selection among millions of chance variations is, as Darwin himself observed, "absurd in the highest degree."[4] It is about as plausible as that the plays of Shakespeare would accidentally assemble themselves out of discarded type in the numerous printing offices of the world.

More than any other structure we know the human brain seems to show that nature does not work by blind and mechanical processes of chance, as some scientists have argued, but involves a cosmic purpose and intelligence that works toward meaning and wholeness. The human brain, regarded as an artifact, is perhaps the most compelling evidence we know of to support the idea that the designing and controlling power of the universe is a creative cosmic being—the God behind all gods. It is, in fact, the eternal, infinite biocosmic mind which the Bible calls "God" or the "Holy Spirit." Modern philosophers and researchers are beginning to see it as an all-pervading reality underlying both mind and matter—an energy from which they both spring and into which they can be resolved.

Yet, even if we grant that such a power could create intelligent hominids and even Celestials million of years in our future, an enigma remains. For such developments take time.

The paleontological record shows that major species changes require hundreds of thousands or even millions of years to accomplish. The rise and fall of dinosaurs, for example, occurred over a period of 150 million years. And our earliest identifiable hominid ancestor, *Homo habilis,* lived at Lake Turkana in northeastern Kenya over 2 million years ago. Yet the changes that separate us from him are insignificant when compared with those that distinguish us from our nearest living cousins, the great apes.

Normally, then, even hundreds of thousands of years are insufficient to produce major changes in a species. Yet in the case of modern man we find a most astonishing exception to this rule. For our ancestors of only a little over 30,000 years ago lived scarcely above the level of the beasts around them. They used only the crudest of tools, made by flaking stones, and lived at an animal level of existence. As far as we can discover they had no religion, no art and no established agriculture. And the fossil record shows they had lived at this same level since they first appeared around 250,000 years ago.

The Modern Human's Celestial Brain

Suddenly, however, about 30,000 years ago, subtly different *Homo sapiens* appeared. Though their fossils look much the same as those of earlier humans the quality of their intellectual functioning shows an incredible leap into the future. For within a bare 25,000 years they had spread throughout the world and lifted their species from a common lot with animals to the level of gods. Within a tenth of the time the species had taken to produce crude tools and a rudimentary use of fire they developed writing, mathematics, religion, literature, philosophy, medicine, agriculture, trade and commerce and the use of money. They left records showing they understood the orbital periods of the planets and their satellites and the cycles of eclipses and comets. They catalogued thousands of pharmaceuticals, mastered techniques of surgery, learned the art of embalming, built pyramids and other wonders that could hardly be duplicated today. The statuary and poetry they created compare with the best in the modern world.

Why did the human species suddenly begin to do all these things? Was it because their brains, produced over eons by the ultimate Creative Power, had suddenly been altered by visiting extraterrestrials? And was their sudden knowledge of science, art and religion taught them by these same godlike extraterrestrials?

The common assumption of anthropologists and historians that we discovered and developed all these refinements in a mere 25,000 years, as a result of biological and cultural evolution, seems, to quote Darwin again, "absurd in the highest degree." Nothing in the fossil record, or our knowledge of developmental biology, suggests that natural evolution has ever produced such profound transformations in such a moment of time.

The conclusion is inescapable. We were fashioned in the image of godlike Celestials. Our incredible brains are not just the result of natural selection operating on chance variations. They required a deliberate and artificial improvement. The mechanisms postulated by biologists to explain our explosion of brain function are simply inadequate to account for the results.

Our achievements cry out for a better explanation. They tell us that we are heirs of the gods and that our minds and civilization are the result of their intervention. To see more clearly how this is so we will now give some final consideration to the unearthly traits we mentioned at the opening of this chapter. These traits, more than any others we have, show the nature of our minds and the extent to which their development has gone beyond the evolutionary needs of our ancestors.

Overendowment

One of the most firmly established principles of modern evolutionary biology is that natural selection cannot equip living creatures with traits they do not need or give them excessive amounts of those which are necessary. Natural selection works only with variations which occur spontaneously in the course of reproduction. It can preserve only those which are necessary for existence—and only in degrees or amounts which are useful for survival.

Overendowment cannot be produced by natural selection alone. If that were the factor that produced our 2-million-year leap from apelike to human intelligence it would have left us at the level of apes. For, for most of those 2 million years, we needed little more than the apes to survive. We lived in the open or in caves, ate raw foods and used only the crudest of tools.

Then, suddenly, we appeared on the pages of history 6,000 years ago in ancient Sumer. And when we appeared we already knew more than we need, even now, to survive in the twentieth century. In fact, it is not demonstrable, in many areas of knowledge, that we know more now than our ancestors knew then. By any reasonable critical standards their reflective thought, their literary expression, their political skill, their moral sensitivity and their spiritual aspirations were the equal of our own. Only in areas of technical and scientific accomplishment is there any real evidence of a superiority on our part.

How did such an unbelievable overendowment occur, and why? Some anthropologists, attempting to explain this anomaly, have suggested that natural selection somehow created a "reserve" of intelligence in stone-age man, beyond what was actually used. So Bjorn Kurten, of Helsinki University, says: "Why should we be able to grasp advanced mathematics and philosophy and enjoy intricate poetry and music—things that cannot possibly have played any part in the life of paleolithic man?" The answer, he says, is quite simple. It is that "untutored brains" use only a small part of their potential. So that paleolithic man could survive, natural selection had to "call forth a vastly greater unrealized capacity, which remains dormant in the savage but can be activated by suitable education."[5]

Unfortunately for Professor Kurten, this argument is simply not supported by the facts. Anthropology and archaeology show, beyond question, that early primitive man was able to grasp advanced mathematical relationships and to philosophize about the great perennial problems of the universe without a formal education. In the Valley of the Kings in Egypt, at Machu Picchu in Peru, at Stonehenge in England and at many other places throughout the world we have overwhelming proof of this. Similarly Paul Radin,[6] early in this century, showed that the myths of contemporary primitives come to grips with the great philosophical questions which preoccupy "educated" men. Clearly it does not require a "good education" to call forth these abilities in Homo sapiens, nor are they dormant without it.

Man's incredible overendowment of intellect, then, is not a reserve created by natural selection. Nor was its creation of civilization, a few thousand years ago, an ordinary historical evolution. The quality of the human mind, and its products, are without parallel in any other species on Earth.

The clearest proof of this lies in the group of intellectual capacities we have called the "unearthly traits"—philosophical reflection, religious aspiration, scientific curiosity and artistic creation and expression. Let us see how this is so.

THE UNEARTHLY TRAITS

It has often been pointed out that the more general forms of metaphysical speculation have little bearing on the conduct of life. Whether the world is ideal or material, machinelike or organismic, is not a matter about which we can do anything or which requires any sort of response. Yet we have always been compelled to puzzle about such questions. Why?

If we are the product of evolution, one of its strangest ironies is that it has endowed us with the capacity to criticize its handiwork. So Bertrand Russell observes, "A strange mystery it is that Nature, omnipotent but blind... has brought forth at last a child... gifted with sight, with knowledge of good and evil, with the capacity of judging all the works of his unthinking mother. In spite of death, the mark and seal of the parental control, man is yet free, during his brief years, to examine, to criticize, to know and in imagination to create. To him alone, in the world with which we are acquainted, this freedom belongs..."[7]

And ironic and mysterious it is if this strange endowment is the work of natural selection. But if it is a gift of the Celestials it is as inevitable as night and day. How could heirs of the gods show less than "divine discontent" and existential despair having their human lot? Could they show less than discontent with the souls of gods imprisoned in the bodies of beasts? Could they feel less than despair, knowing the ties of evolutionary kinship doom them to share, with the beasts of this earth, their dark instinctual urges and their mortal doom? With such a prospect it is small wonder that "*Homo philosophicus*" broods about the meaning of human existence and destiny. His unearthly capacity for philosophical reflection makes it inevitable that he "cherish, ere yet the blow falls the lofty thoughts that enoble his little day."[8]

Yet in spite of his existential tragedy man is also a child of
hope. And among his "lofty thoughts" one persists that is
peculiarly indicative of its givers. It is the curious mixture of
belief and feeling we call religious aspiration, and it is our only
hope of escape from our mortal prison.

It is strange that an endowment which seems to have no
earthly survival value should be our only hope of eternal survival—yet it is so. For religion, in one form or another, has always had, as its central theme, man's possibility of sharing
with the gods. We will defer until later any discussion of
whether all religions discern a common vital truth. But it is
clear, from the most casual inspection of the Bible, that its
central theme is our hope of sharing in the Celestials' secret
of eternal life. In Scripture after Scripture, throughout both the
Old and New Testaments, the hope and the promise of eternal life is repeated again and again. An unbiased study of the
Bible leaves no doubt that immortality is the Celestials' most
prized possession. The first glimpse we catch of them, in Genesis, reveals a tree of life in their midst. And the final, glorious
revelation we have of them, in Revelation, shows a holy city
come "down from God out of heaven" (Revelation 21:2), with
a "pure river of water of life . . . proceeding out of the throne
of God" and the tree of life growing on its banks (Revelation
22:1-2). Wherever Jehovah reveals himself he is always remind-
ing us that he is the "Alpha and Omega, the beginning and the
end, the first and the last" (Revelation 22:13)—who "liveth
for ever and ever" (Revelation 15:7). And the final promise
given in the Bible is the promise of life everlasting: "And the
Spirit and the bride say, Come. . . . And let him that is athirst
come. And whosoever will, let him take the water of life freely"
(Revelation 22:17).

Is this hope, man's oldest and fondest dream, the product
of natural selection? Or was it implanted by a Celestial race
who has every intention of fulfilling it in the future? No other
animal, not even man's closest primate relatives, has any conception of life everlasting or yearns for it. Zoologists and students of comparative psychology have never produced one
shred of evidence to support such an idea.

Humans alone, of all living creatures, aspire to the godlike
condition of immortality. We alone regulate our lives accord-

ing to its otherworldly promise of survival—even when it flies in the face of natural survival as it has for countless martyrs to faith. Is religious aspiration and yearning for immortality the product of nature, or is it a gift of the gods? Will they return to fulfill this aspiration? In a later chapter, we will examine the scientific facts and theories which support such a hope.

The most distinguishing characteristic of man, according to biologists and anthropologists, is his capacity for manipulating symbols with his extraordinary brain. This is why they have named him *Homo sapiens*.

No other animal on Earth has our peculiar ability to use mental representations as indicators of abstractions. As a result, no other animal has the capacity for abstract thought in any but the most rudimentary form.

When thought is tied to the concrete environment around us, it is limited to what is immediate and present. Foresight, planning, multistep problem-solving and creative thought such as theorizing, fantasy and aesthetic composition are all impossible. Humans alone, so far as we can tell, can react to inner images, rather than external stimuli, as symbols of complex relationships and long-range consequences. They alone can conceive of labels for classes of objects and experiences so that generalized thinking about relationships, rather than things, becomes possible.

It is these abilities which have earned us the description of "sapient." Even at their lowest levels they so far exceed what other animals can do that the difference becomes one of kind rather than degree. A rat, or a chimpanzee, can solve simple problems such as psychologists' mazes. But their problem-solving, when compared with that of a chess grandmaster or a theoretical physicist, differs as a horse and buggy does from a moon rocket.

When this ability is directed toward what Francis Bacon called "interrogating nature" it becomes science—the ability to construct abstract inner models, in terms of mathematics or logic, which mirror the structure and relationships of the universe.

Our ability to do this separates us from all other animals. Even more, however, we are separated from them by our desire to do it. Only we have this "disinterested curiosity." A cat or dog or ape will examine something if it shows promise of satisfying an immediate need. But only the sapient human will toil through years of patient research, follow endless blind leads and suffer ridicule, rejection and even privation in the search for objective truth.

This capacity for the disinterested pursuit of truth is one of our most godlike traits, for it elevates us above the merely animal business of surviving and making a "living." It enables us to discover our place in the universe and gives us a sense of identity. It helps us realize our oneness with all things and promotes that largeness of view which makes the immediate problems of life endurable.

And in their unending search for truth the great scientists of the past and present have helped us grasp the immensity of the universe and the intricate harmony of life. They have deepened our sense of kinship with all natural things and given us purpose and hope for the future.

In the infinite patience of the experimenter and the cosmic breadth of the theorizer, pure science represents us at our unearthly best. Only Celestial motivations could have driven Marie Curie to sort through tons upon tons of pitchblende, over thousands of experiments, during long years of privation, because prejudice and her sex barred her from a university position. When she at last glimpsed the faint smudge of radium, too slight even to weigh, glowing in the darkness of her homemade laboratory she regarded the years and sacrifices as completely rewarded. There was no way of knowing her discovery would have practical usefulness, but her Celestial aspiration for truth had been satisfied.

When visitors at the Princeton Institute for Advanced Study would ask Albert Einstein where his laboratory was he would tap his head, and when they inquired about his tools he would extend his pencil. His Celestial brain and pencil-wielding hand were all he needed to probe the depths of the universe as no man before him had done. The beauty and almost divine simplicity of the equation in which he expressed his insight brings it close to the mysterious symbols of the ancients which were believed to indicate the supreme reason underlying all things. To grasp that a simple combination of abstract symbols, $E = MC^2$, could express the ultimate interrelationships of space, time, energy and matter must surely be one of the most profoundly creative intellectual feats ever performed by the human mind.

Did Marie Curie and Albert Einstein inherit the inspirations that drove them to unique heights from millions of chance variations in subhuman ancestors? Could the gradual accumulation of skills permitting the survival of tree shrews and lemurs and apelike primates eventually add up to an ability to unlock the secrets of nuclear energy or to capture the universe in an equation? Could such incredible overendowments be generated by such simple mechanisms? Or were they outright gifts—matured on other worlds over the hundreds of millions, or billions, of years evolution has not had to produce them here?

Perhaps the sense in which we most mirror the gods, the sense in which we best share with them their godlike nature, is our ability to create. Like God the Creator, who called the worlds into existence, like the Lord God who called us into existence, we can call the creatures of our own Celestial mind into being and give them objective expression.

No primate, no ape—not even the chimpanzee—has this ability even in the most rudimentary degree. In humans it is overendowed beyond the widest conceivable limits of usefulness—far beyond. The mind of a Beethoven could conceive symphonies that rival the heavens in their complexity. Shakespeare created hundreds of humans, in his plays, as real as those we meet in daily life—more real, in a deeper sense, for they are quintessential; they embody in their single selves what is most typical of the whole range and diversity of mankind throughout human history. Michelangelo could recreate the creation in such staggering splendor that throughout the ages it remains the event, itself—the infinite captured in finite paint and mortar on the vault of the Sistine Chapel.

Is this strange gift a product of natural selection acquired because of its survival value? Can any accumulation of chance variations over any number of generations for any conceivable practical reason explain the bursting of genius in the mind of a Beethoven, or a Shakespeare, or a Michelangelo? Or is it a blaze of Celestial fire? Do humans create and express their artistic dreams because, like God, they possess a divine creative nature? Do humans compose, paint, sculpt, declaim and poeticize because "The Spirit itself beareth witness with our Spirit, that we are the children of God. And if children, then heirs; heirs of God" (Romans 8:16–17)?

We believe the answer is evident. Yes, man is a Celestial artifact housed in a natural body—the product of a Celestial experiment. As Shakespeare has Hamlet say: "What a piece of work is a man! How noble in reason! How infinite in faculty! In form and moving how express and admirable! In action how like an angel! In apprehension how like a God! The beauty of the world! The paragon of animals!"

If this is so, however, one important question remains. Apart from the Bible, is there any proof that our incredible overendowments of mind and unearthly gifts of spirit are the work of an experimental creation?

We have already referred to the fossil record. Scientists who study this record tell us it documents the evolution of man by gradual and progressive stages to his present state. Is there any point in this record, any discontinuity or gap, where the Celestials could have made their experimental modification in a way that is supported by the fossil evidence? We will consider this important question last.

THE FOSSIL RECORD AND EXPERIMENTAL MAN

The field of paleoanthropology is concerned with the bones, their imprints in stone and the various cultural relics of ancient man. It has been a field of endless controversy and debate since the time of Darwin. From the beginning, imposing theories have rested on the minimum of hard evidence—a tooth, a jaw fragment, a piece of skull or a bit of chipped or flaked stone. Gradually, over the decades of this century, more refined methods of investigation have been brought to bear on the products of the pick and shovel. These include delicate instruments for reassembling bone fragments, casts and models, biochemical analyses, radioactive carbon and potassium-argon dating and computer analyses based on refined measurements. Above all, the fossil finds have continued to pour in from all over the world. The record now contains many fairly complete skulls, relatively intact skeletons and tools of all sorts—cutters, choppers, scrapers and awls.

At the same time, geologists, paleontologists and other specialists have been filling in our knowledge of the early environments in which humans developed—the climate changes, the ice ages, the drift of continents and the rise and fall of land masses.

And out of all this data an increasingly clearer picture of human evolution has been emerging. Yet curious gaps remain. We have never identified our immediate ancestor, though he is much closer, in time, than many others we have found. As a result, we are not sure where modern humans first arose or how they spread throughout the world. Nor have we explained the development of races.

THE HUMAN FAMILY TREE

Yet in spite of this the main outlines of our family tree are clear. As it has been reconstructed by anthropologists it can be quickly summarized. A little over 2 million years ago our first clearly human ancestor, *Homo habilis* ("handy man"), appeared—so called because of his flaking and use of stone tools. He apparently hunted, stood erect and had a brain capacity of around 800 cubic centimeters. Beyond this, little more is known about his way of life. His remains have been investigated, over the last two decades, by the famous Leakey family in Kenya, Africa.

About a million years ago his descendant, *Homo erectus*, took the next step forward in human evolution. Around 5 feet in height, this race had a truly erect posture and used a wider range of tools. In their most advanced form their braincase averaged about 1,100 cubic centimeters. They were originally found in Java and eventually spread to most of the tropical Old World.

Then, around 500,000 years ago, a new type of human destined to become sapient appeared on the scene—the Neanderthal race. At first they differed little from *Homo erectus*, but as millennia passed their braincase expanded to over 1,400 cubic centimeters (larger than our own average). Unlike modern humans they were long-headed, barrel-chested and powerful individuals with curved arm and leg bones in their later sapient form. They used a rich assortment of tools, lived in the open or caves and buried their dead in a way which suggests the beginnings of religious belief.

Around 250,000 years ago another sapient human also appeared on the scene. This race was also large-brained (around 1,300–1,400 cubic centimeters) but actually predated the sapient Neanderthals. Their remains were first found in the riverbed of the Thames, in England, and at Fontechevade, in France. Recent computer analysis of the skull taken from the Thames (called "Swanscombe man") shows that its owner was undoubtedly an early Homo sapiens.[9] Bjorn Kurten believes this race may have been ancestors of both sapient Neanderthals and modern mankind.[10]

However that may be, they spread throughout much of Europe, for similar remains have been found at Steinheim, Germany, and Vertesszolos, Hungary. Though these finds are fragmentary, they reveal an individual that lacked the exaggerated rear brain of sapient Neanderthal and had a high, well-rounded brow like our own.

With these finds the record of a non-Neanderthal Homo sapiens is interrupted until about 40,000 years ago, when a very similar type reappears which anthropologists variously call "Cro-Magnon man," Homo sapiens sapiens or "modern man." Taller than the Neanderthals, this race was, and is, also more slender and graceful. Their high, well-rounded forehead surmounts a braincase that averages around 1,250–1,350 cubic centimeters. From the first they used an extremely wide range of tools, buried their dead and left elaborate cave art. They rapidly carried toolmaking far beyond the late Neanderthal stage and, at the end of the stone age, suddenly developed into communal dwellers.

Within the next 5,000 years they created villages, domesticated plants and animals, and developed metallurgy and pottery. Around 4000 B.C. they produced, at the eastern end of the Fertile Crescent, a full-blown urban civilization with the flowering of all the arts and sciences. This is the account present-day social scientists and historians give of our origins.

ENTER THE CELESTIALS

This brings us back to our original question. Is there any point in this record, any discontinuity or gap, where the Celestials could have made their experimental modification? Even such a brief review reveals one startling discontinuity, or gap. It is the strange appearance, disappearance and reappearance of the non-Neanderthal *Homo sapiens*. Well-known students of human evolution and the fossil record have commented on this puzzling phenomenon. So Theodosius Dobzhansky remarks: "... before Europe was inhabited by Neanderthaleans there apparently existed a race of men more like ourselves than the Neanderthaleans were, and the Neanderthaleans ended by being replaced, *rather abruptly* [italics added], by a race of *Homo sapiens* whose bones were much like our own. So it looks as if *Homo sapiens* appeared, disappeared and reappeared again."[11] Could the conjurers behind this "abrupt" reappearance have been a race of extraterrestrials? Did they refashion this moribund race into a superior type that quickly spread throughout the world and displaced the Neanderthals who had previously bested them?

As we saw in our brief review of human evolution, early *Homo sapiens* spread as far east as Vertesszolos, Hungary. In fact, the specimen found there had the largest brain of the lot —about 1,400 cubic centimeters.

It is a short distance from Vertesszolos to the eastern end of the Fertile Crescent. A migration moving in that direction could well have carried a small population of this race to the Garden of Eden site. And though they declined, as sapient Neanderthal rose to dominance, representatives would, in all probability, still have been there when the Celestials arrived. These large-brained survivors would have been logical candidates for the Celestials' genetic experiment. Is there any scientific evidence that our undiscovered immediate ancestor arose from such a type or in the area we have identified as the Garden of Eden site?

THE MT. CARMEL FINDS

The answer to this question may lie in one more set of fossil clues—probably the most ambiguous ever uncovered. They were found between 1929 and 1934 near Haifa at Mt. Carmel—the general area the Bible assigns to Eden itself. They consisted of two sets of fossils in two caves, Tabun and Skhul. The older set, at Tabun, were Neanderthal and were dated at around 41,000 to 42,000 B.C. The later set, at Skhul, showed a curious mixture of Cro-Magnon and Neanderthal features. This is puzzling, since the Neanderthal type had already disappeared from this area by 35,000 B.C.—the date assigned to these fossils.

The "Ancient Modern"

While various theories were offered to account for the problems these fossils presented, one explanation is of special interest to us here. It proposed that the later Skhul fossils represented descendants of the Tabun Neanderthals—descendants produced by interbreeding with an unknown ancestor of Cro-Magnon man. According to the theory, this ancestor had "evolved" to the east and then migrated to Mount Carmel. Speaking of this, C. L. Brace and Ashley Montagu wrote of a "solution to the puzzle" which assumed the existence of an "ancient modern" who arose "farther east perhaps?"[12]

If this "solution of the puzzle" is the correct one, the "ancient modern" could be the Lord's experimental creation, who migrated from his point of origin "farther east"—the Garden of Eden site. Though the Bible makes no mention of such a migration it is interesting that one of the apocryphal books, *The First Book of Adam and Eve*, tells how, after their expulsion from the Garden, Adam and Eve went to dwell in a "Cave of Treasures" on the western border of the Garden. Could this "Cave of Treasures" have been one of those located on Mt. Carmel such as Tabun or Skhul?

Whatever the answer to this question the ideas suggested by the Mt. Carmel findings are further supported by the Bible itself. To appreciate the full significance of this we must now turn, once again, to the Genesis account. This provides another clue which may link the Lord's experimental creation, Brace and Montagu's "ancient modern" and the Mt. Carmel finds.

God's Sons and Men's Daughters

We have earlier seen how, soon after the Lord's experimental creation of Adam and Eve, their son, Cain, went into the land of Nod and "knew his wife." Could this have been the first instance of the sort of interbreeding C. L. Brace and

Ashley Montagu suggest might have occurred between an "ancient modern" and less advanced races around him?

The idea becomes more significant when we read a little past the Cain story in Genesis and find that "...it came to pass, when men began to multiply on the face of the earth, and daughters were born unto them, That the sons of God saw the daughters of men that they were fair; and they took them wives of all which they chose" (Genesis 6:1–2).

Some commentators have suggested these "sons of God" were angels who were lured into unions with the mortal "daughters of men"—in spite of Jesus' assurance that angels "neither marry, nor are given in marriage" (Matthew 22:30). Others have proposed that the "sons of God" were descendants of righteous Seth and the "daughters of men" the offspring of murderous Cain. Yet they fail to explain how righteousness and ungodliness are inheritable or why God would make such a prejudicial distinction among Adam's innocent grandchildren.

Our space age interpretation offers a better explanation of this most curious passage. The "sons of God" were the descendants of the Lord's experimental creation, and the "daughters of men" were evolved *Homo sapiens* around them.

If this is so, then Brace and Montagu's "ancient modern" was, in all likelihood, the Lord's experimental creation. And the Skhul fossils are those of his descendants, who represent crossings between "God's sons" and the "daughters of men."

WHEN DID THE CELESTIALS' EXPERIMENT OCCUR?

On this assumption we can pinpoint the time of the Celestials' creation rather closely. It could not have occurred after 35,000 B.C., since "ancient moderns" had already ancestored the Skhul descendants.

Allowing them time to migrate from the eastern end of the Fertile Crescent, where they were created, to Mt. Carmel, we can set a somewhat earlier date for their creation. Yet it would not have been long, for their descendants replaced the Neanderthal race only after it was in a decline. Now this occurred around 40,000 B.C. The experimental creation would, therefore, probably have occurred a little while before—long enough to allow the "ancient moderns" to "multiply," to outgrow their subsistence and to move on to Mt. Carmel. How long was this? We have no way of knowing exactly. But their success in competing against Neanderthaleans suggests a very late date in the period of Neanderthal decline—probably a few thousand years at most. Weighing all these considerations, a date between 50,000 and 40,000 b.c. seems realistic.

If anthropologists ever find the remains of the "ancient modern," conjecture will be at an end. Unfortunately this is unlikely because of what anthropologists call the "Sewell-Wright effect." The causes of fossilization are complicated and occur rarely. As a result, small populations seldom leave fossils and the "ancient moderns" were too quickly hybridized to ever have become numerous. Their hybrid descendants, however, left their mark on the fossil record throughout the earth, for they are ourselves—Homo sapiens sapiens!

The Mysteries of Race

One of the major problems in current anthropological investigation is the mystery of race. If Homo sapiens sapiens emerged only 30,000 to 40,000 years ago, how has there been time for them to differentiate into the races one finds today? Our space age view of modern man, as a hybrid, offers a reasonable explanation for this mystery.

Since the "daughters of men" had an evolutionary descent stretching back over two, or more, millions of years, there was ample time to develop racial differences. During the time when the small population of "God's sons" interbred with these "daughters of men" they would quickly have absorbed their racial differences as they spread throughout the earth.

Is there any evidence that racial differences did not arise in Homo sapiens sapiens, but already preexisted in his evolutionary ancestors? The answer is given by Carleton Coon. Speaking of Choukoutien man (an early Homo erectus found in China and dating from 360,000 years ago) he says, "Although definitely Homo erectus they differ from the Javenese specimens racially. Instead of sloping gradually their foreheads stand out sharply from their eyebrow ridges. These persons had cheekbones and jaws which protruded forward . . . their teeth were . . . shaped like shovels. These peculiarities are still seen in mongoloid teeth from China to Cape Horn."[13]

The evidence cited by Carleton Coon, then, makes it clear that races already existed among early humans who were ancestral to *Homo sapiens sapiens*. In them they had the hundreds of thousands of years necessary for natural selection and interbreeding to do their work. When created humans interbred with their sapient descendants they quickly acquired these genetic differences they had not had time to produce on their own.

The Bible seems to offer a confirmation of this theory of racial origins in the story of races beginning with Noah's sons, Shem, Ham and Japeth (Genesis 10). Taken literally, the idea of a man having sons of three different races seems absurd. But, if these sons stand for whole populations, then the idea that they became racially differentiated as they migrated to different locations and interbred with various races of "daughters of men" makes good sense.

AN OVERVIEW

It appears, then, that the present interpretation of the origin of man is consistent with anthropological facts. It further suggests hypotheses which could, if verified, clear up present gaps and mysteries surrounding man's beginnings.

In concluding our examination of the experimental creation, it may help to summarize the agreements between the Bible's account and what science has discovered in the fossil record. These agreements give strong support to our space age interpretation of the Genesis story of man's creation.

1. The Bible says man was "created" to the east of Jerusalem. The Mt. Carmel finds suggest that an "ancient modern" who ancestored us did indeed come from "east" of Jerusalem.
2. The Bible says God created man in his own "image." If modern man reveals that image it is so unlike most of his fossil ancestors as to defy a natural selective explanation. Yet genetic engineering could bridge the gap—if "creation" means modifying something like Swanscombe-Steinheim-Vertesszolos man.
3. The discovery of this type of man, in Hungary, makes it likely that a descendant may have occupied the eastern end of the Fertile Crescent 40,000 to 50,000 years ago. The Bible says the

Celestials created "man" here, and anthropologists have found *Homo sapiens sapiens* fossils nearby that date just after this period.

4. The findings at Skhul Cave suggest the "unknown" ancestor of modern man interbred with Neanderthaloids. The Bible says the "sons of God" took wives from the "daughters of men" after they became numerous.

5. Our interpretation of the Genesis account suggests an explanation of the origin of races which is a problem for more conventional theories.

Our space age interpretation of man's "creation" seems, then, to reconcile the biblical and scientific accounts. In addition, it suggests theories which could fill gaps and clear up puzzles in our present scientific knowledge. Only further fossil finds can establish or refute these theories.

We will now turn away from the scientific record and take up a question which is primarily moral and theological: How did man lose his created estate? Why was he expelled from the Garden? How did the experiment go wrong?

CHAPTER VIII

THE EXPERIMENT FAILS

And when the woman saw that the tree was good for food, and that it was pleasant to the eyes, and a tree to be desired to make one wise, she took of the fruit thereof, and did eat, and gave also unto her husband with her; and he did eat.

—Genesis 3:6

THE "ORIGINAL SIN"

In the grammar schools of colonial New England the Puritans taught their children to read from Bible-story readers. Infants learning the ABCs were greeted with the announcement, "A is for Adam; in Adam's fall we sinned, all."

The English poet Milton composed what may be the greatest literary epic of our language, *Paradise Lost*. Though his imagery and conception were infinitely more elevated than the Puritans' Bible readers, the message is the same.

She gave him of that fair enticing fruit
With liberal hand. He scrupled not to eat,
Against his better knowledge, not deceived,
But fondly overcome with female charm.
Earth trembled from her entrails, as again
In pangs, and Nature gave a second groan;
Sky loured, and, muttering thunder, some sad drops
Wept at completing of the mortal Sin
Original ... [1]

Since its composition Genesis has puzzled thoughtful readers with its telling of this immortal legend. Is it fact or fiction? It has been compared with the Prometheus myth of the Greeks—Titan stealing celestial fire from the gods, incurring their wrath and being chained to a rock eternally with a vulture tearing his liver for punishment.

What do such stories mean? Is the sapient human's wisdom its own punishment, because it enables him, alone of all the beasts, to realize his end is death? Or does the Adam and Eve story have some more factual basis? Did our ancestors commit some actual folly which demoted them, and us, from a higher state of existence? If so, what was it? Was it literally eating an apple? The Bible makes no mention of apples—it only mentions a "fruit." Was the "forbidden fruit" symbolic of some other act? Was it, as Milton thought, sexual intercourse? Did the Lord God have some other plan for reproduction in mind for humans which man upset by his lustful transgression? Could this have been the original sin?

Whatever the "original sin" was, theologians and scholars have been even more puzzled by its relation to us—Adam's and Eve's descendants. The Bible seems to teach the "doctrine of original sin"—the idea, so quaintly put forth by the Puritans, that "in Adam's fall we sinned, all." But how could we be responsible for what Adam and Eve did even if the story is literally true? Yet the Bible does seem to say we are. So the Apostle Paul observes, "Wherefore, as by one man sin entered into the world, and death by sin; and so death passed upon all men ... by one man's disobedience many were made sinners ..." (Romans 5:12, 19).

How could an advanced civilization of Celestials with "lofty moral purposes" reason in this way? Probably no doctrine in the history of Christianity has caused more revulsion among morally sensitive men and women. How could a just God condemn billions of blameless humans to death for the transgression of an ancestor whom they never knew?

A MORAL RIDDLE AND A POSSIBLE SOLUTION

This is the great moral riddle which the story of man's fall poses. It has no answer in terms of enlightened morality and justice. And according to our method this suggests it may be in need of reinterpretation. Isn't it possible the whole Adam and Eve story has been misunderstood by both theologians and mythologists? May there not be another interpretation of it which makes sense and does not outrage our notions of morality and justice?

In this chapter we shall try to discover what the "original

sin" was by analyzing the story in the light of modern thinking about genetics and psychology. Let's start by reexamining the story itself. The first thing to notice is that though Adam and Eve were denied the tree of "knowledge of good and evil" they were denied no other. Presumably they ate from the "tree of life" and were granted immortality. Here are the Scriptures which make this clear.

Early in Genesis we read that "the Lord God planted a garden eastward in Eden" and out of the ground made "to grow every tree that is pleasant to the sight, and good for food; the tree of life also in the midst of the garden, and the tree of knowledge of good and evil" (Genesis 2:8–9). Next, we find the "Lord God commanded the man, saying, Of every tree of the garden thou mayest freely eat: But of the tree of the knowledge of good and evil, thou shalt not eat of it: for in the day that thou eatest thereof thou shalt surely die" (Genesis 2:16–17). Later the "serpent" tells Eve that "God doth know that in the day ye eat thereof [of the tree of knowledge of good and evil], then your eyes shall be opened, and ye shall be as gods, knowing good and evil" (Genesis 3:5). When God discovers they have succumbed to the "serpent's" temptation he counsels with the other Celestials, saying, "Behold, the man is become as one of us, to know good and evil: and now, lest he put forth his hand, and take also of the tree of life, and eat, and live forever..." (Genesis 3:22).

Evidently Adam and Eve "ate" of the "tree of life" from the beginning and shared in the immortality of the Celestials. In "eating" of the "tree of knowledge of good and evil" they did something which destroyed this immortality and gave them another godlike attribute in its place—an attribute the Lord felt they were not ready to receive. To prevent its misuse he barred them from further eating of the "tree of life" so that they could not restore immortality and misuse the godlike power they had stolen.

If this is so, it follows that, while the "original sin" was disobedience to the Lord God's command, the specific act of disobedience involved something more. Its "sinfulness" lay not just in its opposition to the Lord's will but in something it did to Adam and Eve—something which made them and their heirs forever after "sinful" and caused all their descendants to inherit death. What this actually was we will speculate on shortly. In the meantime the important point to make here is that the act—described as "eating" forbidden fruit—resulted in Adam's and Eve's being able, for the first time, to know "good" and "evil."

The Hebrew word used here for "know" is a derivative of *da'ath*, which has the meanings of "cunningly" or "wittingly." Unlike the primary root *yada*, "know," from which it comes, it narrows the meaning to imply purpose. It is one thing to know, but quite a different thing to use knowledge purposefully ("cunningly" or "wittingly") to achieve moral results.

What the "forbidden fruit" gave Adam and Eve, then, was not a mere ability to distinguish between "good" and "evil," as traditional Bible scholars have thought. It was, rather, the power to regulate their conduct according to the knowledge that they already had (they knew they were not to eat of the forbidden tree). What they acquired, in short, was not moral knowledge but moral responsibility—the ability to choose between good and evil.

MORAL RESPONSIBILITY

Up until this time they had been like the evolved animals from which they came. Like our lower animals, their large-brained, earthly ancestor was governed by his animal instincts and conditioning. There is no evidence he regulated his behavior by abstract notions of "right" and "wrong."

The ability to do so is peculiar to modern man and is one more unearthly trait which proves his Celestial origin. For moral responsibility has no survival value. Since it allows us to choose our responses freely, according to abstract notions of right and wrong, it can lead us to go against survival as readily as with it. In fact, moral values often require self-denial and may dictate courses which jeopardize survival.

The Genesis account makes it clear that moral responsibility was evidently a trait which was not included in Adam's and Eve's original equipment. The Lord intended to add it later—after they had been trained to understand the values he wished them to follow. He had created them, like animals or infants, so that they would follow the strongest influence. They had no real ability to choose.

And to protect the experiment he had placed them in a controlled environment where they would receive only the right sort of influences—his and those of his trusted director. We can understand the implications of the situation better by considering how human trainers teach animals. They train them to do "right" by rewarding good behavior and punishing bad. But if they are humane they do not hold them morally responsible for their actions. When they punish them it is because they are trying to change their behavior—not because they are "guilty" of anything. They can have no guilt, since they have no self-control. They merely respond to the strongest influence.

In the same way Adam and Eve were being conditioned to do what was right. Since they had inherited a "bestial" nature from their evolutionary forebears it was necessary to counterbalance it by training them to live according to higher ideals. Since character cannot be inherited it could not be included in their original DNA blueprint. It had to be taught.

But until they had learned it there was danger in allowing them moral choice. They might choose the wrong course and ruin the experiment. If they were to be helpers and eventual citizens they must develop as virtuous beings who were good from choice—not as programmed robots like the cherubim or seraphim. Keeping these distinctions in mind, we are now ready to reinterpret the "original sin" and its consequences.

The "Original Sin"

To do this we must start with the idea that Adam and Eve were in an animal, or childlike, state of innocence before the fall. If we accept this seriously it poses a strange paradox. Since they were "innocent" as infants and animals are—since they could not use "knowledge of good and evil" in regulating their behavior—then they could not "sin" in the moral sense of that term. They were not morally responsible.

Just as animals and infants are not morally responsible for their behavior, so the Lord could not hold Adam and Eve morally responsible for "eating the fruit." They simply yielded to the strongest pressure—Eve to the persuasiveness of the "serpent" and Adam to Eve's example. At the moment these were more powerful influences on their behavior than the fear of punishment by the Lord.

They could only "sin" in the literal and moral sense after they had "eaten" the fruit and acquired moral responsibility. The "eating," itself, was not a morally responsible act. To hold them guilty of a moral offense would be applying what, in law, is called an "ex post facto" judgment—a judgment which could fairly be made only after the fact to which it is applied.

Since this is true, our earlier suggestion that their "sin" and "guilt" were figurative, rather than literal, has to be correct. No other interpretation could vindicate the Lord God of a double injustice—holding them responsible when they were not and holding us responsible for what they did.

They "sinned" in the sense of doing wrong—disobeying a command of their parent. But it was a "sin" for which they were not morally responsible. It was like the "sin" of a naughty infant or a mischievous animal, except that they were adults, and the consequences of their "sin" were enormous. In this respect it was more like an act of murder committed by an idiot. They murdered themselves and us, their descendants, through their lack of moral restraint. The "original sin," then, was not a literal moral lapse. It was, rather, something which gave them, and us, a "sinful" nature—one capable of sinning. And, as Milton put it, it was a "mortal" sin, for it undid their immortality and passed death on to us, their descendants. In this way we literally inherited their figurative guilt and punishment—death.

THE "FATAL APPLE"

Now let's see if we can discover what act they could have performed to invite these dreadful consequences. What did they really do in "eating forbidden fruit" and what were the circumstances surrounding their folly? As in so many passages that refer to the Celestials, it would not have been possible to understand this part of the story before the twentieth century. Only since the development of molecular biology have we gained some insight into the processes by which living creatures develop the structures and traits that make up their natures. The writer of Genesis 3, knowing nothing of this, could only describe Adam's and Eve's fatal misdeed as "eating a fruit."

We know now that to acquire a new trait, such as the ability to exercise choice, we must undergo two specialized developments. First there would have to be a suitable specialization of the cerebral cortex itself—the seat of abstract thought. This would be necessary so that the brain could store memories of rewards and punishments, abstract what these have in common and label their relationships by the terms "right" and "wrong." As we saw in the last chapter, this development had already taken place in the evolution of Adam's and Eve's large-brained ancestors.

But the capacity to use these conceptions to regulate behavior would require a further development having to do with voluntary action. This can perhaps be understood better by considering the case of humans who presently fail to exhibit this further development. Apparently this second specialization which Adam and Eve underwent by "eating forbidden fruit" fails to take place in them. Psychologists and psychiatrists in the early part of this century used to refer to such people as "moral imbeciles." Later they were called "psychopaths" or "sociopaths." Today we often use the phrase "character disorder" or "disorder of impulse." But whatever name is used the nature of their defect is clear and enables us to understand, by negative example, what it was that Adam and Eve acquired in committing the "original sin."

Like Adam and Eve before the fall, and unlike normal human adults, they cannot choose to ignore impulse and self-gratification in favor of higher moral values or long-range interests. They lack the capacity for moral responsibility.

This brings us to the key question. What could Adam and Eve have "eaten" that would stimulate this development in their brains? The field of microbiology gives a possible answer. It lies in the fact that we constantly remanufacture our own bodies according to instructions which are built into the heart of every cell. As our body cells die they replace themselves by means of these instructions—a process called "protein synthesis." This is a natural, built-in sort of replication not unlike the artificial process the Celestials used to create mankind. By means of it we restore our bodies and maintain health and life until aging and death overtake us.

During the last twenty-five years, biologists have been experimenting with improving this natural replicating process. Some studies are concerned with keeping it perfect indefinitely —without the rejuvenation losing effectiveness. These could eventually lead to control of aging and even immortality.

Others have focused on artificially changing the instructions so that the cell does not manufacture a duplicate but makes an "improved" version of the original. This is a start toward genetic engineering. Ultimately, it could lead to feeding an animal or plant specific nucleic acids and producing new traits at will—traits such as moral responsibility. Our own biologists have already taken tentative steps in this direction in what is called "recombinant DNA" research.

This "doctoring" of the code card is similar to what the Lord must have done when he created Adam, except that to produce a whole man outright, he would have needed to use an artificial replicator (such as Arthur Clarke describes).

Once man was created and the model had been tested, however, a desirable trait could be added by simply having him "eat" a prepared "fruit." The substance would be "organ specific" and would replace the part of his instructions which controlled the specialized area responsible for the trait desired.

The "fatal apple," then, was probably a preparation of nucleic acids which stimulated Adam's and Eve's brains to develop moral responsibility. The "tree of knowledge of good and evil" from which it came was most likely a model of the part of the DNA helix which controls the center for moral choice in the human cortex. It would have been similar to the plastic and metal models made by Watson and Crick during their experiments. It was probably in the Celestials' laboratory, in the center of the Garden, and had detachable parts which could be rearranged to represent various codings they considered in engineering this change in man's mental function. In like fashion, the "tree of life" was probably a model of amino-acid combinations which could neutralize the aging genes gerontologists believe exist in all living things, reverse environmentally caused aging and ensure immortality. Biologists have recently begun experimenting with such "nucleic acid therapy" and have used it to extend significantly the life span of lower animals.[2]

Yet, if the Celestials understood genetic engineering and had controlled their Garden experiment as carefully as the Bible says, how did it go wrong?

THE UNFORESEEABLE

The failure of the Garden of Eden experiment seems improbable. If the Celestials were hundreds of thousands, or millions, of years in our technological future, if they had mastered the secret of eternal life, if they created modern man, then how could they have miscalculated his behavior so badly? Why would the Lord have put the "tree of knowledge of good and evil" where Adam and Eve could reach it if he did not wish them to eat from it? Being their Creator, could he have overestimated their ability to resist its temptation?

Many of these problems which obscure the Adam and Eve story become clear when it is reinterpreted in the way we have suggested. The Lord did not miscalculate Adam's and Eve's behavior, nor did he make a mistake in allowing them access to the "tree of knowledge of good and evil." The "mistake," which led to the failure of the experiment, occurred at a much higher level and was made long before Adam and Eve. It was in predicting the behavior of his favorite archangel, Lucifer (or Satan), the director of the experiment. And such a prediction would not have been possible—even for the Lord. The Celestials are free moral agents. Like their image reflector, man, they have the capacity for moral choice. Long before the Garden of Eden experiment, on another world, they had removed the influences from their society which cause humans to misuse their power of moral choice. Theirs was a utopian society without injustice or evil.

It would be natural for the Lord to believe that any member of the Celestial society was beyond doing evil. It had probably been millions of years since a single evil or unjust act had occurred in their civilization. How could the Lord anticipate that it would suddenly appear in his right-hand

Celestial, Lucifer—the one he had trusted with the direction of this vital experiment?

And, indeed, there is no obvious answer. The "problem of evil" (as traditional theology calls it) has never been satisfactorily explained. According to Ezekiel, Lucifer was regarded by the Lord as his created masterpiece. Speaking of him the Lord says, "Behold, thou art wiser than Daniel; there is no secret that they can hide from thee... Thou wast perfect in thy ways from the day that thou wast created, till iniquity was found in thee.... Thine heart was lifted up because of thy beauty, thou hast corrupted thy wisdom by reason of thy brightness..." (Ezekiel 28:3, 15, 17).

The medieval picture of Satan as the Devil—complete with horns, cloven hoofs and pitchfork tail—is obviously not a copy of the portrait given here. This medieval view is the result of later pagan influences that crept into Christianity. The Lucifer (and Satan) of the Bible is a highest-level Celestial, next to the Lord in his intelligence and wisdom, gifted with an exquisite musical voice, beautiful of form; the Lord's favorite archangel—an "angel of light" (II Corinthians 11:14). Why, then, was there evil in his nature?

The only possible answer seems to lie in the nature of moral freedom—the ability to choose between good and evil. It is a fact that we do have the choice between good and evil. The Bible tells us we mirror the Celestials in this respect.

Like us they are free to do either right or wrong. But social planning and moral discipline have eradicated the tendency to do wrong. Where, then, did this wrong come from? How could evil enter their carefully controlled world or the Lord's perfect assistant? The answer is that evil was never absent from their world or ours. It was simply invariably rejected. Understanding the failure of the experiment starts with recognizing that good and evil are ultimate aspects of all reality. Like matter and energy, or gravitation and light, they are, as scientists say, ultimate "data."

All explanations must start with good and evil as given facts in the world—and with the Celestials' ability, and ours, to choose between them. If theories we adopt seem to make them problematic, then it is the theories that are at fault, not the given facts. So it is with the "problem of evil."

The "Problem of Evil"

The fact that evil is a problem cannot be solved by denying it. It is as evident as any other data of experience, such as sights, sounds, smells and tastes which we call "facts." It is therefore real. It becomes a problem, in traditional theology, only because its existence seems inconsistent with the perfection of God. If God is all-knowing, he is aware of evil. If he is all-good, he must abhor it. And if he is all-powerful, he can get rid of it. Why doesn't he, then?

The solution to this problem is provided by our space age distinction between "God" the Lord of the Celestials and "God" the ultimate Creative Power. If by "God" we mean the Lord of the Celestials (and in the Garden story we do), then he is not the infinitely perfect being of medieval theology. He is vastly superior to us but he too "is flesh" and is fallible. He could create a being such as Lucifer, whose conduct he might be unable to predict. It seemed that the Garden experiment was foolproof, but it was not.

"The Best-Laid Plans"

Adam and Eve were created, childlike, so that they followed the strongest influence. The Lord had isolated them in the Garden so that they were removed from every evil influence in the strange new world from which their animal ancestors came. They inherited a "carnal" (or bestial) nature from them, but they had godlike minds capable of controlling it once they had received the capacity of moral choice. This the Lord intended to give them as soon as they were "trained" by him to know the right choices.

As future members of the Celestials' society he wanted them to live morally and justly from choice—not just as programmed robots. Good conduct which is forced has no virtue—and he and the Celestials could welcome only virtuous humans as fellow citizens and equals. The situation is similar to a powerful king, who can command his beautiful subject to submit to his embraces but wants her to love him from choice. Her love means nothing unless it is freely given. So he courts her patiently, trying to win by love, rather than taking it by force.

Perhaps this is why, throughout the Bible, the righteous humans who will eventually be welcomed into the Celestials' society are compared to a bride, and the Lord to the bridegroom. So Isaiah says, ". . . as the bridegroom rejoiceth over the bride, so shall thy God rejoice over thee" (Isaiah 62:5).

The final control was set by the Lord in putting Lucifer, his trusted aide, in charge. He would see that nothing went wrong with the plan for creating a race of intelligent and moral beings who could assist in taming the new world. Afterward they could be welcomed as heirs and fellow citizens.

The Lord could have created more angels for the job as he had created Lucifer and others, perhaps. Replication or cloning would have provided Celestials in any numbers he desired. But the idea of making fellow citizens out of the most superior natives of the new world seemed more appropriate. The motive again was not unlike that of human colonizers who employ or marry residents of the areas they colonize. Adaptation to a new environment is hastened by using the adaptations already present among its natives.

And the only way humans could be trained to prize the good was to give them some opportunity to reject the bad—even though, at first, it might not be a real choice. In the same way, earthly parents train children, even before they have developed moral responsibility, by conditioning them to do what is "good" and avoid what is "naughty." The "That's a good boy (or girl)" and the "No, no!" (with a slap of the greedy hand reaching to touch) can teach the child "moral" values even before he has the actual power to choose them.

So the Lord had set a moral value, obedience to proper authority, as a training feature in the experiment—even before Adam and Eve could really choose. Like earthly parents, he had said, "Don't touch—don't eat," with the threat of death. He could have made the tree of knowledge of good and evil inaccessible, but in a moral vacuum his creations would have had no opportunity to learn the value of obedience before they were given the power to choose or reject it.

As the experiment was set up their obedience seemed guaranteed. All influences worked to ensure it. As an added precaution, however, the Lord inserted an additional control—he had added a "self-destruct" feature to the experiment. As our own earthly scientists build a self-destruction feature for rockets that abort launching, so he had built the possibility of death into this experiment. If they "ate of the tree," in spite of his command (and their bestial heritage did perhaps leave some uncertainty), then their immortality would be canceled out. The Celestials could not permit a race of immortals, prone to evil, to share their world with them. If the "fruit" was "eaten" before the Lord had removed this feature, humans would lose immortality by reacquiring "aging genes" which had been added to the mix. With these, and their exclusion from the tree of life, an experimental failure could be humanely dealt with without endangering Celestial society. Without the tree of life the remodeled humans would quickly revert to the mortal state of animal existence from which the Lord had taken them.

"Thou Shalt Not Surely Die"

But in spite of all these controls, in spite of the Lord's warning Adam and Eve about the self-destruct feature, in spite of the trusted leadership of Lucifer, in spite of the Lord's indulgence and parental guidance, the unforseeable happened. Lucifer, the created masterwork, had been given too much. "Thine heart was lifted up because of thy beauty, thou hast corrupted thy wisdom by reason of thy brightness" was the Lord's postmortem judgment on Satan's defection. Pride, a virtue in moderation, had become a vice when inflated to excess in a being capable of freely making a wrong choice. Satan decided he was the Lord's equal—no, his superior. He was more worthy of the position of leadership.

He would first subvert the weakest link in the Lord's plan. Adam and Eve, the childlike experimental hybrids incapable of moral choice, would yield to the most immediate and powerful influence. He would use all of his brilliance, his charm, his charisma, to dazzle Eve. She, in turn, would subvert Adam. In the first domestic environment her attention had been occupied with matters other than the technical details of the DNA mix. She would be easier to convince that the Lord's caution was groundless. Adam, taught by the Lord and with more understanding of the self-destruct feature, would be harder to persuade. Later, after Eve had eaten and not immediately died, he could be moved by her charms. He would want to believe her and share her experience. Like today's drug enthusiasts she would want to "turn him on." With a little urging he would be only too glad to share her forbidden adventure.

Afterward, once Lucifer had shown that he could flout the Lord's authority in this matter, it would be easy to sway the other Celestials to his side in the power struggle. He would persuade them that the Lord should have made more Celestials rather than creating these undependable humans to do his work. The Lord's fitness to command would be called into question; his pet creation, the humans, would be on the way to extinction, and the field would be clear for a takeover by himself. He would assume the position of leadership to which his gifts entitled him.

His plans laid, Satan made his move. Genesis 3 says, "Now the serpent was more subtily than any beast of the field which the Lord God had made." Going to Eve he said, "Yea, hath God said, Ye shall not eat of every tree of the garden?" Eve replied that they might except for the tree in the midst of the Garden. "Ye shall not eat it, neither shall ye touch it, lest ye die. And the serpent said unto the woman, Ye shall not surely die: For God doth know that in the day ye eat thereof, then your eyes shall be opened, and ye shall be as gods, knowing good and evil" (Genesis 3:1, 3–5).

With skill he seized on the weakest point in Eve's psychology—her vanity. She and Adam had admired and been awed by the brilliance and achievements of the Lord and the other Celestials. To be like them would be the greatest achievement she could imagine. And to be equal to the beautiful creature now flattering her with his attentions would be heaven!

"THAT OLD SERPENT CALLED THE DEVIL"

In the Genesis account the "serpent" appears as a literal snake, possessed by Satan, and used as his mouthpiece. Whether it was actually Satan himself or some automated device or robot through which instructions were ordinarily relayed to Adam and Eve we cannot tell. But it is evident, from the context, that it was not a literal serpent. Eve's succumbing to such a Dr. Dolittle-like device has been traditionally explained by the argument that the "serpent" was far different from its present form—walking upright, beautiful, next to man in intelligence. It is small wonder that such a fable finds little acceptance in the twentieth century.

The word "serpent" used here comes from a Hebrew root, *nacash*, meaning "to hiss" (or whisper a spell, as magicians often did). It is likely then that the original version of this story blamed Eve's misconduct on an enchanter—not a snake. The association of this hissing enchanter with a "snake" came about, later, as editors gradually wandered away from the original meaning.

In view of this it seems likely, then, that the "serpent" was actually Satan, or a robot through whom he spoke, and not a literal "beast of the field" as the Genesis story implies. That he did not magically assume the form of a serpent on this one occasion, as literal-minded commentators have argued, is further supported by the fact that he is referred to, throughout the Bible, as a "dragon" or "serpent" (as in the heading of this section, Revelation 12:9). The curse later put upon him by the Lord also shows that this is a figurative description. He says, "Because thou hast done this, thou art cursed above all cattle, and above every beast of the field; upon thy belly shalt thou go, and dust shalt thou eat all the days of thy life ... " (Genesis 3:14). This seems literal, but is shown to be figurative by the following declaration that "I will put enmity between thee and the woman, and between thy seed and her seed; it shall bruise thy head ... " (Genesis 3:15). Even the most literal-minded Christian interpreters have agreed that this is a figurative reference to the son of Mary, Jesus, overcoming death in the resurrection. The Bible says Jesus died that "through death he might destroy him that had the power of death, that is the devil" (Hebrews 2:14). Thus, he, the seed of a woman, "bruised" the "serpent's" head.

"In Adam's Fall"

And so it was that Satan, "that old serpent," was the direct cause of the fall. Being the director of the experiment he had access to the DNA mix that could confer moral responsibility and death. It was a simple matter for him to beguile the childlike Eve into "eating" the mix (probably by oral administration rather than injection). That accomplished, she involved Adam. Whether it required just one ingestion of the nucleic acids or whether it required a number is not clear. But after they "ate," the "eyes of them both were opened, and they knew that they were naked; and they sewed fig leaves together, and made themselves aprons" (Genesis 3:7). Whether their shame was for literal nakedness or for the nakedness of their guilt is not clear; and whether they literally tried to hide behind "fig leaves" or whether these are symbolic of behavior defenses they used in a futile attempt to conceal their newfound moral perception can only be surmised. Whichever it was, the Lord saw through their disguise. Humanlike, his first reaction was one of shocked disbelief—"what is this that thou hast done?" (Genesis 3:13).

"Upon Thy Belly"

From that point the narrative moves rapidly to a conclusion. The serpent was cursed first. All sorts of fanciful zoological myths have been employed to explain the declaration, "upon thy belly shalt thou go." Imaginative fundamentalists have suggested that previous to this time snakes walked on legs. A more probable interpretation, in view of our claim that the "serpent" was Satan, is that the curse meant that when the other Celestials left Earth Satan and his followers would be condemned to stay here and "eat" the "dust" of this earth with the human hybrids he had corrupted.

To be earthbound, after knowing the freedom of ranging intergalactic space, would be a punishment comparable to earthly sailors marooned on desolate islands by their comrades.

Whether Satan and the other disloyal Celestials were actually limited to this earth or confined within some larger orbit is uncertain. But evidently their "wings" were clipped. They "crawled" upon the earth. The righteous Celestials took their spacecraft with them and apparently set up controls which prevented Satan and his angels from manufacturing others that could reach the Celestials' outer space empire.

The rebellion of the fallen Celestials had led to warfare in which Michael was victorious over Satan. "And there was war in heaven: Michael and his angels fought again the dragon; and the dragon fought and his angels, And prevailed not; neither was their place found any more in heaven. And the great dragon was cast out, that old serpent, called the Devil, and Satan, which deceiveth the whole world: he was cast out into the earth, and his angels were cast out with him" (Revelation 12:7–9).

The peace terms evidently stripped Satan and his followers of long-range spacecraft and confined them to earth as their prison planet. They were compelled to "crawl" and "eat dust" on this world.

"The Prince of This World"

This line of reasoning leads us to a startling conclusion. Satan and the fallen Celestials were confined to this planet. Apparently their quarantine was indefinite—at least until the victorious Celestials' final return.

If this is so, then the fallen Celestials must still be here, and Satan is "alive and well on earth" as a recent best seller puts it.[3]

Where are they, and why are we not aware of them as they go about their nefarious activities? Could it be that, over the centuries, a large population of extraterrestrials has dwelt among us without attracting historic and scientific attention?

The answer to this question is one more surprising disclosure to come out of our space age interpretation. And, though bizarre, it sheds light on one of the greatest mysteries of our time—the UFO enigma. In Chapter XI, *Celestials, Prophets and UFO's*, we will take up this fascinating problem.

In the meantime, however, it is sufficient to note that, according to Genesis, the failure of the Garden experiment changed the destiny of this planet.

It became a prison world—a place of exile for Lucifer and his companions. The Lord's curse of him and his change of name were both symbolic of his degradation. No longer Lucifer, the "light bearer"—the brightest and most dazzling of the Celestials—he became Satan, the "serpent"—a degraded subverter, doomed to wait out the long millennia until the Celestials' return. And while he waited he would "crawl" upon the earth and choke on its "dust."

"How Art Thou Fallen!"

The ignominy of his fate is summed up by the words the Prophet Isaiah attributes to Jehovah when he has him exclaim, "How art thou fallen from heaven, O Lucifer, son of the morning! how art thou cut down to the ground, which didst weaken the nations!" (Isaiah 14:12).

His gifts and leadership experience would enable him still to dominate the other rebellious Celestials who shared his fate. And, together, they could easily influence and dominate a majority of the human hybrids they had duped. So, marooned, stripped of his rank and place among the Celestials, Satan, who had aspired to replace Jehovah himself, would thereafter have to be content with dominating a handful of felons and a degraded population of humans. As the ruler of a penal colony in the trackless backwaters of outer space he could contemplate the irony of Jesus' contemptuous description of him, "the Prince of this World"! And while he did so the human hybrids he had betrayed would work out their destiny by his side. The Lord's curse extended to them, as well.

Sorrow and Toil

Their fate was less inglorious, though equally harsh. Eve was dealt with first as the initial wrongdoer. "I will greatly multiply thy sorrow and thy conception; in sorrow thou shalt bring forth children..." (Genesis 3:16). Turning to Adam he continues: "... cursed is the ground for thy sake; in sorrow shalt thou eat of it all the days of thy life... In the sweat of thy face shalt thou eat bread, till thou return unto the ground; for out of it wast thou taken; for dust thou art, and unto dust shalt thou return" (Genesis 3:16–19).

Even though the curse seems harsh, in view of their childlike innocence and Satan's wiles, it should be remembered that it was built into the experiment—these penalties were automatic, and they had been warned.

That the Lord was compassionate, even in his frustration and disappointment, is evident, for immediately after this he took them both and made them "coats of skins, and clothed them" (Genesis 3:21). This was evidently to prepare them for the harsher weather, outside the sealed environment. Immediately after he "drove out the man; and he placed at the east of the garden of Eden cherubim, and a flaming sword which turned every way, to keep the way of the tree of life" (Genesis 3:24).

The automatic nature of the penalties can be explained readily in our space age interpretation of the original sin. Fundamentalists have speculated on what exactly the Lord did to make women "bring forth children" in sorrow. And zoologists and anthropologists have puzzled over the fact that the human female alone, of higher mammals, seems to suffer greatly in the process of giving birth and is unable to resume normal functions at once.

The answer would seem to be that the Lord did not originally intend human reproduction to be sexual. That he created humans to enjoy sex and express love through it we have already seen. But the possibilities of mutation and genetic accidents, which attend sexual reproduction, would make it undesirable for eugenic reasons. It is more likely that the Lord intended to reproduce humans by the same method used for the Celestials—replication or cloning.

But now that the experiment had been spoiled, they were on their own. Outside they would revert to the method used by their evolved ancestors—sexual reproduction. Unfortunately, the large brains which these ancestors had evolved had enlarged the cranial cavity, as well. As a result the skull was too big for easy passage through the pelvic opening. This had to remain small, because the hips must be close together in a creature that walks upright. Clearly man's large-brained ancestors found giving birth a painful process. This could have been avoided if replication or cloning had been used for Adam and Eve, as the Lord evidently intended. Now, however, they were back to a state of nature, and so the necessity of natural birth, with a painful labor, became an inevitable consequence of Eve's fall. Like her ancestors she and her descendants would ever after pay the evolutionary penalty for developing upright posture and a large brain at the same time. They would "bring forth children" in sorrow.

And with both Adam and Eve the problems of diet and food gathering were built into their physiology. Unlike most animals of Earth they had developed as omnivorous creatures

—living on a varied diet of animal and plant products. This complexity was probably necessary for their more complex brain functions, since the complete range of amino acids are found naturally only in both animal and plant sources.

At any rate it meant their high standard of living would require an elaborate economy involving both hunting and domesticating plants and animals. Unlike simple creatures which can subsist on a single natural source of food, man would ever after earn his bread by the "sweat of his face." Within the Celestials' controlled society these problems had doubtless been solved by the produciton of synthetic foods. They had developed beyond the necessity of "earning a living" and could devote themselves to higher things. On the outside man could subsist only by unrelenting toil until he returned to the "dust of the ground" from which he was taken.

"Cherubim and a Flaming Sword"

And with the Lord's curse upon them Adam and Eve were driven out of the Garden, and the Lord placed "cherubim" and a "flaming sword" to keep them from the tree of life and the restoration of their immortality.

Again traditional interpretation has pictured winged angelic beings standing day and night with glittering swords drawn ready to strike down Adam and Eve if they attempted to return.

As we have already seen, however, the word "cherub" and its plural, "cherubim," refer not to angelic beings, but to servomechanisms, or robots, which perform the drudgery of the Celestials' civilization.

The cherubim posted at the entrance to the Garden of Eden were evidently a sort of erect barrier, armed with "a flaming sword"—a rotating beam (probably a laser) which "turned every way" (Genesis 3:24) and was capable of wounding or killing anything that attempted passage. Such "flaming swords" are currently being used in many industries to cut through metals and other materials resistant to ordinary cutting tools.

But some Bible-wise readers may be objecting. Doesn't Scripture also use "cherub" to mean "angels"? Doesn't Ezekiel 28:14, for example, say that Satan was the "anointed cherub that covereth" in the Garden, and doesn't this prove some cherubs, at least, are Celestials? The answer to this problem can be found in a critical examination of the derivations of the words themselves. And it serves to point up the problems of translation.

In this case the fault lies with the King James translation. The phrase "anointed cherub" is used for the Hebrew word *mimschach*. It is derived from a root meaning "rub with oil," or "anoint," but the primary sense intended is the spreading connected with rubbing oil. For this reason *mimschach* is usually translated as "expanded" or "outspread." This was taken into account when the King James translators added the phrase "that covereth"—"thou art the anointed cherub that covereth." Yet, although the words "anointed" and "covereth" do convey the essential ideas, and the phrase follows the Hebrew word order, a number of modern translators feel they miss the real meaning. Thus the New English Bible gives the passage as "I set you with a towering cherub as guardian." The Jerusalem Bible gives it, "I had provided you with a guardian cherub." And again the New Oxford Annotated Bible gives the same sense when it says, "With an anointed guardian cherub I placed you."

If these modern readings are correct, then the King James translation completely misses the point. Satan is not called a cherub—anointed or otherwise. It is rather that a "guardian cherub" spread its protection over him and his headquarters at the Garden. This guardian cherub was probably similar to the one the Lord set at the gate of the Garden—a laser device which "covered" the experimental headquarters. This was where the director stayed with his precious stores of genetic mixes—the laboratory at the Garden's center. A revolving laser generator on its roof would have "covered" its entire perimeter to keep out intruders. Only Satan could have penetrated it to put Adam and Eve and the forbidden "fruit" together.

Paradise Lost

With these guarding cherubim, then, the access to the Garden and its secret of immortality was permanently shut off for mankind. From the moment of their expulsion Adam and Eve reverted to the state of nature from which their unreconstructed ancestors had come.

Like them they now had to make their way amid hostile predators, alien evolved humans and the fallen Celestials who were imprisoned on their world.

The story of their struggles in the strange and savage world outside the Garden is told in the briefest of narratives in the later chapters in Genesis. It is elaborated, sometimes plausibly and sometimes fantastically, by accounts given in the apocryphal literature. Secular history can tell us little of this period, for it precedes any written records.

In the next chapter we will try to reconstruct the trials and progress—the failures and triumphs—of mankind as they took up a precarious existence in their demoted state.

CHAPTER IX

THE BIBLE
AND HISTORY

...when the sons of God came in unto the daughters of men,
and they bare children to them, the same became mighty men
which were of old, men of renown.

—Genesis 6:4

AFTER THE FALL

"And Adam knew Eve his wife; and she conceived, and bare
Cain, and said, I have gotten a man from the Lord. And she
again bare his brother Abel" (Genesis 4:1–2). With these
lines Genesis picks up the thread of narrative after Adam's
and Eve's expulsion from the Garden. For the next nine
chapters the Bible continues the story we traced in the fossil
record in Chapter VII. No other section in the Bible com-
presses so much in so short a space, unless it is the account of
original creation in Genesis 1. According to our earlier esti-
mate these chapters must encompass nearly 30,000 to 35,000
years of history, for they end with the call of Abraham, after
his migration from Ur, where the ancient Sumerian civilization arose.

The Biblical genealogies and history set this event at around
4,000 years ago.

In these chapters the Bible recounts epochal happenings—
the first murder; the multiplication of men and wickedness
throughout the world; the genealogies of the patriarchs and
their descendants; fantastic life spans of almost a thousand
years; mortals being carried to heaven alive; a catastrophic
flood that destroys all but one family; and the dispersion of
mankind throughout the earth with the development of races
and languages.

GENESIS AS HISTORY

Unfortunately, there is no way to recover an exact historical
record from these legends. It is generally agreed by scholars

162

that the biblical narrative is highly selective. Further, its accounts have doubtless been reworked as countless generations
passed down the oral traditions from father to son. Yet this
does not mean the events are imaginary or the people fictitious. To believe this goes against the informed opinion of
most mythologists and historians. The narrative is essentially
historical, but it is not the kind of history we associate with
textbooks and courses in high school and college. It is folk
history—legend—the record preserved in the consciousness of
the race by the process of parents telling their children of
their heritage and by priests and bards reciting, or singing,
more solemn accounts on ceremonial occasions. If we are to
believe what the Bible tells us it may also be that these narratives reflect the editorial influence of the Celestials themselves. We have its assurance they communicated, to the
writers, those special insights they wished preserved in human
memory as symbols of their redemptive plan.

THE PROBLEM OF THE GENEALOGIES

The real problem in trying to reconstruct a history from
these genealogies is that they are selective rather than complete. Though the Genesis editors tried to make them seem
complete by giving exact lines of descent, ages of parents at
children's births and life spans, these mean little.

Bishop Ussher's attempt, in the seventeenth century, to
add them up to a total, giving the date of creation, was
doomed to failure. Other scholars using the same methods have
arrived at dates quite different from Ussher's.

There are several discrepancies. In the first place, various
genealogies, in several parts of the Bible, show discrepancies.
So we read in II Kings 24:8 that "Jehoiachin was eighteen
years old when he began to reign," but in II Chronicles 36:9
we find that "Jehoiachin was eight years old when he began
to reign."

In some genealogical passages no ages are given at all, and
in different versions of the Bible, such as the Hebrew Masoretic text and the Greek Septuagint, ages given do not always
agree. Further, the Hebrew word for "son of"—ben—can
mean a remote descendant as well as an actual son. So, too,
yolad—"begat"—doesn't necessarily mean "father of" but can

be used for a more remote ancestor.

This can be confusing, as Matthew 1:8 shows. There we read that "Joram begat Ozias." What the passage fails to mention is that three generations passed between Joram and Ozias —Ahaziah, Joash and Amaziah. The Ozias "begat" by Joram was not his son but his great-great-grandson!

This is not an evidence of carelessness on the part of biblical writers—it was custom. Genealogies often mentioned only the more important members of a family tree.

From this it is evident that adding up Bible genealogies cannot clarify whether Adam and Eve were created in 4004 B.C. or 40,004 B.C. Any serious effort to date Bible events must rest on outside evidence such as that of archaeology or the fossil record.

In spite of this there is increasing evidence, from history and archaeology, to indicte that the heroes and places of the Bible are usually based on real lives and actual times and places. Recent finds at Ebla in Syria have unearthed over 15,000 clay tablets which mention such names as Abraham, Esau, David, Saul and even Israel. The time and place of these finds would be right for these Bible patriarchs and kings.

In this chapter we will therefore assume that the biblical narrative is essentially historical. And we will take it for granted that biblical characters, such as Adam and Eve, Cain and Abel, Enoch and Noah, were real in the sense that they represent real people, or peoples, of whom they are representative. Further, we will assume that those they represent were descendants of the Lord's special creation and were real actors in the drama of the Bible.

We believe that the record of their doings is true in the special sense that folk history is generally true. In this chapter we will try to discover the role they played in the development of mankind. More important, we will try to show, in later chapters, the role they played in the larger drama written and directed by the Celestials.

REDEMPTIVE HISTORY

In discussing the doings of the Celestials, up to this point, we have been mainly concerned with what could be called secular history—history of the sort created by the folk process or history that is written by specialists called historians. While much of the Bible began with the first sort of history, and many parts have been reworked into the second, the intent of its writers was to create still a third kind. It is what we may call "redemptive history"—history that reveals God's will to man in order that man may be redeemed by it.

Time and again the Bible tells us it is not just ordinary history and that its purpose is not just to tell a story. In almost every book it directly states, or at least implies, that the stories it contains are intended as revelations and examples. They reveal the Celestials' plan for us and instruct us in how to follow that plan so we may be redeemed. Once again we are reminded of the famous passage from II Timothy which tells us: "All scripture is given by inspiration of God, and is profitable for doctrine, for reproof, for correction, for instruction in righteousness: That the man of God may be perfect, thoroughly furnished unto all good works" (II Timothy 3:16–17).

The attempt to square this claim, made by Bible writers, with scientific history has been a major problem for theologians of the last hundred years. If we cannot know the events told in the Bible actually happened, and if we are not sure the people in its stories were real, how can it reveal anything and how can it make any demands on us to live in a particular way? This has been a central issue in Bible criticism for both religious leaders and skeptical critics (and many recent theologians have been both). An answer to this difficult question has been worked out by certain German theologians over the last two centuries. They call their solution *Heilsgeschichte*—"redemptive history."

According to this notion, things can be really understood only in terms of their history, and their history is complete only if it shows their relation to God. We have already used this concept in Chapter V, *In the Beginning*. If we acknowledge the creative power of nature as God, and our dependence on it as its creatures, then our view becomes a religious one —our history is a sacred one and our participation in that history becomes redemptive.

But even more, we are the product of a special history not shared by the rest of the natural creation. We are the special creation of the Celestials—and their heirs. This special history has placed upon us demands unique in the natural world. We, alone out of all living things, have a special calling to prepare the world for their return and to make ourselves worthy of sharing in their rule of it.

The Bible is a record of this special history. It discloses their purpose in coming to our world and it challenges us to share their plan for its future. As such it is a call to action. And it is precisely this call to action with distinguishes it from ordinary history.

As the Danish existential philosopher Kierkegaard pointed out, it is as though we sit observing a great epic drama on a cosmic stage. Suddenly the principal actor, who is also the director of the drama, steps up to the front of the stage, points at us, and calls out, "You, you're wanted. Come up here. Take your part!"[1]

THE BIBLE AS REDEMPTIVE HISTORY

So it is that the Bible is more than a record of people and events. Through its characters and narratives it reveals a plan and calls out to us to fulfill a special destiny and to prepare for a unique inheritance.

Of course the question immediately comes up, "By what authority does the Bible issue this challenge and hold out these promises?" The answer is given again and again in the story we will follow. It claims that the Lord and his assistants, the other Celestials, not only came at one special time to create us, but have continued a watchful care throughout history. Throughout the entire Bible we will see the repeated claim that they have often directly intervened to produce events serving as types and symbols of their plan for us. At other times they have selected special people, or even whole peoples, to act as emissaries and messengers to tell of their plan and to inspire and reprove humans as they carried it out or ignored it. In many cases these special people were the writers of the Bible. And it is their special relation to the Celestials, and the revealing events in which they participated, that give their writings a claim to inspiration and sacred authority.

HIGHER CRITICISM AND THE BIBLE

Much of the higher criticism of the Bible, during the last two centuries, has tried to show these claims for inspiration and authority are worthless. Critics have argued that parts of the Bible were not written by the people claimed to be their authors; they have attempted to show that the ideas in their writings were taken from folklore and mythology of other peoples whom they knew. They have invoked the folk and myth-making processes to debunk extraordinary or miraculous events of the Bible and to show they were really just ordinary experiences that seemed miraculous to ignorant nomads and illiterate fishermen. Or they have claimed they were the inventions of later copyists and editors who inserted them into the record, after the fact, to support their own pet doctrines and views.

Anyone who examines the Bible carefully and critically cannot doubt these things have sometimes happened. Books claimed to be written by certain authors show usages and name locations which would have been known only to later writers. Bible stories do parallel the myths of other cultures, but this may be because they both come from a common source and not because they influenced each other. Some of these stories are told as though they were of universal, world-shaking events when it is clear, from the context and secular history, that they were only of local importance. And certain passages, in our current translations, are not even found in the earliest surviving manuscripts.

WHAT REALLY MATTERS

All of this is unimportant, however, if we accept the idea that inspiration and authority do not require the Bible to be literally and scientifically true in a word-for-word sense. What does matter is that, in spite of growth and change and the problems of translation, the essential revelation has been retained. With the aid of archaeology and textual analysis, scholars have discovered a solid core of historical fact.

Now our space age interpretation adds a new tool for getting at this core. Its discovery that incredibly advanced extraterrestrials were principal actors in the drama of the Bible gives new dimension to our understanding of its pages.

The inspiration and authority of the Bible does not lie in its word-for-word dictation by Celestials, nor in its literal scientific truth. Neither of these is necessary, or even possible, considering the nature of the record and the people who wrote it. What is essential is that the revelation of the plan is there and that we perceive it and respond to its challenge. For this reason it does not particularly matter whether Adam and Eve were actual individuals or mere symbols of the race created by the Celestials. The message of the Celestials' watchful concern over human affairs is communicated whether the flood was a local event, destroying the small world known to the Genesis writers, or a truly worldwide catastrophe as the record seems to claim. The unique nature and history of the Jews is not changed whether Abraham was called by the angel of the Lord or the inevitabilities of his own life. And the significance and validity of the Mosaic law, as a revelation of righteousness, is not altered whether Moses was the unacknowledged son of a Pharaoh's daughter or a Hebrew slave who was chosen by God to receive a divine revelation on Mount Sinai.

The only value in showing these persons and events were real lies in making revelation more convincing. It is this disclosure of revelation and its challenge which is always the true work of interpretation. And a space age interpretation, by bringing new knowledge to bear on ancient mysteries, unveils their hidden treasures.

In this sense, then, our interpretation of the Bible's meaning is valid. Its explanations make the timeless truths of the Bible timely. Even more, its space age version of the Bible's challenge gives it urgency as we stand on the threshold of the twenty-first century. It says, "They're coming back—now! An advanced civilization will soon arrive here on Earth—a civilization without crime, war, injustice or death. Are you ready for citizenship?"

A LIVING FAITH

But, some readers may be thinking, different interpretations are possible—how can we know which one is right? The answer to this is that none is right, in the sense that matters, unless it speaks to you. If, by looking at the Bible from some particular viewpoint, the Lord steps to the front of the stage, points his finger at you and says, "You, you're wanted. Come up here. Take your part!," then that is the right interpretation for you. And, if you respond by taking your part, you will do so, not because you have been convinced by arguments, but because you have been moved by the power of revelation—a power which challenges you to a personal commitment.

Such a response is based on religious faith, and your action makes it a living faith. Only by a living faith, discovered in this way, can you know that it is true. Without such a practical test, proof is impossible and with it, proof is unnecessary. "The proof of the pudding is in the eating" as the old adage says. The Bible is largely a record of the doings and sayings of people who found the Lord pointing his finger at them and who responded to the challenge with a living faith. Some of the first and most important of these are introduced in the first dozen chapters of Genesis.

MEN OF RENOWN AND MIGHTY EVENTS

The personalities of the first dozen chapters of Genesis are an impressive "Who's Who"—the founders of the present human race, the first murderer, the first human to escape death, the longest-lived human, the only surviving family from a universal catastrophe, and the founder of the most remarkable race in history. The biblical heroes, Adam and Eve, Cain and Abel, Enoch and Methuselah, Noah and his family, and Abraham are figures of epic grandeur.

As we said earlier, however, it is impossible to reconstruct the beginnings of the race from the accounts of their deeds and the genealogies linking them with lesser figures. Their deeds are representative and the genealogies are selective. They leave many questions unanswered.

Where did Adam and Eve go after they were driven from the Garden? When did they, or their descendants, move to other areas? When did settled community living begin, and where? How did the institutions of civilization begin—agriculture, building, art, social and religious ceremony? If these are mentioned at all they are already highly developed when we first read of them in the Bible.

Adam tills and keeps the Garden (Genesis 2:15). His twin

sons, Cain and Abel, carry on the tradition. Cain brings the
fruits of the ground and Abel the firstborn of his flock to the
Lord. Cain murders Abel when the Lord prefers Abel's offering (Genesis 4:2-8). Farming and animal husbandry are already developed arts as the Genesis narrative opens. In Genesis
4:17, we learn that Cain "builded a city"—architecture and
city planning were recognized human skills. In Genesis 4:21,
we find that Jubal "was the father of all such as handle the
harp and organ." Musical art was a recognized tradition. In
Genesis 4:22, Zillah gives birth to Tubal-cain, who instructs
men in the crafts of brass and ironwork. Zillah's husband, Lamech, boasts that he has slain a man who wounded him and
another for hurting him, and asserts that if Cain was avenged
"sevenfold" he will be avenged "seventy and sevenfold" (Genesis 4:23-24). Fighting, as organized warfare, is on its way. In
Genesis 6:14-16, we find Noah building an ark half the size
of a modern ocean liner. In Genesis 11:4, men build a tower
that reaches into the heavens—monumental architecture is
highly advanced. In Genesis 12:1, Abraham is called, by the
Lord, out of a city which modern archaeology has shown was
already highly civilized a millennium before Nebuchadnezzar.

Can any of these developments be set into a chronology?
Archaeologists and prehistorians have estimates as to when the
domestication of plants and animals began, but it would be
much later than the time of Adam and Eve and their two
sons—if the experimental creation was over 35,000 years ago.
If Tubal-cain taught iron and brass work when historians
think the use of these metals began, it would have been
millennia after the Bible genealogies date him in the seventh
generation from Adam. If the Tower of Babel was a ziggurat,
as some archaeologists have contended, it must have been
built when the early civilizations of the Fertile Crescent were
flourishing. Yet this would have been much too late for the
spread of humanity and development of languages which are
linked with its defeat. Clearly, these stories involve tremendous telescopings in time.

GENESIS AND LONGEVITY

And this telescoping involves another fascinating problem—
one of the most puzzling in the Bible. This is the problem of

the incredible ages attributed to the preflood patriarchs. All but one are claimed to have lived over 700 years, and one, Methuselah, is credited with an age of 969!

Are these ages to be taken seriously, or are they merely attempts, on the part of the priestly editor, to close the gaps left by selective genealogies?

It is interesting that later genealogies give ages that drop to more believable averages. For example, until Eber, no patriarch after the flood lived less than 433 years. But now, in one generation, the life span drops to 239 years and never exceeds that amount again. In fact, a steady decline continues, with Abraham dead at 175; Moses dying an old man at 120; and in Psalms 90:10 we find that, by David's time, "three score and ten" had become the expected human span.

Because these genealogies are selective, there is no way to set up any kind of continuous chronology that would permit checking these age spans against one another for consistency.

Yet, if the Adamic race did start with a superior longevity, due to their having fallen from a condition of immortality, the decline Genesis shows is exactly what we would expect as a result of interbreeding with the short-lived "daughters of men."

Lacking evidence independent of the Bible record, then, the case for an extreme life span in the first created humans remains uncertain.

BIBLE HEROES AND OTHER RECORDS

Little more is told about the preflood heroes in Genesis. Beyond the bare genealogical framework, only an occasional human-interest item breaks through from Adam's and Eve's expulsion from the Garden to Noah's building of the Ark. We read of Cain's slaying Abel over the Lord's choice of offering; Enoch's "walking with God" and then ceasing to be; Methuselah's unbelievable durability; Noah's justness and perfection and his "walk with God"—these fill out the account. The richness of detail we find in the folklore and epics of other peoples is notably lacking in these early Bible stories. Unlike Homer's poetic magnificence we have no elaborate descriptions of weapons and costumes, or, curiously, even of the heroes themselves. This lack of personal description is a

strange feature throughout the entire Bible, for there is
scarcely a hint as to the physical image of any important
figure. We have no scripturally based idea of the appearance of
Adam and Eve, Noah, Abraham, Moses, Elijah, John the
Baptist, Jesus or Paul. Our ideas are almost wholly derived
from the conceptions of relatively modern artists such as
Leonardo da Vinci, Michelangelo and Gustave Doré.

Perhaps this is the reason a large body of literature grew up,
in early Judaism, to fill in historical gaps and elaborate on
biographical and descriptive details. By the time the priest
Ezra and his fellow scribes began reconstruction of the Hebrew Scriptures which were lost or scattered during the exile
(around 440 B.C.), there was a much larger body of oral traditions and writing than they actually selected. Much of this
had, at one time or another, been regarded as sacred and set
down in scriptural form. In attempting to reconstruct a text
from these fragments they decided to make a division of the
materials. A part was selected for publication and the rest
was reserved for special purposes. This led to a distinction
between those writings which were officially recognized for
public use (the "canon") and others which were reserved for
use by scholars and teachers.

THE APOCRYPHA

It is probably this idea that the books outside the canon
were to be kept secret, or hidden, which led to their later
designation as "apocryphal" (from a Greek word meaning
"concealed" or "hidden away"). However the term arose, it
was later adopted by the Christians and used to designate not
only books which the Jews had left out but a newer collection
of Jewish and Christian literature that these later church
fathers and councils rejected when they were selecting the
Christian canon of Scripture.

It is this body of apocryphal literature (older and newer)
which has, for both Jews and Christians, served to fill in the
details of the belief system based on the Bible. At first, among
the post-exilic Jews, it was regarded as a source of religious
instruction and wisdom intended to supplement the Penta-
teuch and other canonical books. In the centuries just before
and after the beginning of the present era, however, there was

a tremendous increase in apocryphal literature. This was largely due to the influence of Greek ideas on religious thought of both Jews and early Christians. These Hellenized Jews and Christians were often developing strange ideas in conflict with the traditions of their faiths. They also frequently raised questions which the Scriptures in common use did not answer.

As a result they began to search for the old "outside" books which had been lost, or deliberately destroyed, in the hope of answers. New versions of the old books appeared, and new books were sometimes forged to promote strange beliefs or present new solutions to unanswered questions. To get these forgeries accepted, the writers would often claim them as the work of some famous hero or patriarch or even a Bible writer. Since many of the original outside books had been lost, it was not easy to distinguish between restorations and outright forgeries, and often a given book might involve both processes. This is how the Christian view of apocryphal writings as spurious, or false, teachings arose. As a result, both Jews and Christians developed a mixed attitude toward the apocryphal writings. They continued to cherish and enjoy them for a number of centuries, and both the Septuagint and early editions of the Christian Bible included them. Even the early editions of the King James Version, published after 1611, included some of them. On the other hand, as the Masoretic version of the Hebrew Scriptures and the formation of the Christian canon developed, in the early centuries of the present era, there was a growing tendency to regard them as a source of false doctrine. This led to neglect and avoidance of their use. Gradually they were excluded from most modern versions of the Bible. The common belief that they were rejected as "uninspired" at some specific time by official groups of Jewish or Christian leaders, after prayerful consideration, is simply not true. When such groups made decisions on what was canonical or excluded, they were generally only recognizing what had already been announced by some revered rabbi or early church father or giving official recognition to what had become an unofficial acceptance or rejection.

There was, of course, a general feeling among the Masoretes and the early Christian fathers that outright forgeries were not "inspired." As Christian doctrine began to be unified it was also felt that books teaching "false" doctrines (or views which had been declared "heresies") were not inspired. These views influenced some of the exclusions. But others seem to be without any foundation in reason. Even today it is difficult to see why Esther was received and Judith excluded. As a basis for religious instruction it is hard to show the advantages of Ecclesiastes and the Song of Solomon over the Book of Wisdom or the prophecy of Baruch. It is hard to explain why Jews and Catholics recognize the books of Maccabees while modern Protestants reject them. Yet all three accepted the authority of Chronicles. It is also difficult to explain why Hebrews is included in the New Testament, though its authorship still remains unknown, when other well-authenticated letters to the apostles were rejected.

The Bible a Growing and Changing Work

From this we see that the present canon of the Bible is the result of historical growth in which chance, the changing ideas of people, as well as careful study and prayerful searching all played a part. Some of the Bible's present books have been recognized almost from the beginning. Others, such as Hebrews and Revelation, were doubtful and were rejected by some and accepted by others well into the present era. A few, like the Maccabees, still remain in dispute among Jews, Catholics and Protestants. Of those finally rejected, a number are authentic writings from the hands of Bible writers or principal characters in the drama of the Bible. Others are patchworks of traditional writings combined with forgery. Still others are outright forgeries. Among them is much that is historic, spiritual and wise as well as what is fantastic, absurd and unsound.

There is no sure approach in separating the wheat from the chaff in the apocryphal writings. That they can be useful in rounding out our picture of the Bible's meaning is beyond doubt. But they can also be a source of confusion and misinterpretation, as can conflicting passages in the Bible itself. In the last analysis, it seems the only sure method is one which

the thousands of believers, scholars, fathers and rabbis who
founded our present canon employed. Each student of the
writings, inside or outside the canon, must decide for himself.
We must each repeat the process which those who have gone
before have had to go through if we would experience the
full revelation of the Bible. Whether we find it in the Masoretic text, in a Catholic version with the Maccabees or a
Protestant version without them, or even in rejected books
which speak to us must be a personal decision.

There is no simple rule of thumb which can make this decision for us. Are we to reject all writings not known to come
from the pen of inspired writers? Several of the books in the
canon are from unknown authors. Are we to reject whatever
shows the influence of pagan idolatries and heathen superstition? Some have argued that the account in Genesis 22 of
Abraham's near-sacrifice of Isaac is evidence that Canaanite
child-sacrifice practices influenced Jewish thought. Others have
found the account in II Kings 2:23–24 which implies that God
sent two she bears to destroy forty-two children who mocked
Elisha an evidence of heathen superstition.

An impartial reader must surely agree that it would be odd
if the God of the law were to test Abraham's faith by seeing
if he was willing to engage in the idolatrous practice of his
neighbors. And it is very hard to imagine the God of universal
justice and truth, portrayed in Jewish and Christian belief,
lending himself to child slaughter on the whim of an old
man's annoyance.

From all this it is evident that the Bible is not a fixed body
of words unchanging for all time. It is the product of a history
which will continue into the future. It was not produced, like
ordinary books, by one writer during a single lifetime. It was
written, a book at a time, by many writers over many centuries
and in many places. Even individual books were sometimes
the joint product of several writers over a period of time. The
Bible grew as it passed from Jewish to Christian hands. Its
content and form fluctuated during the centuries its canon
was being fixed, and its outline is still unclear from one faith
to another. It has continued to undergo subtle transformations
as it has passed through successive translations. Today, cha-

meleonlike, it continues to assume different appearances to different viewers in the perspective of various interpretations.

DOUBTFUL DEEDS AND CURIOUS CHARACTERIZATIONS

Returning to the books outside the canon, we find a bewildering array of material to fill in the history omitted from the record in the first dozen books of Genesis. We find, in the books of Adam and Eve, that, after expulsion from the Garden, Adam and Eve crossed the rivers surrounding Eden. These had been frozen when the archangel Michael touched them with a rod. At God's command they went to dwell in the Cave of Treasures. Later, in their despair over losing Paradise, they attempted suicide. In time Cain and Abel, as well as daughters, were born to them, and Cain stirred up enmity in the family circle. After Cain slew Abel, God placed seven curses on him. During all this time Satan continued to appear to Adam and Eve, as well as to their children, and tempted them to further sin. Once he appeared to Adam as a beautiful woman who attempted his seduction.

Later Satan induced Seth to marry away from his family, but Seth remained steadfast and, after Adam's death, became the head of his clan. In Adam's old age he prophesied the coming flood and instructed Seth concerning his death and funeral. As generations passed, descendants of Adam and Eve continued to keep the Cave of Treasures as a family shrine, and leadership passed through a succession of heroes to Enoch.

In the Book of Enoch we learn that this hero was a seer noted for his great wisdom. He instructed humanity with religious teachings and prophesied concerning times to come. He told his son, Methuselah, of two visions he had in which the destruction of mankind by flood was revealed, and the whole human history from his own time to the end laid before him. The chronology of these events, and the signs and wonders which accompanied them, are an interesting hodgepodge of astronomical and astrological lore, as well as an excursion into numerology and angelology (the study of orders and functions of angelic beings). The occult knowledge and prophetic powers claimed for Enoch may be the origin of ancient views which credited him with secret wisdom later attributed to such figures as Thoth, Hermes Trismegistus, Pythagoras and Plato.

The Book of Jubilees goes on to tell how, after inventing writing and instructing the human race in learning, Enoch set down a testament to enable them to know the seasons and keep track of time. Finally he was conducted by the angels, "in majesty and honor," to the Garden of Eden, where he remained to write down "the condemnation and judgment of the world" and "all the wickedness of the children of men." The book then goes on to give the births and biographies of Methuselah, Lamech and his son, Noah. It interrupts the narrative to tell of the death of Adam, after Noah's birth, and states that he was "the first to be buried in the earth." Soon after this it tells how Adam's son, Cain, died when his house collapsed on him, moralizing, "for with a stone he had killed Abel, and by a stone was he killed in righteous judgment."[2]

The account then takes up the life of Noah and begins an elaboration on the story of the flood. And with the deluge we reach a great divide in the biblical story of our race. For after its waters recede, life is never again the same for the Celestials' created heirs.

Life spans are dramatically shortened, races emerge and mankind is scattered throughout the earth. Diverse languages bar communication and the Celestials' role in earthly affairs becomes more remote and dependent on human leaders and prophets.

Bible Legends and Prehistory

And, out of the mists which shroud the antediluvian period, the beginnings of secular prehistory emerge. The attempt to relate the Bible to other legends and myth systems is one of the most fascinating puzzles in the field of historical research. It has also been a recent subject for a variety of provocative books on prehistory.

As we saw in Chapter VII, *Homo sapiens sapiens* emerged on this planet 30,000 to 40,000 years ago. Yet the earliest truly historic records we have go back no further than about 6,000 years. What events bridge this gap that separates early Cro-Magnon man from the recordkeeping priests of ancient Sumer? Was the flood or the building of the Tower of Babel among them? And what of legends from other cultures? What about Atlantis and Lemuria and Mu?

We have already seen that early Genesis chapters plainly state that the first generations of the Lord's creation were adept in most of the arts of civilization. These included animal husbandry and horticulture, skilled iron and brass work, city planning, ship building and music. Though the Bible does not directly state that the righteous Celestials instructed humans in these arts, the apocryphal literature is full of such assertions. In the Secrets of Enoch it tells how Enoch was taken up into each of the ten heavens, and in the last the angel Michael brought him to the Lord. He then commanded Enoch to write down all the "works of heaven, the earth and sea, and all the elements, and their passings and goings and changes of the stars, the seasons, years, days and hours, the risings of the wind, the number of angels, and the formations of their songs, and all human things . . ."[3] It goes on to state that when Enoch was done, after sixty days and nights, he had filled 366 books.

Not only are the Lord and his angels credited with instructing men in the arts of civilization, but the fallen angels are said to have played a part as well. In the section of the Books of Enoch known as the Book of Watchers it tells how they—the watchers (or fallen Celestials)—"taught men to make swords, knives, shields, breastplates, the fabrication of mirrors, and the workmanship of bracelets and ornaments; and the use of paint, the beautifying of the eyebrows, the use of stones of every valuable and select kind; so that the world became altered, impiety increased, fornication multiplied, and they transgressed and corrupted all their ways."[4]

Now, though we do not know the source of these traditions, they are clearly reasonable. If the loyal Celestials left a staff behind to look after the fallen creation, it is logical their duties would have included instructing humans in arts which would make them useful and religious duties which would preserve them from total depravity. And if the rebellious Celestials were doomed to share this planet with humans, it is also probable they tried to win them over by instructing them in wickedness and arts which would make them allies in rebellion.

Prehistoric Civilization

By putting these hints, given in Genesis and the apocryphal books, together with other non-Semitic legends we can fill in a probable prehistory for the later descendants of the Lord's creation. The nonbiblical stories come from very ancient times and tell of advanced civilizations which existed long before ancient Sumer. One of the best known of these was told by the Greek philosopher Plato, who asserted that he had knowledge of such a civilization through an acquaintance, Critias.

In the dialogue which bears his name, Critias tells the history of a fabulous, lost civilization, Atlantis, which sank beneath the sea. According to Plato's retelling of the conversation, the information was given to Critias by Solon, the Athenian lawgiver. He had met a priest of Sais, in the Nile Delta, who told the story, which he claimed was contained in sacred archives of the Egyptians. He described Atlantis as an island with magnificent roadways, bridges, a splendid palace and a long canal 300 feet in width, 100 feet in depth and almost 6 miles in length leading up to an inland harbor.

Another of Plato's dialogues, the *Timaeus*, tells how this island sank beneath the sea in a single day and night in the midst of violent earthquakes and a flood. According to Plato, this event took place about 9,500 years before his time, which would place it around 12,000 years ago. Could such a civilization have existed then, and could the cataclysm that allegedly destroyed it have been the same as, or similar to, the one the Bible calls "the flood"? Numerous attempts have been made to locate the site of the "lost Atlantis." Recent deep-sea observations have convinced some archaeologists that it may have been where its mountain tops remain as the present Canary Islands, off the coast of Spain. According to Plato it lay just west of the Straits of Gibraltar, which would make this location a possible one. And a giant upheaval centering in the Mediterranean could have involved both this area and the Fertile Crescent at its perimeters.

There are many other legends that tell of lost or sunken civilizations in the remote past. Almost everyone has heard of Lemuria, Mu, Hyperboria and others. Most of them are credited with advanced technologies, including monumental architecture, advanced mathematical and astronomical knowledge, control of mysterious energy sources and sometimes flying machines. What are we to make of these stories?

CREATED MAN AS THE BEARER OF ADVANCED CIVILIZATION

Putting together the biblical and pagan legends, we arrive at an obvious explanation for filling the gap of prehistory. It suggests that the created *Homo sapiens* became heirs to a Celestially taught civilization. In the millennia following their expulsion from the Garden they migrated throughout the earth carrying this civilization with them.

As they spread their level of genetic superiority gradually declined because of interbreeding with evolved humans. In the same way their cultural heritage also became fragmented and was eventually lost—partly perhaps through natural calamities such as that recounted in the *Timaeus* by Plato, or those which destroyed Pompeii and ancient Crete. Yet before this occurred, areas to which they migrated became the centers of prehistoric civilizations. These form the factual basis for well-known legends, such as that of Atlantis.

As cultural dilution and fragmentation continued, descendants from these original colonies founded other lesser civilizations. These are the first of which we have direct historical evidence. The Sumerians, the Egyptians, the Indus Valley dwellers, the Chinese, the Druids, the Aztecs and the Mayans were all probably of this sort.

All of these civilizations show a common mastery of certain kinds of advanced technical knowledge. Because of geography it is difficult to suppose these similarities were due to direct influence on one another.

For example, it seems strange that the Sumerians, the Egyptians and the Mayans, separated by continents and oceans, all created very similar types of stepped pyramids. And in view of the quite different functions they served it is even harder to explain why they were all built on similar geometric principles with similar orientations to the stars and solar system. It is also baffling that the ancestors of the Druids, in Great Britain, also built monolithic structures unrelated to pyramids (such as those at Stonehenge) yet followed these same astronomic orientations—as did the builders of stone arrangements at Carnac, in France.

Already, during the third millennium B.C., there were many places, throughout the ancient world, where men shared a common knowledge of cutting, transporting and building with huge blocks of stone. These ranged in size from a ton or two to several hundred tons. They were able, in Sumer, Lebanon, Egypt, North and South America and Easter Island, to move these considerable distances—often many miles across dense jungles and over mountain ranges. In many places they were lifted to heights of hundreds of feet, as in the Great Pyramid in Egypt or at Machu Picchu in Peru, where buildings were erected thousands of feet above the quarries from which their blocks came.

Many of these monuments were arranged with such precision they could be used to measure exact times, to the day, of equinoxes, solstices and other astronomical cycles.

Professor Gerald S. Hawkins, of the Department of Astronomy at Boston University, made a study of the Stonehenge arrangement, using a computer analysis of the data. He found Stonehenge to be a very precise observatory for following the sun's, the moon's and the stars' apparent motions and for predicting such events as eclipses over hundreds of years.

At Stonehenge hundreds of stones are set within a great circular ditch 380 feet in diameter and spaced with an accuracy of inches. Some were quarried over a hundred miles away, and a number weigh as much as 45 to 50 tons. They are set in the form of a circle and a horseshoe with marker stones used for sighting across the arrangement from different viewpoints at its center. Professor Hawkins discovered the alignment of these stones was so accurate that their error today, allowing for the precession of the equinoxes since they were built, would be less than 0.5°. If corrections are made for the settling of the stones the error is reduced to virtually zero.[5]

The point, of course, is not only that it is astonishing that men of four or five millennia ago could do these things, but even more that we would find them difficult to duplicate today with all the technology of modern engineering. Where did prehistoric men learn such skills?

As remarkable as these common threads of accomplishment

are, other specializations are perhaps even more baffling. These are hard to explain except as fragments from a common seminal culture. It would appear that representatives of the parent culture migrated to all available points of the compass, carrying with them, in each case, only a part of the original whole.

It is as though some collection of diverse talents in modern times, such as the Princeton Institute for Advanced Studies, were to be broken up and its specialists scattered throughout the world. One would carry an advanced knowledge of building and architecture here, another of medicine there and a third of space science and technology elsewhere.

A careful study of the earth's early civilizations shows a similar imbalance of specializations. Each is peculiar for some advanced area of achievement which others do not share and that is unlikely in terms of its own general level of accomplishment.

So we find the ancient Mayans and Egyptians had an advanced knowledge of medicine, including surgery and pharmacology, which others did not share. Some, like the inhabitants of Easter Island or the builders of Stonehenge and Carnac, were able to create monumental architecture on a prodigious scale without a highly organized urban life style. Unlike the Egyptians and Babylonians, they left no evidence of having developed temple cultures or grid-pattern cities. The Mayans, Egyptians and Babylonians seem to have had a profound knowledge of astronomical cycles, which they used in orienting their pyramids—a knowledge not shown in other centers where monumental architecture with massive pieces of stone was also practiced.

Could these remarkable technical specializations, which lifted certain ancient peoples above their own general level of achievement as well as their peers, have been the gift of a superior and otherworldly race?

It is interesting that the myths and legends of the ancient Egyptians, Tibetans, Hindus, Greeks, Aztecs and Mayans all tell of gods coming from the sky to teach mankind the arts of civilized living.

These tales contain accounts of what seem to be flying

craft, atomic weapons, advanced communications systems and medical miracles.

The ancient Babylonian historian Berosus tells of written accounts, going back thousands of years, which credit an animal endowed with reason and a fishlike body (but with human parts beneath and below—could it have worn a space suit?) instructing mankind in letters, sciences and every kind of art. This being, Oannes, is credited by Berosus with teaching humans to construct houses, to erect temples, to compile laws and to understand the elements of mathematics and engineering.

Speaking of this and similar stories, Carl Sagan says: "We do not know where the Sumerians came from. Their language was strange: it had no cognates with any known Indo-European, Semitic or other language, and is understood only because later people, the Akkadians, compiled extensive Sumerian-Akkadian dictionaries... I feel that if Sumerian civilization is depicted, by the descendants of the Sumerians themselves, to be of nonhuman origin, the relevant legends should be examined carefully."[6]

In view of these facts, then, it seems probable that the descendants of the Adamic race were bearers of an advanced extraterrestrial civilization. After centuries of cultural dilution and natural disaster the original centers of this Celestially taught civilization all disappeared.

THE DELUGE

A major factor in this disappearance may have been the Noahic deluge.

Scientific criticism of the flood story has generally been based on the assumption that Genesis describes a worldwide deluge. A careful study of the text, however, does not support this view. Though it says the waters covered "the earth," the word for "earth" erets, can mean either land or the whole earth. Since the Lord resolved to destroy "man whom I have created" it seems likely that erets here means only the Fertile Crescent—the land occupied by the experimental humans in the early chapters of Genesis.

One of the strongest evidences that such a destructive flood did occur comes from comparative mythology. Flood legends closely resembling the Genesis account have been found among the most widely scattered peoples, including the Egyptians, Greeks, Chinese, the Druids of Great Britain, Polynesians, Micronesians, Melanesians, Indonesians, Eskimos, Africans, East Indians and American Indians. These generally tell of a calamitous deluge in which a few were saved, in some type of boat or ship, by reaching the top of a high mountain.

Furthermore, archaeology and geology alike show that massive flooding has occurred, in recent times, in the Fertile Crescent. And in view of the fault structure at its western end and the delta at its most eastern, it is likely that it has been the scene of numerous great floods from time immemorial.

If one of these included the deluge of Genesis, stories of it would have been carried by descendants of the Adamic race throughout the world. It is difficult to explain the widespread versions of a flood story on any other basis.

In the Scriptures these descendants are typified by Noah's three sons, Shem, Ham and Japeth. The Bible states that "of them was the whole earth overspread" (Genesis 9:19).

If these speculations are correct it is likely that the descendants of the created race who remained closest to the site of the creation retained the purest and least fragmented form of the Celestials' civilization.

AFTER THE FLOOD

It is well known that the earliest historical civilization did, in fact, emerge at the eastern end of the Fertile Crescent. It was here that the ancient Sumerians first appeared about 6,000 years ago. We have already commented on the fact that their appearance is unique, among civilizations, in that it seemingly had no development. In the fourth millennium before Christ they appear in the pages of history, by what seems to be a sudden leap from stone-age ancestors to a full-blown urban civilization. This includes grid-pattern cities, a highly inflected written language, money and a developed economy, and complex and subtle literature, philosophy and art as well as an advanced knowledge of mathematics and astronomy.

If our speculations are valid it seems likely the Sumerians

were the direct lineal descendants of the "unknown ancient modern" who ancestored us all. As the "next of kin" to the "sons of God" they would have preserved much of the material and technical civilization their ancestors had been taught, as well as the Celestial religion.

This was not, of course, the popular religion later elaborated by the Babylonians, but the patriarchal religion described in Genesis—the religion of Adam and Eve, of Enoch and of Noah. It was this religion which was later carried by Abraham out of Sumer to Canaan, where he founded the people to be known as the Hebrews.

In the next chapter we will see how it was that this people was chosen, by the Lord, for a special destiny in the redemption of mankind. We will examine the Genesis record to discover how their genetic and cultural purity was preserved through the creation, by the Lord, of a social laboratory—an experiment in righteous living. We will see how their descendants were given the law which embodied the essentials of the Lord's plan for saving his fallen creation.

CHAPTER X

THE PEOPLE
AND THE LAW

And I will make of thee a great nation, and I will bless thee,
and make thy name great; and thou shalt be a blessing.

—Genesis 12:2

STARTING OVER AGAIN

Many generations had come and gone since the deluge. In
their dispersion the descendants of the flood's survivors had
strayed ever further from the Celestials' teaching. Everywhere
the Lord saw new signs of the corrupting influence of the
fallen Celestials.

He could not afford further delay in setting up his social
laboratory. Since the Celestials' Earth base had been removed,
visits to earth had been infrequent, but the time for another
was now approaching.

The schedule called for a stay of several centuries in the
area of the galaxy containing Earth and other potential colonies. During this time the Lord would gather his chosen ones,
select a leader and supervise their resettlement. Once they
were established in their new land he would give them the
law. And, in between times, he could visit other neighboring
colonies to confer with melchisedecs and inspect their progress.

The genealogical records and sample data showed the
purest strain of his creation was still concentrated near the
original Garden site, as he expected. It had developed an impressive civilization based on the Celestials' training of its
ancestors. The Celestial religion had been corrupted almost
beyond recognition. It flourished in the great urban centers,
where its priests ruled the people in an exploitive theocracy.

But here was the genetic material the Lord needed for his
"chosen" race. Once a sample had been removed he could

186

renew his covenant with them and begin their training as a "holy" people.

THE PATRIARCHS AND A DELIVERER

Few portions of the Bible have aroused more controversy, among historians and other scholars, than the chapters and books describing the Lord's next moves. As they stand in Genesis and Exodus, the call of Abraham, the saga of his heirs, their exodus from Egypt and the giving of the law to their deliverer, Moses, seem straightforward enough. Countless generations of Jews and Christians have taken them as pure history. And the colorful stories which surround them are the substance which has nourished and inspired innumerable generations of the Lord's chosen people as they struggled for survival.

Taken as a simple narrative, their "history" centers on the lives and deeds of a handful of principal actors. The Lord's call comes to Abraham, who is dwelling with his family and flocks in Haran. Tough and independent nomads, they have migrated from Ur, one of the major cities of Mesopotamia, to this crossroads on the greatest caravan route of the ancient Near East. The Lord's word is short and to the point. "Get thee out of thy country, and from thy kindred, and from thy father's house, unto a land I will shew thee" (Genesis 12:1).

Though he is already seventy-five, Abram sets out with his wife Sarai, his orphaned nephew Lot, and his flocks and herds. As the dust of the trail rises around them the promise of the Lord rings in his ears: "I will make of thee a great nation, and I will bless thee, and make thy name great..." (Genesis 12:2).

Already their course has arched hundreds of miles up through the Tigris and Euphrates valleys. Now it drops southward through Damascus into Canaan. After a sojourn in Egypt, during a famine, Abram and Lot return to Canaan and settle permanently—Lot near Sodom and Abram at Hebron, an unusually fertile region about 20 miles south of Jerusalem.

Here the Lord renews his promise to Abram, whom he renames "Abraham." He promises his "seed" will possess the land "forever" and become as numerous as the "dust of the earth" (Genesis 13:15–16). As a token of this new covenant he institutes the rite of circumcision for Abraham and his descendants. He also promises the barren Sarai (whom he re-names "Sarah") a son. Soon after this Isaac is born to brighten Abraham's and Sarah's final years.

As the saga unfolds, generations pass. Isaac fathers twins, Esau and Jacob. Jacob returns to his grandfather's homeland, "across the river," to find a wife among his Uncle Laban's daughters (Genesis 31:21). He works to pay the bride price for Rachel, whom he loves, but is first compelled to marry her older sister, Leah.

The twelve sons which come from these unions found the twelve tribes of the Lord's people. They are called the "twelve tribes of Israel," because Jacob has also been given this new name by an angel of the Lord with whom he wrestles.

Later Jacob's favorite son is sold into slavery by jealous brothers. This son, Joseph, gains his freedom and rises to power in the land of Egypt. When another famine strikes and his brothers seek refuge in Egypt, he forgives them, and the family is reunited.

And with this reunion a large-scale migration of Abraham's descendants begins. For over 400 years, Israelites dwell in the land of the Pharaohs. When the Egyptians overthrow their Hyksos invaders, a native pharaoh is reestablished on the throne. He and his successor enslave the immigrant Israelites and force them to work on cities and monuments they build to glorify the new dynasty.

Moses, the son of Levite slaves, is born and hidden among the reeds of the Nile to escape a pre-Hitlerian program of genocide. The pharaoh's daughter rescues Moses, and he is reared in the Egyptian court as a prince. As he matures he is disturbed by the mistreatment of the Israelites. Finally, in a fit of rage, he slays a particularly brutal overseer and flees Egypt to save his own life. He goes to live in Midian and marries Zipporah, a priest's daughter. While he is living in Midian the call of the Lord comes to him to deliver his people from Egyptian bondage. He returns to Egypt as a wonder-working prophet and calls down God's wrath on a reluctant pharaoh.

The Lord visits a series of plagues on the Egyptians, culminating in a dreadful night when he "passes over" the children of the Hebrews but slays the firstborn of all the Egyptian families and flocks.

After this disaster a bereaved pharaoh at last lets the Israelites go. In a mass exodus they miraculously pass through the Red Sea while a pursuing pharaoh, who has changed his mind, is drowned, along with his army.

Moses leads the Israelites for forty years in the wilderness, with the Lord guiding them in a "pillar of a cloud" by day and a "pillar of fire" by night (Exodus 13:21). Finally they are led to Mount Sinai, where the Lord gives Moses the commandments and the law.

Such is the Bible's story of how the Lord chose his people. Is it fact or fiction? Is it sacred history or national paranoia? Did God really choose the Jews or have they simply promoted themselves? These and similar questions have provoked endless controversy among scholars and theologians ever since the accounts were first set down.

Myth and the Bible

Higher critics have eagerly seized on the seemingly supernatural elements in these stories as evidences of their absurdity—a barren Sarah conceiving at ninety, the miraculous parting of the seas in the Exodus, guidance by a pillar of fire, and the commandments, written by the finger of God, on tablets of stone.

Yet, out of the welter of scholarly controversy and popular debate, a solid core of supporting evidence has emerged which argues the essential historical accuracy of the biblical record. Like the preflood heroes, the early Hebrew patriarchs and Moses are not mentioned in any historical documents other than the Bible (with the possible exception of those found at Ebla which await translation).

As with other legendary heroes, however, it seems probable their characterizations were based on real lives. Abraham, Sarah and Lot, like Noah and his "sons," may be used, in Genesis, to typify whole populations of migrants. But this does not mean they are unreal. Just as a few outstanding officers, or heroic enlisted men, are used by historians to create the picture of a battle, so the birth of the Hebrew nation is typified by the deeds of Abraham, Isaac, Jacob and Moses.

What they did and felt, what they suffered and achieved, is made to stand for the experiences and accomplishments of the whole group for whom they stand.

Viewed in this way, there is good reason for supposing Abraham and Sarah were members of the migrant population historians say did move from northwestern Mesopotamia to Canaan about 4,000 years ago.

And though the human-interest items that breathe life into the Bible's stories cannot be documented in the same way, customs and rites, supported by the findings of archaeologists and anthropologists, can tell us much. We can know, for instance, that the Genesis characterizations are ones which would have been correct for people in those times and places.

In this way we know that Jacob's going to Haran, "across the river," to pick a wife among his Uncle Laban's daughters is how a good son of 4,000 years ago, in that part of the world, would have behaved. Archaeologists and anthropologists verify that cross-cousin marriages were then, and still are, preferred among Bedouin tribes in the Near and Middle East. And as the daughters of his mother's brother, Rachel and Leah would have been Jacob's cross-cousins. Also the custom of paying a bride price is one which has been practiced in that part of the world for millennia.

Further, research into Egyptian records shows that the Hyksos pharaohs held Canaanite tribes as vassals and allowed them to cross Egypt's borders in times of famine. And historians tell us their amiable and protective policy toward the Israelites changed when the native dynasty was reestablished.

Yet, in spite of such considerations, there is good reason to think the stories of the Hebrew patriarchs and Moses have been embellished by mythic elaborations. Unlike the preflood heroes, who are often reduced to little more than genealogical skeletons in Genesis, the lives of the Hebrew culture heroes are fleshed out to an extent mere oral tradition and early recordkeeping could hardly have provided. It seems probable, on the face of the matter, that these stories have been enlarged and reworked in the process of handing down and retelling. What we know of human nature and the folk process make this inevitable.

Further, studies of these stories by comparative mythologists make it clear they show remarkable parallels with culture-hero stories around the world. Yet they tell of events which happened too late to have been spread so widely by diffusion.

So Moses, as a culture hero, follows a well-defined path when his survival is threatened in infancy; he is hidden to preserve his life, is reared by a family not his own and returns to become the leader and deliverer of his people. Variations on this "culture-hero" myth are found throughout the world and in forms which predate the Moses legend by millennia.

Yet, again, this does not mean Moses did not exist. Nor does it imply he was not called by the Lord and did not receive the law in a special revelation.

Myth as Redemptive History

Modern students of mythology know that myths are true—not in the way that textbooks in history are true but in a deeper and more profound way. Though they may contain embellishments that are contrary to fact, they are like figures of speech. Their truth lies in their hidden revelation, rather than their surface detail. Just as it communicates the truth more powerfully to say a man is a "tower of strength" than to describe him as "dependable," so a mythic description evokes commitment and purpose from its hearers which a merely factual narrative cannot. In this sense it is a form of redemptive history and defines for its hearers their deepest values and commitments.

Of this Joseph Campbell observes, "Man, apparently, cannot maintain himself in the universe without belief in . . . myth . . . Whence the force of these unsubstantial themes, by which they are empowered to galvanize populations, creating of them civilizations, each with a beauty and self-compelling destiny of its own? And why should it be that whenever men look for something solid on which to found their lives, they have chosen, not the facts in which the world abounds, but the myths of an immemorial imagination . . ."[1]

So it is that the half-mythical, half-historical materials of the patriarchal legends have informed the Lord's people of their special calling and inspired them to fulfill a timeless destiny.

It is this ability of redemptive myths to elicit living faith that most sets them apart from mere secular history. The im-

portant thing about the Genesis stories of the patriarchs and
Moses is that they have provided a living faith which has sustained the Jews through 4,000 years of unparalleled survival,
and have provided spiritual sustenance for half the Gentile
world, as well.

THE JEWS AND REDEMPTIVE HISTORY

And what is it these stories reveal? What is the hidden
meaning they conceal amid their trappings of Middle Eastern
myth and imagery? The Bible, and the identity and survival
of the Jews, are unanimous on this point—the Jews are a
chosen people with a divine calling.

Every fragment of the Genesis legends and sagas points up
this assertion. By it, and it alone, the "truth" of their biblical
history must be judged.

And what is the verdict? Are the Jews God's chosen people?
Is the law a redemptive plan given them by divine revelation?
The Bible says it is so, and our space age interpretation justi-
fies its claim.

Traditional interpretations have strained the credulity and
offended the common sense of Jews and Christians alike. Why
would a just and benevolent God arbitrarily single out an
obscure people for an unfair favoritism? This attitude is
cynically reflected in the oft-repeated aphorism, "How odd of
God to choose the Jews." Even more, having singled them out
and unilaterally imposed a covenant on Abraham's descendants,
why would he allow his chosen ones to suffer the exclusions,
persecutions and even exterminations which the Jews have
undergone? Assimilated Jews, who have rejected their Jewish-
ness, are particularly prone to raise such questions—but so
have the faithful. Is it possible to give an enlightened explanation of the idea of a chosen people, a special covenant and the
law?

A SPACE-AGE VIEW OF GOD'S "CHOICE"

The starting point in an enlightened understanding of the
Lord's "choice" of the Jews is to recognize when he chose
them. If our interpretation of the experimental creation is
correct, it was not when he called Abraham, even though the
mythic account seems to say this. It was not even earlier when

he singled out Abraham's ancestor, Noah, for salvation from the flood. No, the Lord chose those who would become the Jews when he re-created them from an evolved *Homo sapiens.* His choice of them was not a moral or a theological one—it was essentially genetic. The ancestors of Noah and Abraham were "chosen" by the Lord when he chose to create them. They became his "people" when he designed them to be the people they are.

The later choices, when he covenanted with Noah and Abraham, were not instances of arbitrary favoritism—they were simply recognitions of an inbreeding population that had remained closest to what he originally designed.

THE JEWS AS A "LIVING FOSSIL"

The term "living fossils" is used, by paleontologists, to designate species that have existed through vast ages, while most others have become extinct. During this time they remain virtually unchanged and seemingly extinction-proof.

Earlier, in Chapter VII, we quoted C. L. Brace and Ashley Montagu, who point out that fossils of the "ancient modern" who ancestored *Homo sapiens sapiens* have never been found. And in the strictest sense this is, of course, true.

In another sense, however, there is good reason for believing the Jewish people are "living fossils" of the Lord's experimental creation. For in spite of some miscegenation and assimilation, they have endured as the people of his law. Over millennia, while all the civilizations that were their early contemporaries vanished, they have remained virtually unchanged in their essential culture—without a national identity, without a homeland and without even a common tongue.

Like the coelacanth and ginkgo tree, which have defied the biological laws governing the life of species, the Jews have defied historical laws that govern the life of civilizations.

In this sense, of course, their fossilhood is more figurative than real. There is substantial evidence, however, to support the idea that, as a gene pool, they also show a more literal kind of fossilhood.

We have argued the created "ancient modern" was superior to contemporary humanity in intelligence and civilizational achievement. If the Jews represent a fossil survival of this gene type, they too might be expected to show superior capacity for intellectual and civilizational achievements. Is this, in fact, the case? The answer is an undeniable affirmative.

"AND THOU SHALT BE A BLESSING"

One of the most remarkable and inexplicable aspects of Jewish identity is its extraordinary record of intellectual and creative achievement. One has only to examine a roster of eminent men and women in almost any field of intellectual or artistic endeavor to verify that Jews are represented out of all proportion to their numbers.

Since they were first instituted in 1896 by Alfred Nobel, a Swedish chemist, the Nobel prizes have been, perhaps, the world's most prestigious recognition of civilizational achievement. They are awarded annually to the most outstanding contributors in physics, chemistry, medicine, literature and peace. Though Jews constitute only about .3% of the world's population they have received an astonishing 12% of the total of all Nobel prizes ever given; and in Germany alone, in the period preceding World War II, though they made up only 1% of the total German population, they won 50% of all Nobel prizes awarded.[2]

Not only do Jews swell the ranks of eminence out of all proportion to their numbers, but the most sweeping intellectual revolutions in history have, to a remarkable degree, been the work of Jews. Though only one person out of every 300 is a Jew a predominance of Jewish names comes to mind when we think of the great intellectual upheavals that have shaped western civilization and shaken the world—Moses, Jesus, Marx, Freud and Einstein are examples.

The fields of philosophy, religion, science, the arts and philanthropy scintillate with Jewish genius. Sociologists tell us that Jews enter the learned professions more frequently, in proportion to their numbers, than do members of any other ethnic or religious group. Yet in America, though they constitute 3% of the population, less than .1% are imprisoned for crimes of violence.[3]

Such statistics inevitably call to mind the Lord's promise to Abraham: "And I will make of thee a great nation, and I will bless thee, and make thy name great; and thou shalt be a blessing... and in thee shall all families of the earth be blessed" (Genesis 12:2–3).

In the face of such evidence we are compelled to admit the Lord's promise has been abundantly fulfilled. Wherever Jews have gone, in their worldwide dispersion, they have brought honor and glory to their adopted homelands and bestowed on them the gifts of civilization.

It has been argued by some that Jewish achievement is not the result of genetic superiority but rather of an in-group culture which stresses achievement to an extraordinary degree. And undoubtedly this emphasis is present in the childrearing practices of many Jewish families. Sociologists agree it has been a primary cause of Jewish survival.

But this will not explain why, in tests of intelligence (which most psychologists agree is primarily genetic), Jews also showed marked superiority to most other ethnic and religious groups— even at an early age.

For example, in 1922 Lewis Terman made a survey of 168,000 elementary-school children in California and qualified 649 as "gifted," using the Stanford-Binet Intelligence Test. (He defined "gifted" as scoring at, or above, 140 IQ). Of this group (drawn from the cities of Los Angeles, San Francisco, Berkeley and Alameda), he found Jews represented 10%. Since Jews were estimated at only 5% of the population of these cities this means they were twice as likely to be gifted as their incidence in the general population would have suggested.[4]

THE SOCIAL LABORATORY

This leads us to an inevitable question. Why? Why have Jews survived when all their early contemporaries have disappeared? Why do they excel in business and professional achievements? Why do they swell the ranks of genius and civilizational accomplishment, out of all proportion to their numbers?

Is it because, as an inbreeding group in a direct line of descent from the experimental creation, they have retained an unusual amount of their original endowment? Is it, as C. P. Snow has suggested, because they are a "superior genetic pool"?

If our space age interpretation of the creation is correct, they are the most direct descendants of the Lord's original experiment. And because they were chosen by him for a unique social experiment they have retained, over the millennia, the isolation and control necessary for maximum reinforcement of their genetic superiority. As those specially selected to spearhead the Lord's redemption of humanity they have remained in a social laboratory throughout the centuries —a social laboratory designed by the Celestials to preserve genetic superiority and reinforce excellence and righteousness in the human gene pool.

A laboratory, in a scientific experiment, can be defined as an isolated and controlled environment in which a scientific objective can be achieved. The isolation and control of the Lord's social laboratory was defined by the rules handed down to Moses—the law!

The Law

Scholars have debated the origin of the law. In reality it matters little whether the Lord gave it directly to Moses or it arose in some other manner. Its content is its own proof of Celestial origin. As a legal code it is unrivaled in wisdom and unique in the aims it seeks to accomplish. No other system devised by mankind has equaled its record of endurance, shown its adaptability to all the vicissitudes of the human condition, developed the subtleties and elaborations it has engendered or attempted the range and completeness it possesses.

As an instrument designed to make a people peculiar, separate and holy it has no parallel among other past or present legal systems. No aspect of life, however great or small, escapes its purview. In its historic embrace it has been careful to define standards of barbering, methods for cleansing dishes and utensils, menstrual hygiene, modes of dress, family obligations, business practices, sound nutrition, patterns of work and rest and rituals of worship.

According to Genesis it began with the Ten Commandments written by the finger of the Lord on Mount Sinai. Ultimately, as its revelation unfolded, it culminated in the Torah —the first five books of the Bible: Genesis, Exodus, Leviticus,

Numbers and Deuteronomy. According to the Scriptures it
is the legislation of Moses inspired by the guidance of the
Lord. According to Jewish tradition it embraces 613 commands.

Over the millennia, since it was first given to the chosen
people, it has undergone endless analysis, refinement, elaboration and application. Like any other system of laws its own
content has been dwarfed by the mountainous structure of
rulings and interpretations which have been erected on its
foundation. The essence of these has been captured for students of Judaism, in a monumental multivolumed work known
as the Talmud. For the scholars and teachers of the chosen
people it has been the Encyclopaedia Britannica and Black-
stone of Judaism rolled into one. Basically it is a legal com-
pendium, but it is like no other ever put together. For whereas
most legal compendiums are dry as dust, the Talmud constantly elaborates the closest legal analysis with a bewildering
array of illustrative and atmospheric detail involving tales,
poems, prayers and anecdotes all reminiscent of earlier times
and conjuring up vibrant pictures of Judaism over the centuries.

Yet the heart of the law remains the Torah. And with the
Torah we reach the second major artifact which proves the
Celestials were here.

In the chapter on the creation of mankind, and earlier, we
pointed out that humanity, itself, is the most convincing
single piece of hard evidence which shows that members of a
Celestial civilization once walked the earth. With our unparalleled strangeness and our unearthly brains we cannot
adequately be accounted for by the mechanisms of evolution.
Only the assumption that our development was interrupted
and drastically improved, within an incredibly short period
of time, can offer a sufficient explanation for our speculations,
spiritual strivings, theorizings and creativity.

In the same way the Torah is a second piece of evidence
which, on its face, bears the stamp of Celestial origin. We
have seen, here and there as our space age interpretation has
unfolded, that bits of knowledge disclosed in the Scriptures
show unmistakable influence of an advanced civilization.

It is as though we are reading some epic or saga, supposedly handed down from the Greeks and Romans, and suddenly come upon a passage stating, "And so Neil Armstrong set foot on the moon." We would, at that point, quite reasonably assume the documents in our hand were not entirely the work of Greek and Roman authors.

In the same way when we suddenly read, in the Psalms or Job, that a "thousand years is as a day" with the Lord, or that "Arcturus with his sons" is "guided" through the heavens, we have evidence that millennia ago Bible writers knew things which we have heretofore believed to be our own discoveries.

In the Torah, we have a blueprint for human living which exhibits precisely the same sort of evidence. Throughout the five books which make up its structure, there is an unending stream of ordinance and counsel proving those who composed it had scientific knowledge surpassing our own in the twentieth century. In its insight into the human condition, its grasp of social psychology, its implied knowledge of biochemistry, nutrition and preventive medicine, it is unrivaled by any other ancient or modern code. The fact that it defines a life style which, alone among those of other ancient civilizations, has survived the ravages of four millennia, including conquest, exile, dispersion and holocaust, suggests there is something special about it.

Scholars have pointed out that many of its laws and prescriptions show parallels with the codes of other Near or Middle Eastern peoples. Some have even suggested that Moses largely borrowed the Ten Commandments of the Decalogue from Hammurabi, an earlier Babylonian lawgiver.

And these parallels do exist. But what these theories minimize, or neglect altogether, is the uniqueness of the law of Moses. Every society which has reached any significant level has had laws for the protection of life and property, for the compensation of the injured by those who injure them, and for the punishment of those who threaten it and the protection of those who are innocent of wrongdoing.

Yet most ancient codes, like that of Hammurabi, are forms of class legislation which guarantee special privileges to the rich and powerful and strip those who lack status of basic human rights. Even our own constitution, in its original form, failed to protect the basic human rights of women and slaves.

The Torah, on the other hand, gave equality, before the law, to all persons—including "foreigners"—over 3,000 years ago.[5]

Few codes, until modern times, have adequately recognized that health and nutrition, as well as a wholesome environment, are responsibilities of the state. Yet the Torah, 3,500 years ago, embodied pure-food laws and public-health measures which are more enlightened than those enforced by many modern governments, including our own.

The claim that most of these were simply borrowed from surrounding civilizations has no real plausibility. There is nothing in the records of the ancient Egyptians or Babylonians that even faintly suggests the extraordinary insight the Torah shows in forbidding foods rich in fat or high in uric-acid level. Only now, in the twentieth century, are biochemists beginning to prove the nutritional link between these dietary imbalances and degenerative diseases such as heart attacks, cancer, diabetes and gout.

Early in this century, Sigmund Freud wrote a series of essays attempting to prove that the law of Moses, as well as Moses himself, were of purely Egyptian origin. Arguing largely from a psychoanalytic study of comparative mythology, he claimed that circumcision, Abraham's covenantal mark of the chosen people, was borrowed from the Egyptians and was not a part of the original covenant. He argued that Moses was probably an Egyptian priest who had been discredited as a follower of Akhnaton—the heretical pharaoh who worshipped one god. His religion was swept away, after his death, in a palace revolution. He proposed that Moses had carried this discredited religion into exile, taking a group of rebellious Hebrew slaves with him. Finally he suggested that Moses had imposed the worship of one God and a patchwork of Egyptian legislation on his followers in an attempt to exalt his own ego and perpetuate the immortality of his name.[6]

Apart from the scholarly questions which Freud's views raise (and they have been severely challenged by recent scholarship), such an explanation of the law simply cannot account for its remarkable scientific insight and endurance. The Egyptian civilization, which supposedly spawned it, has long since disappeared, even though its peoples were not dispersed and have, throughout history, retained a national identity and homeland. How could Moses have extracted anything from it that would explain the unique endurance of the Jews? And, though the Egyptians were remarkably advanced for their times in their knowledge of medicine, surgery and pharmacology, there is no evidence they had a modern understanding of nutrition.

Yet the Torah, in passage after passage, displays the most advanced insights into the relation between diet and health. For example, in Leviticus we read: "Ye shall eat no manner of fat, of ox, or of sheep, or of goat. And the fat of the beast that dieth of itself, and the fat of that which is torn with beasts, may be used in any other use: but ye shall in no wise eat of it" (Leviticus 7:23-24).

Not until the last half of this century have laboratory and clinical studies clearly demonstrated the rationale behind this ancient prohibition. Biochemists now know that fats combine with oxygen, both in the bloodstream and outside the body (as with rancid meat), to produce free radicals—a process called "peroxidation." Clinical and experimental studies show these may attack blood-vessel walls and genetic material to cause cardiovascular diseases and hasten aging.

Further, a high intake of saturated animal fats (the ones forbidden in Leviticus) has been directly linked, in numerous studies, to an increase in the incidence of heart attacks. The best known of these studies is the Framingham, which was sponsored by Boston University Medical Center and followed 5,000 residents of Framingham, Massachusetts, over a twenty-five-year period. It showed high blood fat levels increased the risk of heart attack as much as 600%.

While the relation between diet and blood fat is not yet entirely clear, numerous studies have recently shown nations having diets low in fat also tend to have significantly lower cardiovascular death rates, less incidence of cancer and less diabetes and joint disease.[7]

These conclusions are only now becoming well enough established to win the support of government and other health agencies—3,500 years after the ancient Hebrews received them in Leviticus. So the Senate Select Committee on Nutrition and Human Needs recently recommended a 25% reduction in American consumption of fats. Endorsements of this stand have also recently been given by Gio Gori, of the National Cancer Institute, and David Hegsted, of the Harvard School of Public Health.

How did Moses, or the Hebrews of so long ago, know a high fat intake is a grave hazard to human health? Was it because this law was given to them by Celestials who studied human physiology in the light of a nutritional science more advanced than our own?

And how did the writers of the law know that shellfish can be harmful? What was the insight that prompted the writer of Leviticus to say: "... all that have not fins and scales in the seas, and in the rivers, of all that move in the waters, and of any living thing which is in the waters, they shall be an abomination unto you ..." (Leviticus 11:10)? Could Israelites of 3,000 years ago have guessed these forbidden sea animals would be linked, in our time, to increased risk of joint and kidney disease because of a high uric-acid content? Or had a race with higher biochemical wisdom already communicated this discovery to them?

"A SPECIAL PEOPLE"

And what of the remarkable sociological and psychological insights built into the law? Dissenters and assimilators in Judaism often chafe at the restrictiveness of Jewish kosher laws or the awkwardness of sabbath observance in a society which rests and worships on Sunday. And these aspects of the law are indeed irrational to outsiders, and they do make it difficult for Jews to work for, or even socialize with, Gentiles. But that is a part of their point. As the Lord observed to Moses, so long ago, "For thou art a holy people unto the Lord thy God: the Lord thy God hath chosen thee to be a special people unto himself ..." (Deuteronomy 7:6).

The ingenuity involved in the Mosaic system of cleanliness and holiness taboos, and of special observances, lies precisely in the fact that it does make it difficult for Jews to work for anyone but Jews, to marry anyone but Jews and to go on vacation or have dinner or to worship with anyone but Jews.

The law is unique in its aim of isolating a people from the possibility of influence or assimilation by outsiders and of making them unique and peculiar in their isolation and dedication to a legal code.

Other legal systems aim at equity and justice. The law of Moses includes these but also aims at the higher ideals of righteousness and holiness. To be sure, the Jewish people have not always, or perhaps even often, lived up to these unearthly aims. But enough have aimed at them consistently enough so that the chosen people endure today, after 4,000 years—a miracle of survival.

As novelist Herman Wouk puts it: "Historians and social scientists, speculating on the staying power of our people, all converge on one element of our life that marks us off from other nations: the Mosaic law. In the religious system by which we have lived so long, the modern mind finds an institutional system, a web of habits of thought and conduct, remarkably calculated to enable a small nation, even when fragmentized among other nations, to go on existing against all odds, under all possible adversity, from millennium to millennium.

"The traditional view starts at the other end as it were. It holds that the survival system is the law of God, the law is to be obeyed because it is the will of God, and the eternal people survives by the Grace of God."[8]

The Law as "Schoolmaster"

Yet, important as its survival value has been to the Jews, the Bible teaches that the law has a wider and higher meaning for the world at large. This value resides in the fact that the law is not just a compilation of rules; it is also a training device whose prescriptions and observances are types and symbols. In its symbolic function the law points to a higher way of life practiced on another world—a way of life which is the foundation of the Celestials' civilization. As such it is intended to disclose ultimate realities and values which lie beyond it. And the highest of these is the Celestial religion. The types and symbols of the law prepare the way for a new revelation of this spiritual heritage which was made by the Redeemer. So the Apostle Paul remarks: "Wherefore the law was our schoolmaster to bring us unto Christ, that we might be justified by faith" (Galatians 3:24).

As the stories of the patriarchs and Moses are redemptive

history, so the rituals and observances of the law are redemptive symbology. In their ceremonial detail they foreshadow higher Celestial realities which will one day be established on Earth. So the writer of Hebrews remarks: "It was therefore necessary that the patterns of things in the heavens should be purified with these [sacrifices]; but the heavenly things themselves with better sacrifices than these" (Hebrews 9:23).

The types and symbols of the law, then, prefigured higher realities of the Celestial religion for which it is a training.

Its demand for covenantal obedience points the way to a living faith which can ultimately fulfill and replace it. Its sacrificial rituals foreshadow the redemptive power of divine cosmic love exemplified in the life and death of the Redeemer. Its feasts and observances imitate the institutions and objectives of the Celestials' civilization which will one day be established on the planet Earth.

In this sense the law is not just a life style for a "peculiar" people, but a preparation for Celestial citizenship—not only for Jews but for the world at large! Though a great part of its legal structure pertains only to the chosen people, and to certain periods in their development and history, others of its parts have universal relevance and embody the preparation and training the Celestials require of all who aspire to membership in their future utopia.

As we will see, the chosen people continue to occupy a special place in the Lord's plan and will have a special role at the time of the end and in the Celestials' future civilization. Yet in his fulfillment of the law the Redeemer opened up the plan embodied in the law to humanity at large.

In later chapters we will examine how the distinction may be drawn between those requirements that pertain peculiarly to the chosen people and those that are binding on us all. In the final chapter we shall examine in detail that most unique of all the law's observances, the sabbath. In it we shall discover a hidden meaning which places it at the heart of the Celestials' civilization and makes its observance the highest training for humans aspiring to Celestial citizenship. We shall see how the tools of space age interpretation can reveal its awesome potential—not just as a religious occasion for rest and worship, but as the very key to the Celestials' most prized possession, the secret of eternal life!

Before attempting to grasp the ultimate secrets of Celestial civilization, however, it will be helpful to take a closer look at some of their more practical achievements. Throughout much of the Bible, and particularly in the books known as "prophetic," a space age approach reveals startling similarities between what our own engineers and scientists have produced and what the Celestials revealed to those chosen as the Lord's human messengers. In the chapter which follows we will take a closer look at the hardware of the Celestials' civilization and the light it may throw on one of today's most profound mysteries.

CHAPTER XI

CELESTIALS, PROPHETS AND UFO'S

To him that rideth upon the heavens of heavens, which were of old; lo, he doth send out his voice, and that a mighty voice.

—Psalms 68:33

On July 20, 1969, U.S. astronaut Neil A. Armstrong became the first man to set foot on the moon. As he started on his historic moon walk he said, "That's one small step for man, one giant leap for mankind." And it was a giant leap—a leap toward the stars, which have glimmered like mysterious beacons through the long ages humans have struggled upward from savagery.

Twenty-five centuries before Neil Armstrong took his historic "small step," a young Hebrew priest stood beside the River Chebar, an irrigation canal emptying into the Euphrates near the Persian Gulf. He had been recently deported from Jerusalem by the Babylonian king, Nebuchadnezzar. As he stood there musing about his exile and longing for his family and friends he suddenly heard a roaring noise overhead. Looking up, he saw a huge cloud of smoke with jets of fire stabbing downward from its center. Slowly, out of the cloud, four long columns began to descend. As they cleared the smoke he noticed each was surrounded by a whirring blur like that of rapidly moving wings. The blurs were located about halfway up the columns. As the descent of the strange creature continued it reached a point just north of the priest, where it hovered as though searching for a landing site. This gave him a chance to study it more closely. To his surprise the columns looked like men except that they were constructed of a brass-like metal.

The top of each column was surrounded by what looked like heads facing the four directions. As he checked them he could see each had the same four faces. And, to him, they resembled the faces of an eagle, an ox, a lion and a man. The one nearest him showed the manlike face and created the illusion of a mechanical man. About midway down each column he could see the strange blur of whirling motion where winglike blades moved around a rotating shaft.

Below these, on each side of the column, were what looked like arms with hands except that these, too, seemed to be made of some brasslike metal.

As his eyes slid on down the columns he noticed that two short metal rods projected from each side. These terminated in round metal pods like brass feet. As he took in the whole column facing him it did, indeed, look like a metallic man with wings.

And now he could study those strange stabs of lightning-like flames. They darted from one place, then another, in the midst of the four columns. Their succession was almost too rapid for the eye to follow. And as this irregular lightning continued to shoot out the whole structure shifted this way and that as though seeking a place to touch down.

Suddenly, almost without his seeing the maneuver, it settled and the feet touched ground. Now the sound of roaring diminished as the engine was cut to idling, and the darting flames stopped. The whirling wings rotated slowly, and he could see there were four on each shaft joined at the center.

Then to his surprise something descended out of the base of each shaft which was at last familiar—wheels! The leg pods retracted, and the whole craft began to move about on the wheels.

He had never seen a wheeled chariot move without animals to pull it before, and the sight unnerved him now. But his intelligence came to his rescue. It must be that the manlike metallic creatures were alive, after all, and each one was pulling his own wheel!

But now once again he was thrown into confusion by the creature's strange behavior. He was used to watching chariots and had often seen the slow arc of the wheels when the chariot rounded a corner. These wheels were doing something he had never seen before! The creature had come up against a slight obstruction ahead and, instead of turning to go around it as chariots did, it had simply shifted sideways and moved ahead. The wheels had, all four, gone to the side without turning!

The creature was now nearing him again, and he could see it in greater detail. He strained his eyes to study these strange wheels more closely—no wonder! They seemed to have smaller wheels inside them!

"A Wheel Within a Wheel"

Each wheel had a number of barrel-shaped wheels mounted so that they rotated sideways using its main rim as their axis. As a result it could roll forward smoothly (since the barrels were small and closely mounted), or it could stop and simply roll sideways on them without the main wheel turning at all!

Now, at last, the strange creature seemed to find what it was looking for and settled in a place where all four columns were exactly level. The blades slowed and came to a stop, then two folded upward and two folded downward to rest beside each column.

Now for the first time the priest directed his attention upward above the four columns. From where he stood the cone-shaped underside of the dome, to which the four columns were attached, looked like a greatly flattened child's top. It was supported, around the edge, by the four columns. From his viewpoint the huge flaring undersurface looked like the silver-gray vault of the sky. Up above this "firmament," as he called it, was a small, clear capsule which glistened prismatically in the sunlight. Inside, on a high-backed, thronelike chair, sat what looked like a man. As he watched, the manlike being seemed to notice him, and he prostrated himself as he knew was proper with Babylonian monarchs. As he lay stretched on the ground, face down, a loud commanding voice came from the firmament up above. The being spoke to him.

What Ezekiel Actually Saw

Had Neil Armstrong been standing beside this priest, on the River Chebar, he would have had little difficulty in understanding what he saw. Some of it was incorporated in the Apollo 11 Moon Mission which had taken him on his historic flight. Other features were on drawing boards at NASA as part of the plans for future space missions. Still others were unknown to him, but his training in engineering and astronautics would have enabled him to grasp their principles easily.

He would have recognized the "creature" as an atmospheric entry craft of advanced design. The four columns, containing helicopter units, gave the lift and braking necessary for take-offs and landings in an atmosphere. They could be jettisoned to become modules and to fly independently.

The arms and hands under the blades were similar to ones he had seen handling radioactive materials, by remote control, in atomic reactors. He would have known these were planned for use in future U.S. space shuttles.

The lightninglike stabs of flame came from a rocket engine which produced slight amounts of thrust to maneuver and stabilize the craft during landings.

The sliding legs, mounted to shock absorbers, cushioned the landing to protect delicate precision instruments. The broad leg pods increased the area of contact so that the heavy craft would not sink down into soft earth. A design similar to that of the main body had been tested at NASA's Langley Research Center in developing a body design for entry craft with maximum air drag and minimum weight.

He would have understood that the cowl of the command capsule glistened like a rainbow because its plastic cover acted as a prism in breaking up sunlight.

He would also have known the commanding voice came from a loudspeaker.

The wheel which could go in any direction without turning would have interested him most. He would readily have grasped its principle and felt admiration for the designers who had produced it. For it brilliantly solved a problem that had bothered NASA's engineers in planning for soft landings—how to construct a wheel that could move in any direction in soft earth (or the deep dust that had been anticipated on the moon) without the difficulty of turning the whole wheel. It also provided a way to maneuver in very tight spaces where there was not room to go backward or forward for conventional turns.

The priest, whose name was Ezekiel, had no Neil Armstrong to explain his strange experience, however. As a result he had to try to understand what he saw in terms of his own knowledge. He used analogies and comparisons to which he was accustomed in trying to describe the strange creature that had disturbed his exile.

Let's examine his own version of the experience:

"And I looked, and, behold, a whirlwind came out of the north, a great cloud, and a fire infolding itself ...

"Also out of the midst thereof came the likeness of four living creatures. And this was their appearance; they had the likeness of a man.

"And every one had four faces, and every one had four wings.

"And their feet were straight feet; and the sole of their feet was like the sole of a calf's foot: and they sparkled like the colour of burnished brass.

"And they had the hands of a man under their wings on their four sides....

"Their wings were joined one to another ...

"As for the likeness of their faces, they four had the face of a man, and the face of a lion ... and ... the face of an ox ... [and] ... the face of an eagle....

"As for the likeness of the living creatures, their appearance was like burning coals of fire, and like the appearance of lamps: it went up and down ... and the fire was bright, and out of the fire went forth lightning....

"Now as I beheld the living creatures, behold one wheel upon the earth by the living creatures ...

"The appearance of the wheels and their work was like unto the colour of a beryl ... and their appearance and their work was as it were a wheel in the middle of a wheel.

"When they went, they went upon their four sides: and they turned not when they went....

"And the likeness of the firmament upon the heads of the living creature was as the colour of the terrible crystal, stretched forth over their heads above....

"And when they went, I heard the noise of their wings, like the noise of great waters ...

"And there was a voice from the firmament that was over their heads, when they stood, and had let down their wings.

"And above the firmament that was over their heads was the likeness of a throne, as the appearance of a sapphire stone: and upon the likeness of the throne was the likeness ... of a man ...

" ... I saw as it were the appearance of fire, and it had brightness round about.

"As the appearance of the bow that is in the cloud in the day of rain, so was the appearance of the brightness round about. ... And when I saw it, I fell upon my face, and I heard a voice of one that spake" (Ezekiel 1:4–28).

Since it was set down almost 2,500 years ago, Ezekiel's famous "vision" has been challenged by scholars and theologians. Most have assumed it was simply a mystical experience and have looked for obscure "spiritual meanings." Others, less concerned with its religious significance, have concluded the chariot was wholly imaginary—the figment of a diseased mind. Comparative mythologists have suggested Ezekiel borrowed his "vision" from myths and symbols around him. They have pointed out that the four faces of his "living creatures" are reminiscent of the Assyrian karibu—a sculptured effigy often used at the entrance to palaces in Babylon.

It remained for a NASA engineer to recognize, in Ezekiel's description, elements which link it with experimental designs being developed in our own space program. Josef F. Blumrich, former chief of the Systems Layout Branch of NASA, set out to write a book debunking the idea of ancient astronauts. In the process of studying Ezekiel's "vision" he became convinced that what Ezekiel saw was an entry craft remarkably similar to models being considered by NASA. The idea was confirmed when he realized the "wheel within a wheel" was an ingenious solution to a problem which had perplexed Apollo Space Mission planners.

Critics of this view have argued that Ezekiel's visions were just that—visions or hallucinations. So Clifford Wilson argues: "Visions are not necessarily literal phenomena ... Ezekiel clearly shows the vehicle ... is in fact a symbolic presentation."[1] Unfortunately, for Professor Wilson, the Hebrew text does not back him up. The word Ezekiel uses for "visions" is *mareh*, commonly used for ordinary perception—the act of "viewing" or "seeing." It is not the word employed elsewhere in the Old Testament when a hallucination or revelation is intended. That word is *chazown*—a "dream" or "revelation." Indeed, everything in Ezekiel's account of this "chariot" suggests this intelligent priest was a remarkably sharp observer and possessed a keen, critical intelligence. Speaking of his description, J. F. Blumrich concludes: "The results obtained show us a space vehicle which beyond any doubt is not only technically feasible but in fact is very well designed to fulfill its function and purpose. What remains fantastic is that such a spacecraft was a tangible reality more than 2,500 years ago!"[2]

THE BIBLE AND SPACE CRAFT

Ezekiel's "chariot" is, perhaps, the best-known example of a spacecraft in the Bible. Numerous exponents of the ancient-astronaut theory have seized on it as proof of extraterrestrial visits to Earth. And, in its detail, it is probably the most convincing. Its mention of "wheels" that "lift up" at takeoff and the accompanying noise of its flight—"like the noise of great waters" (Ezekiel 2:19, 24)—hardly sound like descriptions of a mystical vision. They are much more suggestive of twentieth-century space hardware.

Yet Ezekiel's "chariot" is only one of many strange flying objects which appear in the Bible. And along with them we find descriptions of equipment and settings which are much more suggestive of space age technology than of religious symbolism.

An analysis of these would easily require another book, in itself. But it will be useful here at least to sample their range.

In Old Testament times the spacecraft of the Celestials were so commonly seen they apparently were taken for granted and occasioned little or no excitement. So we find that during the time of the Exodus and wilderness experience the children of Israel were led, and visited, by an object which is variously described as a "pillar of fire" (Exodus 14:24), a "cloud" (Exodus 24:15), a "devouring fire" (Exodus 24:17), and a "cloudy pillar" (Exodus 33:9). On one occasion, the Book of Exodus reports, "Mount Sinai was altogether on a smoke, because the Lord descended upon it in fire: and the smoke thereof ascended as the smoke of a furnace, and the whole mount quaked greatly" (Exodus 19:18).

Almost 500 years later the Prophet Elijah is reported to have been carried alive, into heaven, by a fiery "chariot." Strangely it is suggestive of Ezekiel's craft, for it, too, involves "living creatures" which are described as "horses" by Elijah's companion, Elisha. So II Kings reports: "And it came to pass, as they still went on, and talked, that, behold, there appeared a chariot of fire, and horses of fire, and parted them both asunder; and Elijah went up by a whirlwind into heaven" (II Kings 2:11).

Reacting to this remarkable exit, Elisha cried out, "My father, my father, the chariot of Israel, and the horsemen thereof!" (II Kings 2:12). Apparently the Lord's craft was well enough known, by then, that it was commonly recognized as "the chariot of Israel."

A little earlier, Israel's great King David tells how the Lord "rode upon a cherub, and did fly: and he was seen upon the wings of the wind" (II Samuel 22:11). This theme is a continuing one with the poet of the Psalms as the verse opening this chapter indicates.

Interestingly, "a cherub" is how Ezekiel also describes the strange "living creatures" with "wings," "arms" and "faces," which made up the helicopter units of his "chariot." So the Lord instructs a technician who is servicing his "chariot": "Go in between the wheels, even under the cherub, and fill thine hand with coals of fire from between the cherubims, and scatter them over the city" (Ezekiel 10:2).

We have already seen that "cherubs" are servomechanisms which can take many forms, including that of flying craft. And the instructions for servicing this "cherub" sound suspiciously like some sort of waste-disposal procedure preliminary to refueling.

Other prophets, too, report on flying objects. Isaiah tells how he saw the Lord sitting upon a "throne" which was "high and lifted up." Like Ezekiel's craft a loud, commanding voice issued from it which caused the "posts of the door" to move. And like the Exodus "cloud" it filled the house with "smoke" (Isaiah 6:1, 4). The prophet Zechariah also tells of a "vision" in which he saw a "flying roll," over 30 feet long and 17 feet wide, which had humanlike figures "in its midst" that "lifted"

it up "between the earth and the heaven." Again they are
strangely reminiscent of Ezekiel's manlike helicopter units,
though Zechariah describes them as "women"—rather than
men—with "wings like the wings of a stork" (Zechariah 5:1–
9).

Later he tells how he saw "four chariots" come out from
"two mountains" that were "mountains of brass" (Zechariah
6:1–3)—a good description for the most common form of
"flying saucers." Like Elijah's "fiery chariot" these chariots had
"horses" which could be jettisoned and in which pilots, as in
David's poetic description, could "ride on the wings of the
wind."

This unusually precise description of a mother ship dis-
gorging small craft, or modules, is reminiscent of J. F. Blumrich's conclusion about Ezekiel's chariot when he says: "Both
the layout of the spacecraft, as well as the analysis provide a
sure indication that it was designed to serve as a shuttle between a mother ship and the surface of the earth."[3]

Finally, in the New Testament, John the Revelator describes a "vision" (probably a televised view) of a command
center we have already examined in Chapter VI, *Colony
Earth.* The context of the description makes it clear that the
center is not part of a fixed base, but is actually itself a craft
remarkably similar to Ezekiel's. Like his chariot it has a central "throne" flanked by four "beasts" with the "faces" of a
lion, a calf, a man and an eagle. Like Ezekiel's beasts these
have wings; "Seven lamps of fire" burn before its "throne,"
reminiscent of Ezekiel's "appearance of lamps" which emitted
lightninglike flames. A manlike being sits on its throne and
"thunderings and voices" come from the "throne." And, like
Ezekiel's craft, the command capsule of this "throne" is surrounded by a "rainbow" (Revelation 4:2–8).

It appears that this command center is much larger than
Ezekiel's, since it accommodates twenty-four "elders," and it
may be housed in a mother spome which is probably the "New
Jerusalem," docked on Mazzaroth.

The four "beasts" with "eyes and wings" are clearly similar
to Ezekiel's "living beings," since they have "faces" that resemble animals and men to these early writers. Yet, as we
saw, in Chapter VI, they apparently contain computers as well

as helicopter units. The presence of mechanical arms and leg pods combine to suggest still another function of these ingenious "living creatures." When attached to the main craft they obviously "lift it up," as Zechariah suggested. When jettisoned they can fly independently and serve as modules in which passengers can "ride on the wings of the wind."

But they also have nonflying functions on the ground. When the craft is taxiing, and they are attached, they can collect samples or move obstacles out of the way with their mechanical arms. Their wheels "full of eyes" (as Ezekiel describes them in 1:18) transmit a continuous panorama, by closed-circuit television, of the terrain and obstacles which cannot be seen from the command capsule above.

When they are detached, on the ground, they become independent automata, or robots—the Bible's familiar "cherubim" with wings. Equipped with heads that contain computers and are studded with eyelike sensors, possessing mechanical arms and leg pods, these "likenesses of men" can range out from the craft and perform whatever chores are assigned to them by the commander from the capsule. When it is convenient they walk, and at other times they fly with their wings.

The different animallike faces they possess are doubtless due to the fact that they are programmed for different functions. The difference in appearance makes it easy for controlling Celestials to recognize their programming and capabilities at a glance when they send them out. They may also be the result, in part, of the designs of their different computers which give different configurations to their "faces." The Bible supports this idea of different types and functions, among the "creatures," by calling some "cherubim" and others "seraphim."

Various biblical prophets tell of encounters with these manlike "creatures." So the writer of the Book of Daniel tells how he had a "vision" by the River Hiddekel (Tigris), in which he saw a "certain man." Like the familiar cherubim of Ezekiel its "arms and feet" were "like in colour to polished brass." When the creature spoke to him Daniel went into a "deep sleep," but later was awakened when its "hand" touched him and set him "upon my knees and upon the palms of my hands."

His comment upon its overall appearance is that it was "like the appearance of a man" (Daniel 10:5–18).

Similarly the Prophet Isaiah tells how, after the doorpost moved and smoke filled the house, a "seraphim" flew to him "having a live coal in his hand, which he had taken with the tongs from off the altar" (Isaiah 6:6). This seraphim had previously "stood" above the "throne" of the Lord which was "high and lifted up" (Isaiah 6:1–2).

The confusion of these automata with the Celestials themselves, over the centuries, eventually gave rise to the winged angels of medieval art. It is ironic that these mythical representations, which the artists regarded as depicting creatures next to God himself, were actually prompted by mere mechanical contrivances rather than the noble beings that designed them!

From all these instances the picture of a space technology emerges which clearly has much in common with our own. Interstellar travel is accomplished by city-sized spomes such as the one called "Eden," or the "new Jerusalem." Contact between it and secondary bases is maintained by "chariots," such as Ezekiel's, which act as shuttles. These chariots are also used for point-to-point transit over the earth, as are the smaller modules Elisha and Zechariah describe as "horses."

Patrol and surveillance functions are most probably carried out by the smaller modules, as well. So Zechariah is told by the "angel that talked with me": "These [the "horses"] are the four spirits of the heavens, which go forth ... into the north country ... and ... toward the south country" (Zechariah 6:4–6).

The recurrent imagery in the Bible's descriptions of these craft, over so many centuries and by such widely scattered writers, make it highly probable that they were all part of a common technology. Analyses like J. F. Blumrich's add to the near certainty that this recurrent imagery was prompted by concrete engineering achievements—not the random wanderings of unhinged minds or the overheated imagination of religious visionaries. The unambiguous references to folding "wings" that make "noises like great waters," of wheels that "lift up" on takeoff, of "coals of fire ... between the wheels," and manlike creatures with metallic arms and legs are too specifically mechanical, and too often repeated, to be mere coincidences of language.

The Bible and UFOs

So far our discussion of the Celestials' space technology has been confined to occurrences which took place in biblical times. Yet the Bible seems to suggest that the Celestials used spacecraft very like those present-day investigators describe as unidentified flying objects. Could there be a connection? Could the "pillar of fire" of the Exodus, Ezekiel's "chariot" or Zechariah's "flying roll" have any relation to modern-day UFO sightings?

The answer to this question is, perhaps, the most bizarre discovery to come out of our space age interpretation of the Bible. For it throws light on the greatest and most inexplicable enigma of our time—the UFO mystery.

We have already seen that the Lord's curse of Satan confined him and his followers to this planet. Now this raises an interesting question. If the fallen Celestials were imprisoned on our planet, and if they are immortal, then they must still be here. That being the case, where are they?

Why has their presence not been detected and reported in historical documents or scientific literature? Could a large community of highly advanced extraterrestrials have dwelt among us, over the centuries, and gone undetected? Even though they are flesh and blood, and closely resemble us, could they have existed all this time, under cover, without giving themselves away by their futuristic hardware or advanced accomplishments?

When the matter is considered in this light it suggests an obvious answer. And it is that historic and scientific literature do contain numerous references to them. It is just that these references have not been recognized, in the past, for what they actually are.

Undercover Extraterrestrials

We have argued in Chapter IV, *Who Are the Celestials?* that the Bible makes it clear that Celestials are not visibly different from us. The Scriptures give many examples of their being observed and mistaken for ordinary humans until some extraordinary action gave them away (as in the case of Lot entertaining angels and Jacob wrestling with one). If this is so it would be a simple matter for fallen Celestials, with superior intelligence and knowledge, to carry on covert, or "undercover," activities among us. In fact it would probably be easier than for intelligence agents of one of our own foreign powers.

And fallen Celestials, imprisoned on our alien world and devoted to our subversion, would be in almost exactly the same position as agents of a hostile foreign power.

The need for secrecy would be the same. The use of false identities, as covers, would be the same. The need for communication with fellow agents would be the same. Only one important difference would exist. Being very numerous and being used to the convenience of advanced technology, they would require hidden bases where large communities of their members could live and hide the equipment they would want for transport and communication.

Falllen Celestials and "Flying Saucers"

Throughout the ages, aerial objects have been reported which resemble "saucers," "flying rolls," "pillars," or other shapes. As we have seen, some of the most interesting of these are found in the Bible.

In recent times, with our increased use of airspace and radar tracking, these reports have greatly increased. In fact, they have increased until government and scientific investigation have seemed warranted.

While many of these "unidentified flying objects" have been shown to be the result of misinterpreting natural phenomena or man-made objects, and others have involved detectable fraud, a solid core of unexplained UFOs remains. Many of these have involved multiple sightings by trained observers, or have been tracked on radar, photographed or even pursued by conventional aircraft. Their real existence, as unexplained phenonema, is accepted by large numbers of reputable scientists.

Speaking of this, Allen J. Hynek, one of the world's foremost astronomers and official consultant to the Air Force's

Project Blue Book, says: "We can start with the knowledge that the UFO phenomenon is global, that UFO reports persist in this and other countries despite the Condon Report and the closing of Project Blue Book, and that many small groups of scientifically trained people, especially young scientists, are expressing interest in the subject and dissatisfaction with the manner in which it has been treated in the past."[4] Even more pointedly, a subcommittee set by the prestigious Institute of Aeronautics and Astronautics to study the UFO phenomenon reported: "Taking all evidence which has come to the subcommittee's attention into account, we find it difficult to ignore the small residue of well documented but unexplainable cases which form the hard core of the UFO controversy."[5]

In view of these and similar pronouncements, made by reputable scientists throughout the world, it seems obvious that the UFO mystery remains. Something is, and has been, going on, for thousands of years, in our skies which cannot be explained by known principles of science; neither can it be simply debunked as the misconceptions of the gullible or the deceptions of the fraudulent.

The consensus of evidence on the "hard-core" unexplainable UFO cases suggests that they are flying craft which follow patterns of intelligent control. Report data indicate their performance exceeds the best man-made aircraft or spacecraft can do. They defy known principles of aerodynamics. They apparently can fly at many times the speed of conventional aircraft; they are capable of right-angle turns or reversals of direction at high speeds and can hover or ascend vertically. In fact, their maneuvers closely resemble those described, in Chapter II, by Arthur C. Clarke when he speculates on the behavior of craft employing a "gravity shield" and "inertialess drive."

If they do employ inertialess drive it is obvious they are not of human origin. Yet the ETH ("extraterrestrial hypothesis") seems unlikely, too. If they are from other worlds why have they not made official and public contact with world leaders over the centuries? If they are just investigating or observing us, why do they not follow regular patterns of flight as our own satellites and military spy planes do? And in all this time, why have they not completed their investigation and either left for good or proceeded to become more involved with us? Above all, why do they not focus on points of strategic importance such as military installations, cities and technological facilities? Why are they so often sighted in rural and desolate places or high above the earth or over the seas?

Yet, if they are not of human design and are not from other worlds, then what are they? How can they have unearthly capabilities yet not be of extraterrestrial origin? Could they be of earthly origin made under conditions of difficulty and limitation, by marooned extraterrestrials who are confined to this planet? This would explain their advanced design, yet frequent crudeness of appearance in photographs. It would also explain why so many are reported as of very small size. It would offer a reasonable explanation as to why many are reported as too small to make an extraterrestrial origin likely. It would also explain why they are usually sighted in desolate places and seem to avoid contact, since they would wish to remain undetected.

Occasional sightings would, of course, be inescapable. But they would more frequently be in out-of-the-way places. And they would generally occur only when secretive extraterrestrials ventured abroad to replenish supplies or search for mineral and other resources in undeveloped areas.

What this theory suggests, then, is a fusion of the two leading hypotheses which take UFOs to be real. Like the ETH, it assumes they are the product of an extraterrestrial civilization greatly advanced beyond our own. Yet it agrees with those who point out that sighting locations and flight patterns do not suggest an actual extraterrestrial origin. Though extraterrestrial in technology and design, some UFOs, at least, are probably earthly in origin. They are manufactured and based on this planet, under conditions of privation and difficulty, by extraterrestrials who maintain a hidden existence.

Like Robinson Crusoe, who manufactured crude replicas of outside civilization on his lonely island, the fallen Celestials manufacture small, short-range flying craft which are allowed under the terms of their "quarantine." These show a paradoxical "homemade" appearance, combined with sophisticated performance, because they are put together under conditions which require secrecy and restricted access to tools and materials!

Of course, since the fallen Celestials are confined to this planet, this explanation compels us to assume that victorious Celestials maintain some sort of surveillance and patrol, as well. This means there are other UFOs patrolling our skies which are of sophisticated manufacture and genuine extraterrestrial origin. In all probability they are based on the moon, or some nearby planet—or perhaps even a neighboring solar system. Various Scriptures in the Bible and apocryphal literature do suggest that the victorious Celestials maintain a surveillance and security force for this world. Often they are referred to as "watchers"—a term also employed in apocryphal literature, such as the Book of Enoch, for fallen Celestials who mingle among us. In the Book of Daniel we read that "the king saw a watcher and an holy one coming down from heaven..." (Daniel 4:23). And, again, in Jeremiah, that prophet warns, "publish against Jerusalem, that watchers come from a far country, and give out their voice against... Judah" (Jeremiah 4:16). The Hebrew words used in these passages are *iyr* and *nâtsar*, which refer to guardian angels and carry the meaning of observing and protecting as well as concealment. Evidently, then, the writers of these prophetic books believed Celestials maintain a constant vigilance over the affairs of this world. This idea is also supported by UFO reports coming from no less prestigious a source than the Apollo space missions. It was common knowledge, among those closely associated with the Apollo Moon Mission, that our own astronauts were closely monitored while going to and from the moon. Though such reports were not disclosed to the news media, a number of those involved have since made disclosures in articles and books. One of these, an aerospace engineer who designed and built communication and data-processing equipment for the project, comments on these strange events in his recent book *Our Ancestors Came from Outer Space*. Speaking of the missions he says, "It seems that the Apollo and Gemini flights were followed, both at a distance and sometimes quite closely, by space vehicles of extraterrestrial origin—flying saucers, or UFOs...I think that Walter Schirra, aboard Mercury 8, was the first of the astronauts to use the code name 'Santa Claus' to indicate the presence of flying saucers next to space capsules...James Lovell, on board the Apollo 8 command module, came out from behind the dark side of the moon and said for everybody to hear: 'We have been informed that Santa Claus does exist!' ...James McDevitt was apparently the first to photograph an unidentified flying object...Frank Borman and James Lovell took magnificent photographs of two UFOs following Gemini 7....Finally, when Apollo 11 made the first moon landing on the Sea of Tranquillity...two UFOs hovered overhead. Edwin Aldrin took several pictures of them. Some of them have been published in the June 1975 issue of *Modern People* magazine. The magazine does not tell where it got them, vaguely hinting at some Japanese source."[6]

That the victorious Celestials, as well as the fallen ones, keep a close surveillance on this planet seems warranted by both the biblical evidence and UFO reports, then. Indeed, the report data, when viewed as a whole, seem to suggest two different sorts of UFOs. It is almost as though unidentified flying objects are of two totally distinct origins. Some are small, crude and "homemade'" in appearance—obviously short-range craft; others are massive and possess elaborate and refined equipment and accessories—the sort that would be suitable for outer-space travel. Both types seem to avoid human contact for the most part. This would be expected if the victorious Celestials are here primarily to police the fallen ones and prevent their access to outer space.

"CLOSE ENCOUNTERS OF THE THIRD KIND"

In his previously quoted book, Professor Hynek classifies UFO encounters according to the visual character of the sightings and the absence or presence of observed occupants. He reserves a final category, "close encounters of the third kind," for those sightings in which "animated" occupants are reported or actually interact with human observers.[7] His name for this category has recently become the title for a highly successful science-fantasy movie on the subject.

Reports in this category are, however, by no means new. The Bible is full of them, as we have already seen. In the second phase of the Celestials' colonization program, when they monitored mankind closely, many such "encounters" were reported.

The Prophet Ezekiel has an unusually lengthy and detailed report of going for a visit to a base of the Celestials in the flying craft we studied earlier in this chapter (Ezekiel 40). Later in the New Testament, Jesus has an encounter with a strange lighted object ("a bright cloud" which "overshadowed") while he is gathered with his disciples on a mountain. Two occupants, reported to be "Moses and Elias [Elijah]," descend and converse with him, and he is transfigured—his face shines "as the sun" and his clothes become "white as light" (Matthew 17:1–5 and Mark 9:2–7).

The important point here, however, is that the explanation of UFOs we have offered covers not only remote sightings but more intimate ones, as well. And it covers them all—which the ETH and "misinterpreted natural phenomena theory" cannot.

With regard to the fallen Celestials it also explains why a small proportion of close encounters appear to be malevolent. Report literature contains a number of instances in which UFOs, or their occupants, have forcibly abducted humans, subjected them to frightening or incapacitating energies, scorched their cars or homes with laserlike beams or perhaps even destroyed them. In the latter group is the much-debated incident involving Captain Thomas Mantell, an Air Force pilot, whose plane crashed, or was disintegrated, while pursuing a UFO.

And for encounters with craft of both victorious and fallen Celestials the possibility remains that occupants sighted are not the Celestials themselves, but cherubim or seraphim—robots with artificial intelligence. This would account for the descriptions given by some contactees, which say occupants lack features or possess anatomical proportions that seem improbable for living creatures.

THE FALLEN CELESTIALS' HEADQUARTERS

One of the most interesting questions still remains to be answered. Since the fallen Celestials need earthly bases, where are they located? Why has the Air Force, or other investigative groups, not tracked them to their lair? Where could a community—or communities—of extraterrestrials hide for centuries? There are, of course, still unexplored areas on the earth. The most extensive and logical of these would be the depths of the seas. Almost three-fifths of the earth's surface is under water, and the depths of the oceans have never been systematically explored. Nor are they likely to be for some time to come.

It would be a simple matter for advanced extraterrestrials to construct a spome on, or under, the ocean's floor where they could form unearthly societies and store the equipment and craft of an advanced civilization. This idea acquires added plausibility when we consider that our own scientists are already designing underseas communities. Plans are now underway for building large submerged laboratories where numbers of scientists and technicians would live and work, in underwater communities, for prolonged periods of time.

If the fallen Celestials are headquartered underseas, it would be likely that many reports would place UFOs in or near water. And, indeed, this is the case. Geologist Ivan Sanderson, in his best-selling book *Invisible Residents*, cites a large number of excerpts from ships' logs which tell of UFOs entering or coming out of water. In the appendix he also lists, and analyzes, approximately a hundred such sightings. He also suggests that the earth is host to alien "invisible residents" who may have underseas communities.[8]

If an aquatic base is the answer to the invisibility of the fallen Celestials, are there any clues as to where it might be located? Is there a single base, or are several situated throughout the world?

Fallen Celestials and the "Devil's Triangle"

In the last few years much attention has been focused on the triangular area in the Caribbean bounded by imaginary lines running from Miami, Florida, to a point somewhat north of Bermuda and to another somewhat southeast of Barbados. This area has been variously referred to as "the Bermuda Triangle," the "Hoodoo Sea" or the "Devil's Triangle." According to many investigators of UFO reports it has been one of the most concentrated areas of sightings in the world. Coincidentally, and more notoriously, it has also been the scene of an astounding number of complete and inexplicable disappearances of planes, ships and men over a long period of time. In his book *The Bermuda Triangle*, Charles Berlitz states that since 1945, more than a hundred ships and planes have completely vanished from the area and that, in the twenty-six years preceding publication of his book, the Triangle had claimed over 1,000 lives—all without leaving a single body or a piece of wreckage![9]

There have been numerous attempts to debunk the reports on which these statistics are based. Generally these take the line that the area is meteorologically hazardous and that a "myth" has grown up about it which feeds on sensational publicity. The fact remains, however, that the number of disasters which have occurred is statistically much too great to be easily explained by natural causes such as turbulence and sudden squalls. Besides, many of the disappearances have involved radio contact until the moment of disaster when weather was normal. Even more, the frequent lack of wreckage and bodies—the total disappearance of so many of the victims—is improbable. Further, the fact that whole ships have been found in the area, apparently intact and in working order, but without crews or passengers, remains one of the Triangle's greatest mysteries. Finally, and perhaps most significant for our theory, is the fact that a great many UFO reports from the area state that they are seen entering or leaving the water! Could the Devil's Triangle be the site of the fallen Celestials' major base on this planet?

One other area with an equally grisly reputation exists on the opposite side of the world southeast of Japan. Its boundaries are defined by the Bonin Islands, Iwo Jima and Marcus Island. Like the Devil's Triangle this "Devil's Sea" has claimed an extraordinary number of ships, planes and human lives and has been the subject of government-sponsored investigations. Could the Devil's Sea be the site of a second base? If so, why the extraordinary toll of vessels and lives in both areas?

Did the fallen Celestials select these sites because they are hazardous, and they assumed humans would avoid them? Or do they increase their hazard by deliberately destroying craft and lives to protect the secrecy of their bases? Or do they, perhaps, follow some even more sinister policy of abducting humans for their own use? Are they perhaps made into cyborgs (part robot, part living creatures such as our own "bionic" television heroes) to pilot their craft and perform unpleasant or hazardous duties? Or do they simply enslave them to labor in Dantesque underseas communities? With limited technological facilities such a scheme might be simpler than attempting the mass production of robots, and would be consistent with their hostility toward humans.

There are passages in the Bible which seem to imply that the seas are one of the habitations of Satan and his followers. So John the Revelator says, "Woe to the inhabitors of the earth and of the sea! for the devil is come down unto you, having great wrath, because he knoweth that he hath but a short time" (Revelation 12:12).

In a similar manner reports of unidentified submarine objects have been given which support the idea suggested here. In this connection Charles Berlitz quotes an interesting U.S. Navy report. It concerns an underwater object, moving at over 150 knots, first tracked by a destroyer and later by a submarine. It was detected during maneuvers southeast of Puerto Rico in 1963 at the edge of the Triangle. At first it was thought to be a part of the exercise, and thirteen other Navy craft noted it and made entries in their logs. It was tracked for four days and penetrated depths of 27,000 feet while maintaining its incredible speed. The real nature and identity of the object were never ascertained.[10]

Interestingly, the Old Testament prophet Jonah also is reported in the Bible as having had a close encounter with a similar type of craft (Jonah 1:17). So close, in fact, that it is reported as having "swallowed" him. And though it is called a great "fish" in the King James translation, the Hebrew word *dag* simply means something that moves through the sea by means of a "vibratory action of the tail." This, combined with the statement that it was specially "prepared" by the Lord and that Jonah survived "three days in its belly," strongly suggests it was an artificial object rather than the whale traditional theology has taken it to be. Higher critics have ridiculed the whale theory, pointing out that the average whale could not swallow a man, nor could he survive three days in its "belly" without being digested. A submarine, however, would be quite another matter. Could the "great fish" which "swallowed" Jonah and the unknown craft Berlitz mentions be different versions of the same device?

Whatever the answer to these questions may be it seems evident that the history of disasters in these "Devil's" areas and the frequency of sightings of unidentified objects suggest some common mystery they share. Charles Berlitz points out one further coincidence which could explain the link. Both sites are located on the two meridians of longitude, west and east, where true and magnetic north coincide, and the mariner's compass points to both at the same time.[11] Could these locations, on opposite sides of the earth's magnetic alignment, have some special significance? Were they both chosen as bases because the fallen Celestials use geomagnetic lines of force as an energy source for bases or as energy sources to propel their craft?

Yet if fallen Celestials do maintain bases in the depths of the seas it makes it all the more likely they must frequently venture onto land. Being land-inhabiting, by background, they would surely find it both attractive and necessary to leave aquatic bases for frequent visits to the earth's surface.

Do Celestials Walk Among Us?

One of the most eerie possibilities suggested by this theory is that fallen Celestials may commonly walk among us. And, if they do, it would follow that intelligence agents of the victorious Celestials may do so, as well. For just as they would have to patrol our skies to confine fallen Celestials to earth, so they would police them on land to prevent their sabotage of plans for redeeming mankind. And both sides, like our own earthly intelligence agents, would doubtless find it desirable to remain undercover.

In doing this they would, in all probability, adopt human "cover." Since they are physically indistinguishable from humans they could assume human identities and move freely in populated areas.

This possibility may explain some of the strangest of "close encounters" in which reports claim UFO occupants have kidnapped humans and subjected them to inexplicable tests and examinations.

If these humans had unwittingly become suspect as Celestial agents, the opposite side might attempt to unmask them as our own fictitious agents often do in movie spy "thrillers."

By the same token, strange accounts, in history, of unearthly or wonder-working humans may be indications that extraterrestrials have walked the earth.

In this connection legendary figures such as Hermes Trismegistus, Simon Magus and Apollonius of Tyana come to mind. The last, thought to have been a contemporary of Jesus, was also credited with healing the sick, defying laws of nature and even raising the dead.

Similarly the Count of St. Germain, in recent times, has baffled historians by the wonders attributed to him, by usually reliable diarists, including incredible linguistic, musical, artistic and scientific accomplishments, as well as feats of alchemy. Most puzzling of all is his apparent longevity, since he was reported, all over Europe, as a contemporary by diarists writing from 1710 to 1822. And throughout most of this period he was reported as "appearing" to be "about forty-five years of age."[12]

Such evidence does not, of course, prove that alleged wonder workers of the past were extraterrestrials. If they do indeed dwell among us they would be more likely to conceal than to display their superiority. Yet there might be circumstances when the role of a wonder worker would be a useful "cover," or would be inescapable because of the mission to which they were assigned.

In the next chapter we shall consider, in depth, the most extraordinary case in all of history in which an extraterrestrial identity was claimed for one who walked among us.

CHAPTER XII

THE REDEEMER

For I know that my redeemer liveth, and that he shall
stand at the latter day upon the earth ...

—Job 19:25

In 1742, George Frederick Handel set Job's immortal confession of living faith to immortal music. Opening the concluding part of the great oratorio, "I know that my redeemer liveth" rises to spiritual heights that are almost celestial in their elevation.

Speaking of Handel's magnificent achievement one modern critic observed: "... the opening sections of 'Messiah' are already touched with radiance. Only a composer drunk with inspiration could proceed from this point to ever higher levels of greatness."[1]

Yet the artistic tributes to the carpenter of Nazareth are dwarfed by the sheer impact of his existence and its consequences. There are some who question his reality. Even his most devoted chroniclers did not agree entirely about his deeds and sayings.

The records of his life indicate he had little or no formal education; he never married or had a family; his only job skill was rough carpentry; he never owned a home or a decent wardrobe; his ministry scarcely carried him beyond the neighborhood where he was born; he was never appointed to a political post or office; and he died at thirty-three, a convicted criminal, by the most hideous form of capital punishment the ancient world could devise.

Yet more books have been written about him than any other man who ever lived. His name is probably more widely known than that of any other human being. His followers today number in the hundreds of millions. That most famous of world conquerors, Napoleon, had this to say about his existence: "Alexander, Caesar, Charlemagne, and myself founded empires; but on what foundations did we rest the creations of our genius? Upon force. Jesus Christ founded an empire upon love; and at this hour millions of men would die for him."

THE PROBLEM

Over 60,000 books on Jesus are said to have been written in the last century alone. The literary flood has swollen in our own time. Most of these have been concerned with establishing the facts of life or the meaning of his message.

Yet they have arrived at no consensus. Scholars and followers alike cannot agree on what Jesus did or believed or taught.

The problem lies in the records of his life. Like Noah and Abraham and Moses he is a legendary hero. He exists, like them, not in the pages of scholarly history, but in the redemptive prophecies and legends of the Bible—and in the living faith of his followers. Unlike them, the Scriptures and his followers credit him with a unique mission and identity. This claim is simply, and starkly, that he was, and is, God!

Of course, many religions, and even some political systems, claim their founders, or leaders, were gods. Some even regarded them as being immortal, and, when they proved they were not, reinstated them by proclaiming they had risen from the dead.

But the religion founded by Jesus and his followers is different. It proclaims a resurrected Jesus—the Christ—as living in the world today, through the invisible church of his followers. The ancient rivals of his church—the mystery religions, Mithraism, Gnosticism—have all disappeared. Their leaders and gods—resurrected or otherwise—are no longer followed or worshipped.

But the cosmic Christ continues in the lives of his followers who live in and through him. So the Apostle Paul eloquently expresses this mystical insight of the indwelling Christ, ". . . I live; yet not I, but Christ liveth in me: and the life which I now live in the flesh I live by the faith of the Son of God, who loved me, and gave himself for me" (Galatians 2:20). And again, more poetically and with sublime simplicity, this former archenemy of Christianity confesses, "For to me to live is

Christ..." (Philippians 1:21). How did a man as obscure as Jesus achieve such a hold on the hearts and minds of men and women throughout the ages? The problem is without historic parallel.

THE HISTORICAL RECORD

The record of Jesus' life is contained in the first five books of the New Testament—the four gospels and the Acts of the Apostles. The writers are held, by tradition, to have been disciples—Matthew, Mark, Luke and John, the Beloved. Luke is generally also credited with authorship of Acts. He undoubtedly speaks for all the writers when he says their purpose was "to set forth in order a declaration of those things which are most surely believed among us" (Luke 1:1).

His declaration makes it clear that in the gospel record, once again, as all through the Bible, we are dealing with redemptive history—not just the usual textbook variety. It was not the purpose of the writers simply to give a factual narrative of events. They have selected and arranged and interpreted the facts for the purpose of emphasizing their redemptive message. As a result there are differences of emphasis, minor discrepancies and doctrinal divergencies which distinguish these several accounts.

There is a general agreement that the four gospels achieved their earliest written form in the last third of the first century. Mark is thought to be the oldest (about 70 A.D.) and John the last (probably 95 A.D.). Matthew and Luke are believed to have borrowed heavily from Mark. Because these three gospels share many incidents in common they are called the synoptic gospels (from the Greek, "seen together"). John, on the other hand, omits the parables contained in the other gospels and presents Jesus and his teaching in a more philosophical and mystical light.

THE LIFE OF JESUS

Since these records are somewhat divergent in detail and point of view, and may have passed through many hands, some New Testament scholars seriously doubt their accuracy. This is especially so where the accounts show strong parallels to the myths of other cultures or to "types" and "symbols" which are supposed to foreshadow them in the Old Testament. Elaborate parallels of this sort suggest literary tampering. Some have even gone so far as to argue that this prevents our knowing anything for sure about the historical Jesus.

Yet, we must once again remember that the weight of present-day scholarship is against this position. As we have already seen, culture heroes are usually developed out of the lives of real people. As Abraham and Moses were probably real, so, even more, is it likely the gospels disclose a real Jesus. For Jesus is much nearer our own time, and the picture we get of him is accordingly more detailed and vivid. And in its vividness and psychological probability it carries a conviction of truth.

Besides, secular history is not silent concerning Jesus as it is for Abraham and Moses. Historians and social critics of his day, or soon after, speak of him—Pliny, Tacitus, Suetonius, the Jewish historian Josephus, and even the Talmud. And, significantly, even those most opposed to Christianity did not question his existence or his centrality to the new faith.

The narrative of the gospels is simply told. An angel appears to Mary, who is "espoused" to Joseph. The angel tells her she will conceive of the "Holy Ghost." In due time she becomes pregnant though still a virgin, according to the custom of the day, which required a waiting period before consummating marriage. She and Joseph journey to Bethlehem, from Nazareth, for a census count. While there Jesus is born (probably in the year 6 B.C.).

Herod, the king, hears his throne is endangered by a newborn "king." He orders the death of newborn infants, and Joseph and Mary flee to Egypt with their child. After Herod's death they return to Nazareth, where Jesus is apprenticed to Joseph and learns the carpenter's trade. Apparently he also studies the law, for at twelve he is examined in the Temple at Jerusalem, where his parents are celebrating Passover, and astounds its teachers with his knowledge.

His later youth is unchronicled until he appears at the River Jordan, in his thirtieth year, to be baptized by his cousin, John the Baptist. He undergoes a profound spiritual experience, withdraws for forty days of solitude and meditation, then begins his ministry.

He gathers a group of twelve disciples about him and begins a career of teaching and healing which extends from Galilee to Judea. He preaches in synagogues, proclaiming the coming kingdom of God. He heals the sick, exorcises evil spirits and even raises the dead. He walks on water, feeds 5,000 with a few loaves and fish and proclaims an unworldly ethic in the Sermon on the Mount. Yet his tolerance of sinners, his outspoken manner and his popularity antagonize the influential pharisees. A later Herod hears of his teaching and miracles, and fearing he is the Messiah or John the Baptist returned to life, plots with the leaders of the pharisees to kill him.

Jesus flees, with his disciples, to Judea. After preaching there for several months he makes a final visit to Jerusalem for Passover. He is given a hero's welcome by the common people. A large procession accompanies him to the Temple, where he cleanses it of sacrilege by overturning the tables of money-changers and driving out the vendors of sacrificial animals.

On the eve of the Passover, Jesus celebrates Seder with his disciples. Afterward he retires to the Garden of Gethsemene, where he is arrested.

He is tried before the Sanhedrin, the Jewish high court, and convicted of blasphemy for claiming he is the son of God. Since the Sanhedrin cannot carry out the death penalty, they bring him before the Roman governor, Pilate, who extracts an admission from him that he is "a King." With this evidence of treason to Caesar, Pilate sentences Jesus to die by crucifixion. The order is carried out, and he dies an agonized death on the cross.

On the following Sunday morning a group of women who have been close to him come to his tomb to pay their last respects. The stone is rolled away and a person who is nearby says, "Be not affrighted: Ye seek Jesus of Nazareth, which was crucified: he is risen; he is not here: behold the place where they laid him" (Mark 16:6).

Afterward Jesus appears to his close friend, Mary Magdalene, and the disciples. He commissions them to "preach the gospel to every creature" (Mark 16:15) and shortly after ascends into "heaven."

Such, in essence, is the gospel story, with some variations from one gospel to another.

Only Matthew and Luke give infancy stories, and Luke does not mention the flight to Egypt. Only Luke deals with Jesus' later youth. John, as we said before, omits the parables which form such an important part of Jesus' teaching in the synoptic gospels. When it comes to the great central event of Christianity, the resurrection, there are the usual divergences one expects when several witnesses are reporting an emotionally charged event. Matthew says an "angel" rolled the stone away and spoke to all the women who came to the tomb (Matthew 28:2–5). Mark says it was a "young man" who actually sat in the tomb and spoke to them (Mark 16:5). Luke says "two men" in "shining garments" addressed the women (Luke 24: 4–7), and John says it was "two angels" who spoke to Mary alone (John 20:12–13).

Yet, in its main outlines, the story is remarkably consistent considering it was set down nearly half a century, or more, after the events and by at least four different writers of diverse backgrounds. The picture of Jesus and his followers is extraordinarily vivid. And it rings true psychologically. A clever novelist might have created some of the habits and mannerisms and motivations of the principal characters, even including Jesus. But four different writers could hardly have achieved the consistent and fleshed-out portraits that emerge. They have the feel of reality about them. And historians and archaeologists have verified that many of the background circumstances and events recounted are actual or characteristic for that time.

The "Good News"

From this story the apostolic church gathered its central articles of faith—the redemptive message. This was the gospel they preached—the "good news." It focused on the three pivotal events of Jesus' life—his birth, his death and his resurrection. In his birth they proclaimed God became man—"the Word was made flesh, and dwelt among us" (John 1:14). In his death they proclaimed he atoned for the sins of the world: "But God commendeth his love toward us, in that, while we were yet sinners, Christ died for us" (Romans 5:8). And in his resurrection they proclaimed he conquered death so that we all might have eternal life: "... our Saviour Jesus Christ... hath abolished death, and hath brought life and immortality..." (II Timothy 1:10).

This was the good news that sustained the early church through savage suppressions and incredible persecutions. It is the faith on which it has endured for 2,000 years.

Are its claims valid? Do they proclaim historic fact, or are they outmoded mythology? This question has been a growing concern in Christian theology of the last two centuries. With the advance of science and the rise of higher criticism of the Bible, increasing numbers of Christians have come to question the fundamental beliefs on which historic Christianity was built.

Speaking for many of them, the German theologian Rudolf Bultmann has expressed the central problem of twentieth-century faith. So he says: "All this [the gospel story] is the language of mythology, and the origin of the various themes can be easily traced in the contemporary mythology of Jewish apocalyptic and the redemptive myths of Gnosticism. To this extent the kerygma [the gospel message] is incredible to modern man for he is convinced that the mythical view of the world is obsolete.... Man's knowledge and mastery of the world have advanced to such an extent that it is no longer possible for anyone seriously to hold the New Testament view of the world."[2]

The solution to this problem, Bultmann believes, is to "demythologize" the good news. Unlike earlier higher critics he is not willing to dismiss the whole gospel record as the superstitions of a bygone age. Rather, he feels that underneath its surface incredibilities lies a core of genuine revelation. This can be disclosed, he says, by removing the mythic "envelope" that surrounds it.

And what is the revelation that remains when the "envelope" is removed? Though his explanations are somewhat difficult his point seems to be that Jesus of Nazareth was just the starting point for an ongoing historical process. This process is a sort of Christ event consisting of the central idea of the Christ himself as it emerges in history, and all the con-

sequences it has produced. It is this event, not the historical
Jesus, which "incarnates" God. It is this event, not Jesus'
atoning death, which has redemptive value. It is this event,
not a physically resurrected Jesus, that still lives in the world
as it unfolds in the hearts and minds of believers. And it is
this unfolding which constitutes the return of Christ to rule
over his invisible church of true followers—not a future return of the historical Jesus to rule a literal earthly kingdom.

This for Bultmann, and his followers, is the "good news,"
sanitized of mythology. And what of the historical Jesus himself? Bultmann says we simply don't know. The revelation
contained in the Christ event is not based on the credentials of
Jesus. It is its own evidence. If we accept it at all we do so by
an act of existential faith. The Jesus of history was lost in the
mists of oral tradition. When we look at the gospel record
critically we are forced to admit that "We can, strictly speaking, know nothing of the personality of Jesus."[3]

Recovering the Jesus of History

Yet other theologians have been much more optimistic
about knowing the real Jesus. So Bernhard Anderson comments
on recent New Testament criticism: "This does not mean
that we are driven to skepticism about the historical Jesus,
for we would face a similar problem in dealing with, say,
Socrates, who left no writings and is known only by his impact
on others. As a matter of fact the fragments of the oral tradition are invaluable to us, for in many cases they give vivid
glimpses of Jesus in action, small tableaux of the various
episodes in his ministry. Moreover . . . it is possible to reconstruct . . . the broad features of his career and the essential
aspects of his message."[4]

So it is that, once again, our space age approach to the Bible
offers a prospect of bringing new light to bear on ancient
truths. By focusing on the language of the texts, and those
"vivid glimpses" and "small tableaux" of which Bernhard Anderson speaks, we have discovered a new perspective on the
historical Jesus.

And in this perspective he emerges not as the first-century
cult leader and magician some recent scholars have made him

out to be.[5] Nor does he fit the portrait of nineteenth-century higher critics who saw him as a psychotic with fixed delusions of messiahship and divinity. He does not even fit the sympathetic portrayal of Albert Schweitzer, who attempted his rescue from nineteenth-century criticism.[6] For he emerges as more than the good man and great teacher who reasonably, though mistakenly, believed he would fulfill the messianic expectations of his age.

Surprisingly he is recovered much as he appeared to the apostles and those who proclaimed the "good news" in the early church. He appears simply and plausibly as the Lord's promised Redeemer.

"Demythologizing" Demythologized

The difference between our space age view of Jesus and Bultmann's lies in what is to be taken as mythic. We have no desire to minimize the value and the contributions of recent New Testament scholarship. And it has successfully shown that the gospel record emerged by stages and from a variety of sources. And there can be little doubt that in the process the remembered deeds and sayings of Jesus underwent some reworking and even mythic elaboration.

But this does not mean the gospel story is a "mythological envelope." Nor does it mean its cardinal claims are "incredible," or that "it is no longer possible for anyone seriously to hold the New Testament view of the world."

The problem with Bultmann's program of "demythologizing" is that it rests, itself, on a mythic world view—the view of late-nineteenth-century scientific materialism. And what Bultmann failed to realize was that, even before he wrote *Kerygma and Myth*, this world view had already been refuted by developments in twentieth-century science. Bultmann's judgment that the New Testament view of the world was obsolete was made from the perspective of his own world view which, itself, had become obsolete.

For twentieth-century discoveries in physics, astronomy, medicine and psychology have thoroughly invalidated his assumptions that the incarnation, the resurrection, a literal heaven and the advent of Celestials to our world are "incredible." Let us see how this is so.

Is the "Good News" Scientifically Plausible?

We have already seen, in our opening chapters, that modern "miracles" such as teleportation, resurrection and even immortality are already being predicted for our own future by scientific researchers. We have also seen that the Scriptures show Celestials had already mastered these secrets when the Bible was written.

If these things are so they mean the claims made in the "good news"—the incarnation, the miracles of Jesus' ministry, the resurrection, his ascent into heaven and his ultimate return in the clouds—are not incredible. In themselves they are perfectly credible if we attribute them to a civilization considerably more advanced than our own. What made them incredible to Bultmann is that the gospels seem to claim them for a first-century carpenter in an insignificant outpost of the Roman Empire.

But if Jesus was not just an obscure human carpenter—if he was an advanced extraterrestrial sent on an undercover mission to Earth—then all the things Bultmann finds incredible about his life would be quite credible.

It would be logical and necessary that he would be "landed" on Earth in a way that would give him a believable "cover." And by being born into a human family of a human mother he would have the most perfect "cover" possible. No one could reasonably question his humanity.

It would also be probable he would exhibit advanced knowledge and powers that would seem "supernatural" to his contemporaries and "mythological" to modern critics.

The only thing that is improbable in the gospel record, if he was a Celestial, is his death. We will consider the remarkable reasons for it later in this chapter. We will only note here that it requires some extraordinary explanation. For if he were a Celestial he could surely have avoided it, or those who sent him could have rescued him from it.

Once it occurred, however, his resurrection would be a matter of course, as would his removal from our world when his mission was finished. And it would be likely that it would be by some sort of "airlift" involving technological wizardry.

All of these things would follow as a matter of course and

would be in no way remarkable if Jesus were a Celestial.

The real issue, then, is not the wonders and miracles that surround Jesus' life. It is the nature of Jesus himself. Is there any real evidence that he was not just a simple first-century carpenter, but was rather an undercover extraterrestrial?

WAS JESUS A CELESTIAL?

The evidence, if there is any, would have to lie in the gospel records, for these are all we know of Jesus. Yet they could not be the gospel claims themselves, for, as we have seen, these are not scientifically or historically verifiable.

What then would do? The only convincing evidence would be statements or claims, made in the records, which involve unworldly knowledge. If the gospels make claims about Jesus or his message which would only be known to an advanced civilization, then the very content of the statements would be evidence. Even if what was claimed could not be proved the very fact that it was claimed would be evidence of extraterrestrial influence.

For example, suppose the records, known to be set down toward the end of the first century, said Jesus had a vitamin C deficiency. This would be proof someone connected with their composition had twentieth-century knowledge of nutrition, whether the claim was true or not. It would be good evidence that an advanced civilization was involved in the events surrounding Jesus' life.

Do the records contain any knowledge of this sort? We believe the answer is yes. The evidence is of two sorts. One concerns Jesus' birth; the other concerns his message.

JESUS A CLONE

The key to the mystery of Jesus' birth lies in certain statements he made about himself. These are found in the Gospel of John. The occasion is one of the most touching in all the gospels. The disciples are gathered in Jerusalem for their final Passover with Jesus. He has commended them to humility and has urged them to love one another. After washing their feet as a demonstration of humility and love, he tells them that the time has come for him to leave them. He assures them he is going to his father's "house" to prepare a place for them. Philip, one of the first Jesus had called to his circle and a leader, says, "Lord, shew us the Father . . . " and Jesus replies, "Have I been so long time with you, and yet hast thou not known me, Philip? he that hath seen me hath seen the Father; and how sayest thou then, Shew us the Father?" (John 14:8–9). Earlier he also tells them, "I and my Father are one" (John 10:30), and still again, "the Father is in me, and I in him" (John 10:38).

On the surface these seem to be extraordinary statements. If Jesus is just saying he is his father's representative, why would he tell Philip that to see him is to see the father? The point of his remarks here seems to be that he looks exactly like his father. And who was his father—Joseph?

Both Matthew and Luke agree that Mary was a virgin and that Jesus was conceived by a nonhuman father, through the agency of the "Holy Ghost" (Matthew 1:18, Luke 1:35). Could such an extraordinary statement be true?

In the mid-1960s, John Gurdon, a biologist at Oxford University, succeeded in reproducing frogs using one parent only. The technique he used is called "cloning." It involves using the genetic material of a single parent, rather than the sexual method of combining genetic material from two parents. The technical name for nonsexual reproduction is "monogenesis," and cloning is one sort of monogenesis.

The gospel writer John tells us that Jesus was the "only begotten" son of God (John 3:16). The Greek word he uses for "only begotten" is monogenēs—the same word from which the English word "monogenesis" comes.

Could it be that Jesus was the monogenetic son of Jehovah, rather than the son of a human father? This is clearly the claim the gospels make.

How to Tell a Clone

The significant evidence of cloning is that the offspring is an identical twin to its parent. Since a single parent is used, the offspring's genetic type can only come from that parent. It must therefore be an exact duplicate of the parent—an identical twin except for age!

Now let's consider again the extraordinary statements John attributes to Jesus. He says that if you have seen him you have seen his father. He says he and his father are "one." He says his father is in him, and he is in his father.

Is there anything these statements could mean other than that Jesus is a duplicate of his father—a look-alike who has an identical constitution? If this is what they mean, then Jesus is saying, in effect, that he is a clone of Jehovah—a claim that fits extraordinarily well with what Matthew and Luke have to say about his conception.

For a virgin can give birth to a clone. And she can do so without "knowing a man," as Luke has Mary claim. And even though we can't verify the claims of Matthew and Luke, the question remains, how did they know about cloning? How did they know a virgin could give birth without "knowing" a man? And how did John know a son could be an identical twin to his father? Until John Gurdon's experiments it had never happen before—or had it? Did Celestials solve the problem of human cloning before the first century A.D.? And did they use some form of radiant energy which "overshadowed" Mary, as Luke claims (Luke 1:35), to impose Jehovah's DNA blueprint on the genetic material of her ovum? The Greek word used for "overshadow" is episkiazo and has the meaning of "a haze of brilliancy."

If they did then Jesus was indeed a clone of Jehovah—his identical twin. And the extraordinary statements he made about himself then make sense. As the clone of Jehovah he was, as the writer of Hebrews puts it, "the express image of his person" (Hebrews 1:3)—the literal, biological "Son of the Lord God." The mystery of the incarnation—God become human—is solved. Jesus was a human, but of extraterrestrial origin. He was, in fact, a Celestial!

And being a Celestial, sent on a mission to Earth, the extraordinary claims of the "good news" then fall into place. His unusual birth, his miraculous powers, his contact with a UFO on the Mount of Transfiguration, his resurrection, his ascension—all are predictable and make good scientific sense!

Yet one fact in the "good news" remains which does not fit. This is Jesus' death. An examination of the gospel record shows it cannot be accounted for by the mere fact that Jesus was a Celestial. Quite the contrary. For, if he were a Celestial, we would expect him to have escaped death or to have been rescued. Why, then, did he die?

JESUS' MISSION

To understand this unexpected turn of events we must now examine the reason for Jesus' mission. As we pointed out in Chapter VI, *Colony Earth*, it had two objectives. The first was to live among men and women to teach them about the Lord's coming kingdom and to exemplify the way of life the Celestials require for citizenship in it. In short, he was to teach, in as pure a form as possible, the Celestials' own religion. The second was to form a church which would carry this "good news" throughout the world.

And what was this religion he was to exemplify? As we have seen, it centered around the Celestials' discovery and use of the ultimate Creative Power of the universe as the basis for their moral, spiritual and even material civilization.

They had long ago recognized that the ultimate Creative Power is a kind of psychic energy which, as Sir James Jeans put it, has "something in common with our own individual minds." They knew it underlies both mind and matter and is the directing and controlling force in the universe. They called this cosmic intelligence, or power, the "Holy Spirit."

Long before Jesus' birth they learned how to open up their lives to its influence and guidance. They called this experience the "baptism of the Spirit." Once they had received this indwelling "Spirit" it guided their individual and communal life with the same cosmic intelligence with which it directs the course of biological and cosmic creation. Further, it conferred powers on them which we would call "paranormal." By means of it they could accomplish feats of telepathy, clairvoyance, healing, resurrection, control of material objects and even the neutralizing of "laws" of nature, such as gravity. The most important discovery they made about it was that it had something in common with our own human experience of "love." That is to say, it is not just cosmic intelligence, or "logos," it is a cosmic force for good, for fulfillment, for healing and for progress and elevation. It is the creative and constructive and organizing force of the universe.

And it was Jesus' mission to bring the gift of the Holy Spirit to humanity. To understand it was so far above their current level of development that the work could not be carried out by human prophets and teachers. The abortive attempt to teach it in the Garden had left a fragmentary knowledge which had been carried, by descendants of the Adamic race, throughout the world. Something of it was known and used in many religious traditions. In Taoist and Buddhist cultures it was called *chi* or *ki*. Hindu yogis knew it as *prana*. Polynesians called it *mana*, North American Iroquois called it *orenda*, and Ituri pygmies called it *megbe*.

But these fragmented versions of the original Celestial teaching produced uncertain results. Training in its use was long and arduous, and only those who were specially adept and persistent ordinarily experienced a genuine "baptism," or acquired paranormal powers which they could use for good.

Jesus' assignment was to use his gifts for teaching and his development as an adept to explain and demonstrate the gifts of the Spirit to mankind. By exhortations and parables, geared to their level of understanding, he would teach humans the use of cosmic love and its place in the coming "Kingdom of God." By a ministry of healing, therapy of character disorders (exorcism) and good works he would exemplify the power of Cosmic Love.

And he would gather around him a special band of followers whom he would initiate into the "baptism of the Spirit." They would form the nucleus for his "church" which would carry the "good news" to the world.

Yet all of this would leave the outcome uncertain. Jehovah had tried the first phase of his plan already, with his people and the law, and the outcome had been less than encouraging. Humanity, even those closest to his original design, had proved a corrupt and undependable lot. What was needed was some ultimate demonstration of Cosmic Love and its redemptive powers which would become a supreme symbol to this unpredictable race for all time.

THE ATONEMENT

So it was decided Jesus must die. The mystery of the atonement has eluded theologians and apologists since the foundation of Christianity. The early apostles attempted to explain it in terms of the Judaism they knew. Some used the metaphors of temple worship and spoke of Jesus as a worthy "sacrifice" sufficient to appease the wrath of a condemning Deity. Others used the language of the law and spoke of a "redemption price" necessary to buy back mankind's Edenic state. Neither seems very logical or morally acceptable to the modern mind. How could a just God require the death of an innocent person—especially his own son—before he would forgive his fallen heirs? What could the death of an innocent person have to do with buying back favor for the guilty?

Yet with a space age interpretation of the atonement the true reasons behind Jesus' death become clear.

As mankind's moral and spiritual exemplar he was the representative of the ultimate Creative Power—a son not only of his biological father, Jehovah, but a "son" of the highest God, the Creator and Ruler of the Universe. As he was the biological incarnation of Jehovah, so he was the revelational incarnation of the logos—Divine Love.

His death, an innocent person, would therefore be the supreme act of love. If he died not of illness or accident but deliberately, his death would be the ultimate expression and example of the love he taught. Nothing else would do equally well. If he died, when he could have escaped, because he persisted in carrying out his ministry of love, and justifying it by his credentials as the "son of God," the point would be ultimately made for all time.

And it was. The terror and passion of the atonement have gripped the hearts and minds of men and women as no other event in human history has done. The incomprehensible love that would impel an innocent man—a Celestial—to live among degraded humans, to sacrifice every human comfort and pleasure to his mission and finally to die by a hideous form of capital punishment has gripped human imagination as no other event has ever done. It has inspired supreme works of poetry, of music and of art. It impelled a handful of followers to proclaim the "good news" in the face of savage persecutions, until they had convinced half the world. Ultimately the Roman Empire itself bowed to the carpenter of Nazareth and embraced the religion he founded. Through the ages the cross has remained the symbol of all that is highest and best for untold millions of men and women. Jesus' act of redemptive love fully vindicated his mission. Since Golgotha he is known throughout the world as the Redeemer.

JESUS' MESSAGE

Two aspects of Jesus' ministry show an unearthly strangeness. One is his mode of ministering—his attitudes and outlook; the other is what he taught.

Nothing is more indicative of Jesus' unworldly background than his attitude toward death. To most men and women death is that "last, great, final enemy." To Jesus it seemingly had little of this meaning or finality. This is brought out very forcibly in John's account of the resurrection of Lazarus.

Jesus has been preaching on the eastern side of the Jordan near the place where he was baptized by John. A messenger comes from his closest friends in Bethany, not far from Jerusalem. The two sisters, Martha and Mary, and their brother Lazarus have provided the nearest thing to a home Jesus has had in his wandering ministry. Martha has tended his physical needs and shown exceeding concern for his comfort and rest. Mary, the younger, has found a special place in Jesus' affection. Without fully understanding his unusual nature and mission she has, with rare intuition and insight, grasped his loneliness and sense of isolation. She has supplied the sympathy and small attentions which a woman's understanding can give a man whose vocation requires dedication and self-denial. Lazarus he has loved as a brother.

The word tells him Lazarus is gravely ill. It urges him to come at once. Because his ministry is not yet finished, and reasoning that the illness is probably not as serious as they fear, he lingers two days before starting for Bethany. When his disciples ask him about the delay he assures them it will all work out "for the glory of God, that the son of God might be glorified thereby."

"LAZARUS, COME FORTH"

When he finally arrives in Bethany, Lazarus has been dead four days. Martha meets him desolated with grief. He comforts her, assuring her, "Thy brother shall rise again." She replies, "I know that he shall rise again in the resurrection at the last day." Jesus reassures her with one of the most famous utterances in all the gospels: "I am the resurrection, and the life: he that believeth in me, though he were dead, yet shall he live."

By that time Mary has arrived. She falls at his feet, prostrated by her anguish, and cries out, "Lord, if thou hadst been here, my brother had not died."

At this Jesus undergoes a strange alteration. Before he has been composed and sure of his ability to handle the situation. Now he suddenly groans "in the spirit," and is for the first time "troubled." Suddenly he breaks down and weeps uncontrollably. Continuing to groan, he moves to the grave, which is in a cave. Requesting that the stone be moved away, he calls out, "Lazarus, come forth." And the dead man, "bound hand and foot with graveclothes," appears (John 11: 1–44).

What caused Jesus' sudden change? The only obvious explanation is that until his confrontation with Mary, he had looked on the whole affair from the Celestial point of view. Death was no problem. Resurrection could easily take care of it. It would be an opportunity to help the friends he loved and to reveal his heavenly father's power at the same time.

Now suddenly, because of his special empathy for Mary, her appearance confronts him with the human point of view —a point of view essentially foreign to him. He is compelled to look at death in terms of the desolation and suffering it has brought to those he loves, for four agonizing days. For the first time he experiences the grief and hopelessness they have had to endure because of his delay.

Only then does he look at death in the normal, human way, and, sharing their suffering and bereavement, he groans and is overcome with weeping.

This unearthliness of attitude and outlook is frequently found all through Jesus' ministry. In his priorities of concern in his career, in his attitudes and behavior at his trial and crucifixion and in his sense of mission and message an otherworldly outlook prevails. It is most evident of all in his ethic.

"My Kingdom Is Not of This World"

The ethic of Jesus has been a subject for unending debate. Some take it for granted that it is the ethic of Christianity. Others doubt that much of Jesus' outlook and spirit survives in the church he founded. Critics point to the contrast between the simplicity of Jesus' life and message and the pomp and panoply of his church, with its sectarian division and dogmatic pretensions. How, they ask, can followers of Jesus believe the Sermon on the Mount and erect pretentious churches and cathedrals? How can they support institutions that exploit the poor and racial minorities? Why are they uncharitable toward fellow Christians who have different interpretations of his teachings? Why have they condoned force and violence and ask God's blessing on their "right" side in most wars? Perhaps this is why George Bernard Shaw once said that Christianity is probably a good idea, but it is hard to tell, since no one has ever tried it.

Yet, throughout history, there have been those who have earnestly tried to live the ethic of Jesus. Some have even pushed it to its extremes and used it as a tool of social change and revolution. And where they have it has changed the course of the world.

Indeed, no more revolutionary doctrine has ever been taught. In its unworldly approach to social relations and worldly aspirations it strikes at the heart of all that is corruptive and abusive in human living. More than this, it proposes an unearthly method for healing human hurts and woes. For it urges us to curb those natural and instinctive responses we inherit from ancestors who followed the law of the jungle.

The Ethic of Jesus

For the ethic of Jesus says: "Blessed are the poor in spirit: for theirs is the kingdom of heaven. . . . Blessed are the meek: for they shall inherit the earth. . . . Blessed are the peacemakers: for they shall be called the children of God. . . . Blessed are ye, when men shall revile you, and persecute you, and shall say all manner of evil against you falsely, for my sake" (Matthew 5:3–11).

In the same vein, Jesus advised his disciples: "Bless them

that curse you, and pray for them which despitefully use you. And unto him that smiteth thee on the one cheek offer also the other; and him that taketh away thy cloak forbid not to take thy coat also" (Luke 6:28–29).

The unearthliness of these teachings lies precisely in that they run counter to everything that is encoded in our evolutionary heritage, they run counter to everything that is institutionalized in our society, and they run counter to our philosophy of worldly success.

Recognizing the unearthliness of his outlook on human relations and his concept of community, Jesus observed: "My kingdom is not of this world: if my kingdom were of this world, then would my servants fight... but now is my kingdom not from hence" (John 18:36).

And in this utterance Jesus put his finger on what is strangest in his teaching. It is his attitude toward the handling of evil in the world.

No part of his teaching has been more disparaged than his advocacy of nonviolence in the face of evil. The German philosopher Nietzsche ridiculed it as a morality of weaklings. Pacifists who have tried to follow it have been branded cowards and felons and imprisoned in the wars of this century.

Yet when it has been tried it has renovated societies and overturned empires. Early Christians walked unresisting to martyrs' deaths in the arenas of ancient Rome. Yet in the end the mighty Roman Empire knelt at the cross and embraced the faith of the founder it had crucified.

Mahatma Gandhi's followers fell unresisting under the steel lathis of the native policemen who enforced Britain's Salt Act. Speaking of their sacrifice, Gandhi said, "Hour after hour stretchers carried back a stream of inert bleeding bodies."[7] Yet in the end the little holy man who inspired them was invited to negotiate with the empire's viceroy, and Britain relinquished her control of 350 million Indians.

In our own civil-rights struggle, Martin Luther King, Jr., locked arms with black men and women all over the South. Singing "We shall overcome," they marched, unresisting, and children lay bleeding on the streets and languished in and children lay bleeding on the streets and lanquished in jails. Yet in the end segregation in schools and buses was ended, and civil-rights legislation was enacted.

Speaking of the difficulty of living up to Jesus' precepts, King wrote: "It is not simple to adopt the credo that moral force has as much strength and virtue as the capacity to return a physical blow; or that to refrain from hitting back requires more will and bravery than the automatic reflexes of defense..." But he goes on to add, "The argument that non-violence is a coward's refuge lost its force as the heroic and often perilous acts uttered their wordless but convincing rebuttal..."[8]

JESUS AND LAW

It is not just Jesus' precept of nonviolence but the tenor of his whole ethic that goes against the grain of human nature. The beatitudes are a litany of unearthly ideals. Blessedness lies in poverty of spirit, in meekness, in pacifism, and in being persecuted and reviled in a good cause. Giving is better than receiving. Loving one's enemies is nobler and more effective than fighting them.

Human legal and ethical systems are based on the worldly ideals of equity and justice—getting what one deserves. The penal codes of most civilized nations rest on some form of the *lex talionis*—the "law of the claw." An eye for an eye; a tooth for a tooth. Let the punishment fit the crime. Even Hillel, one of the greatest teachers of the law, summed up its essence as a negative form of the golden rule. "What is hateful to thee, do not to thy neighbor." But Jesus viewed the law differently and so fulfilled it, for he stated the same rule in its positive form: "...whatsoever ye would that men should do to you, do ye even so to them: for this is the law and the prophets" (Matthew 7:12).

Jesus was not interested in mere equity or justice—his guiding principle was love. Love does not ask what is deserved but what it can give. So Jesus says: "And whosoever shall compel thee to go a mile, go with him twain.... Ye have heard that it hath been said, Thou shalt love thy neighbor, and hate thine enemy. But I say unto you, Love your enemies, bless them that curse you, do good to them that hate you, and pray for them which despitefully use you..." (Matthew 5:41, 43–44).

And in teaching this law of love Jesus transcended human ideals of righteousness and revealed his Celestial nature. Only the son of Divine and Cosmic Love would have the audacity to urge his followers, "Be ye therefore perfect, even as your Father which is in heaven is perfect" (Matthew 5:48).

What are we to make of such teaching? Even if we grant the value of these ideals how is it humanly possible to live up to them? Jesus' answer was the one he gave to Nicodemus.

"Ye Must Be Born Again"

According to John, Nicodemus was a ruler of the Jews who came secretly to Jesus, by night, for spiritual counsel. Jesus responded with one of his most famous injunctions: "Verily, verily, I say unto thee, Except a man be born again, he cannot see the kingdom of God." Nicodemus, astonished, asked him, "How can a man be born when he is old? can he enter a second time into his mother's womb, and be born?" Jesus answered, "Verily, verily, I say unto thee, Except a man be born of water and of the Spirit, he cannot enter into the kingdom of God" (John 3:1–5).

And with this strange interchange, at the outset of John's Gospel, we come to the central purpose of Jesus' mission on earth—the bringing of the baptism of the Spirit to humanity. The first birth by "water"—the breaking of the amniotic sac in childbirth—leaves humans with a nature incapable of living up to Jesus' ideals. Without spiritual transformation we cannot live up to the Celestials' requirements for citizenship in their coming "kingdom." The second birth—the birth of the Spirit—accomplishes the needed transformation. Jesus taught that by surrendering one's life to the indwelling of the Holy Spirit, and accepting its regeneration and guidance, humans could be restored to the possibility of righteousness.

New Birth and Jesus' "Baptism"

Like Nicodemus, many people find the idea of being "born again" incredible. Some reject it as completely absurd, and others see it as some sort of mystical hocus pocus.

Again, recent discoveries in parapsychology throw new light on this ancient teaching. What exactly was Jesus talking about? Some have supposed his "baptism" was water baptism.

Yet speaking of the charge that Jesus baptized more followers than John the Baptist, John says, "Jesus himself baptized
not." (John 4:2). He adds that only Jesus' disciples baptized.

Morton Smith, a New Testament scholar, has speculated
that Jesus' baptism was a secret magical rite in which he used
hypnosis to induce possessionlike states in hysterical or schizo-
phrenic disciples. He has even suggested that Jesus induced
hallucinations of literal ascent into the "kingdom of God" in
his followers.

Yet fifty days after Jesus' death, at Pentecost, over 3,000
people are reported, by Luke, to have received this same baptism of the Spirit. Jesus himself was no longer present, and no
cult leader or "magician" was there to take his place as a
hypnotist. Further, the phenomena of Pentecost, which we
will examine in the next chapter, are not those typical of
hypnosis. Nor is it likely that 3,000 hysterics or schizophren-
ics would have assembled by chance. Twelve might be collected, over a period of time, by one charismatic cult leader,
but 3,000, at one time and in one place and by coincidence—
never!

Yet there can be little doubt that the "baptism of the
Holy Ghost" reported in the book of Acts at Pentecost is the
same "baptism" Jesus practiced. It was his own cousin, John
the Baptist, who told his followers, "I indeed baptize you
with water unto repentance: but he that cometh after me
is mightier than I . . . he shall baptize you with the Holy
Ghost, and with fire" (Matthew 3:11). We shall have more
to say about this peculiar association of "fire" with the baptism
of the Holy Spirit in the chapter which follows. But the point
here is that Jesus' "baptism" was evidently the same "birth by
the Spirit" which he recommended to Nicodemus and the
"baptism of the Holy Ghost" which was experienced by 3,000
at Pentecost.

THE NEW BIRTH AND CONVERSION

To many people today the term "born again" is associated
with images of skid row rescue missions, sawdust trails, and
Bible Belt evangelism. In spite of the fact that many enter-
tainment celebrities and national leaders claim "born again"

religious experiences, the impression persists that spiritual rebirth is not quite respectable. In many ways this is strange, since some of the world's greatest spiritual teachers have received their calling and inspiration in dramatic "rebirth" experiences. Among them were Moses, the Buddha, the Apostle Paul and St. Augustine.

Perhaps a part of the problem lies in what Christopher Frye called the "domestication of the enormous miracle"—the making of something that is sacred and special into what is commonplace and trivial. There has been a confusion of conversion, as a psychological experience, with spiritual rebirth, to which it sometimes leads.

While many religious "conversions" produce beneficial and lasting changes in the converts, others are of short duration and produce little evidence of a genuine growth in moral and spiritual sensitivity.

As a result controversy has developed, among Christians, concerning the value of religious conversion. Conservative, evangelical Protestants continue to feel it is the only valid entree into the religious life. Liberal Protestants and most Catholics question its long-range benefits. They feel true spiritual development comes about gradually by searching, study, prayer and instruction.

A SPACE AGE VIEW OF THE NEW BIRTH

With the insights of space age psychology Jesus' teaching can now be set in a clearer light. What mattered for Jesus was that the individual undergoes a spiritual transformation —a rebirth. The "birth of the Spirit" brings this about.

Genuine spiritual rebirth requires profound changes in our beliefs, attitudes and values. For some people these are achieved by a conscious process of study, work, self–examination and seeking. Their progress is gradual, and they experience it as spiritual awakening or growth. For others, especially those who are deeply conflicted about spiritual matters, changes may be largely unconscious or even denied. Only when their conflict becomes overwhelming do they admit the other side of their "divided self," and acknowledge it in a sudden "decision" or "conversion."

The spiritual rebirth can be real in either case. If it is, it will prove itself by a change in their lives which is lasting and for the better.

But if a conversion experience is brought on by mere techniques of manipulation, such as fear and mass hysteria, without the necessary spiritual preparation, it will not last or it will produce no real change for the better. The individual may undergo an emotional experience, and he may profess new beliefs and values, but his conduct will not change, or it will soon return to its former pattern.

SPIRITUAL REBIRTH AND CELESTIAL CITIZENSHIP

What Jesus taught, then, is that those who wish to become citizens in the Celestials' civilization must follow the way he taught and exemplified, and without a spiritual rebirth this is not possible.

The proof of rebirth is not a conversion experience. (One may be converted to anything—atheism or a true spirituality.) What really matters, Jesus taught, is that one undergoes "baptism of the Spirit." Whether this comes by gradual or sudden conversion is immaterial.

It is not necessary that one belong to any particular church, or even that one be a professing Christian, to have this baptism. There have been righteous men and women in every culture throughout the ages. Many of them never heard of the historical Jesus or set foot in a Christian church.

In the chapter which follows we will examine this baptism of the Spirit, and the Spirit itself, more closely.

CHAPTER XIII

PENTECOST AND BIOCOSMIC ENERGY

And there appeared unto them cloven tongues like as of
fire, and it sat upon each of them. And they were all filled
with the Holy Ghost ...

—Acts 2:3–4

Fifty days had passed since Jesus celebrated his last Passover with the disciples. In the interim they had plumbed the
depths of despair and reached the peaks of joy. Jesus, their
leader, had been arrested, tried and crucified. One of their
number, his betrayer, had committed suicide. In the terror
of those events they had been scattered by the impact of the
tragedy and its aftermath. John, the Beloved, had taken Mary,
the mother of Jesus, to a place of safety and retirement. Peter,
stricken with grief and overwhelmed with shame at his denial
of Jesus, had gone into seclusion. Others of the disciples had
fled the city. The women who were to visit the tomb on
Easter morning had remained close by, but had lost touch
with the disciples.

Then the incredible had happened. The three women,
Mary Magdalene, Mary the wife of Cleophas and Salome,
were the first to know of it before dawn on Easter Sunday.
The tomb was empty! A stranger, or strangers, told them
Jesus had risen. Soon after he appeared to Mary Magdalene
and still later to two followers on the road to Emmaus—
about 4 miles outside Jerusalem. Still later he appeared to the
assembled eleven and allowed them to see and feel his
wounds.

Now, seven weeks later, they were all assembled together
for the first time since those momentous events. The gathering included the disciples, family and friends of Jesus and
most of his other close followers—about 120 in all. They

had collected, probably in the same upper room where he celebrated his last Passover, to share the summer festival, Shavuos—the feast of Pentecost. And, though they did not yet know it, they were also about to celebrate the founding of Christianity.

Luke tells the story in the book of Acts. In the opening chapter he repeats the account of Jesus' ascension into heaven—taken up into a "cloud" which received him out of their sight (Acts 1:9). Just before he is "taken up" the bewildered disciples ask if he will now finally assume his role as Messiah: "Lord, wilt thou at this time restore again the kingdom to Israel?" Jesus responds cryptically that it is not for them "to know the times or the seasons." Seeing their disappointment he then adds: "But ye shall receive power, after that the Holy Ghost is come upon you: and ye shall be witnesses unto me both in Jerusalem, and in all Judaea, and in Samaria, and unto the uttermost part of the earth" (Acts 1:6–8).

Now the time for the fulfillment of that promise had arrived. Luke moves swiftly to the central event in the second chapter. "And when the day of Pentecost was fully come, they were all with one accord in one place. And suddenly there came a sound from heaven as of a rushing mighty wind, and it filled all the house where they were sitting. And there appeared unto them cloven tongues like as of fire, and it sat upon each of them. And they were all filled with the Holy Ghost, and began to speak with other tongues, as the Spirit gave them utterance" (Acts 2:1–4).

With these words Luke lifts the curtain on the strangest, but most portentous, part of the entire gospel story. For in this aftermath to the life of Jesus he introduces the principal actor in the drama—Jesus' Cosmic "Father," the Holy Spirit. Throughout the four gospels Jesus speaks of his "Spirit," and in the Gospel of John he speaks of him as a "Comforter" who will watch over and guide the disciples when he is gone.

The "Third Person" of the Trinity

In the first centuries of the church early theologians had trouble identifying this "Spirit," or "Comforter." Was it a person separate from Jesus and his Father? Or was it just an aspect of one or the other? Were they also just aspects of one another?

Didn't Jesus say he and his Father were "one," and didn't he refer to the "Comforter" as *his* "Spirit"? Perhaps they were all one in some mysterious way. Yet Jesus also spoke of them as though each had a separate identity and a distinct role.

At first a variety of opinions prevailed on this question. Eventually those favoring the three-in-one view won out. The doctrine of the Trinity was established as the correct one by church edict, and other views were declared to be heresies.

This stopped most of the argument, but the problem remained. The church had spoken. There were three persons in one—but how? Philosophers took over where theologians left off and tried to provide explanations to account for the mystery.

In the meantime ordinary believers, who had difficulty following both theological disputes and philosophical explanations, were formulating their own ideas. Jesus they could understand. After all, he was incarnated—a man. Of course, there were no photographs and the gospels didn't give a physical description, but church artists filled the gap. The familiar bearded figure—the "pale Galilean" of Swinburne's poem—was beginning to take on a standard artistic expression.

God the Father was another problem. Not until Michelangelo would he, too, become the heroic, bearded Semite of *The Creation*. Until then he remained a shadowy sort of superhuman king, Jesus' "Father," who bore an uncertain resemblance to the Old Testament Jehovah.

The Holy Spirit remained, however, wholly "without form and void." The Scriptures gave no hint as to his, or its, appearance. Some artists were content to picture it as a dove descending on Jesus at his baptism. Others made it just a beam of light—a sort of off-stage spot—highlighting dramatic events in the New Testament.

The fact that prayers and salutations were never addressed to him, or it, in the Scriptures increased the difficulty. God, the Father, was often addressed as "Our Father." Jesus was addressed as "Lord." But no one, including Jesus himself, ever seemed to address the Holy Spirit directly.

When the King James version appeared and used the expression the "Holy Ghost," things looked more hopeful. But hope faded as the language of the translation fell into disuse. Today, the term is of no help at all. A ghost is just something in a white sheet that is left over from a dead person. It doesn't seem a very appropriate label for the third person of the Trinity.

A Problem of Semantics

Why has the Holy Spirit been such a problem in Christian art and theology? Why, as one of the principal actors in the New Testament, has he, or she, or it, remained so nebulous and insubstantial? Especially since the baptism of the Holy Spirit was the central event in Jesus' teaching and in the early church. Why did the gospel writers and Jesus leave the agent, whose baptism qualifies us for admission into the kingdom of God, in a semantic limbo?

The answer to this question is again one of the major discoveries of our space age interpretation of the Bible. To our surprise it has rescued the Holy Spirit from the obscurity into which Christian theology had let it fall and restored it to the central role it played in the thinking of Jesus and the apostles.

As we have implied, a great deal of theology's neglect of the Holy Spirit seems to be due to a semantic dilemma. The language used to describe it, in the Bible, does not fit the theological notions early churchmen had about it. It was easier to ignore the whole matter than to revise their thinking.

Describing the Indescribable

The Greek term used for Holy "Ghost," in Luke's account of Pentecost, is *pneuma*. This literally means a "breath" or "wind"—a moving current of air. But the figurative use is clearly the one intended in Luke, and this is abstracted from the action of breath or wind. It suggests a power or "spirit." Like the wind, the Holy Ghost is an invisible "power." Further, the figurative use of *pneuma* also carries the meanings of "life" and "mind." This invisible power has something in common with our own lives and minds—it is an intelligent, vital principle.

The English word "ghost" is totally misleading, for it suggests a sort of astral double—the theological "soul." So early modern Protestants were misled by the King James translators into thinking of the Holy Ghost as a sort of soul of Jesus and God—a "soul" they shared, since they were "one."

When the King James translation says a human "gave up the ghost," however, "ghost" is used for a different Greek word, ekpneo. Clearly the "Holy Ghost" is not the immortal soul of Jesus or God, nor is it their apparition, in spite of some modern theologians who insist both Jesus and God are dead.

One other Greek word is used in the New Testament for the Holy Spirit. It is the word parakletos and it is used only in John's Gospel. It means simply an "intercessor" or "consoler." For this reason the Holy Spirit is sometimes called the "Paraclete." John uses the term when Jesus tells his disciples he will send the "Paraclete" to take his place and comfort them. So he says to them, "But when the Comforter is come, whom I will send unto you from the Father, even the Spirit of truth, which proceedeth from the Father, he shall testify of me..." (John 15:26). And again he tells them the Comforter will "teach you all things, and bring all things to your remembrance, whatsoever I have said unto you" (John 14:26).

Putting these meanings together, we arrive at a very abstract notion. The Holy Spirit is an invisible power. It has the qualities of life and mind and, as a "comforter," can teach all things and "bring to remembrance" the teachings of Jesus—which were principally those of love.

Conceiving the Inconceivable

Four words stand out, then, in these characterizations of the Holy Spirit—power, life, truth and love. And remembering that it is principally John who gives us these attributes, we are drawn back to the opening verses of his gospel. In these he says: "In the beginning was the Word, and the Word was with God, and the Word was God.... All things were made by him... In him was life; and the life was the light of men.... And the Word was made flesh, and dwelt among us..." (John 1:1–4, 14).

The Greek word translated "Word" in these passages is *logos*—a term which almost defies translation into English. Though it is often translated "word" or "thought," it has a much broader meaning in Greek. This use is indicated by its frequent addition, as a suffix, at the end of scientific terms. So we get geology (geo-*logos*), a systematic knowledge of the earth; biology (bio-*logos*), a systematic knowledge of life; and psychology (psyche-*logos*), a systematic knowledge of mind.

Some New Testament scholars believe John was influenced, in his use of *logos*, by the Greek philosophy of stoicism. The stoics used *logos* to mean the ultimate reason which underlies all things and explains all existence. So he tells us (speaking of the "Word"): "All things were made by him; and without him was not any thing made that was made" (John 1:3).

Bible scholars have generally understood John's "Word" to be Christ. As the Cosmic Christ he was "made flesh" and "dwelt among us." Jesus' pre-existence of his own birth in Bethlehem is assumed to be that of the Cosmic Christ.

Yet Paul tells us that this Christ "dwells" within him and that he lives through this Christ—and Jesus said he would send the "Comforter" for just these purposes.

If these things are so, then John's Word and the Cosmic Christ and the Comforter are all one and the same.

The Holy Spirit As Ultimate Creative Energy

So we come to a startling conclusion. The Holy Spirit is not the pale shadow of the other two full-bodied members of the Trinity. It is the principal actor. John says it made the world. Jesus said it was his Spirit which existed before him and would replace him, after his departure, in the hearts and minds of his followers.

Granting this, then the Holy Spirit is the being whom we called "God, the Creator," in Chapter V. The Holy Spirit is the Divine Logos, the Cosmic Christ, the Word—the ultimate Creative Power. And as we said in Chapter V, it is at the very least a person and a God. It is, in fact, the God behind all gods—the God worshipped by the Celestials, themselves, including Jehovah and Jesus. They are divine to the extent that they express its power, and we, too, become sons and daughters of God through its "baptism."

This is why Jesus speaks of it as his "Spirit" (power), for it was the source of all his power. The miracles attributed to him in the gospels were performed by means of it.

And this is why Jesus speaks of it as the "Spirit" (or power) of his Father, Jehovah. By means of it the Lord God performed the wonders attributed to him in the Old Testament.

It is the universal mind Sir James Jeans referred to when he spoke of the "Mind in which the atoms, from which our minds have grown, exist as thoughts."[1]

Yet it is more than a cosmic mind or intelligence. It is also Cosmic Power. It is that mysterious Being which underlies the "mind stuff" and "other entities of the physical world," and of which they both are manifestations. Its relation to them is the link which astronomer V. A. Firsoff sought when he spoke of a "modulus of transformation" which could relate mind and matter and transform one into the other.[2]

Ancient spiritual disciplines recognized it as *chi* or *ki* or *prana*. Modern researchers in paraphysics and parapsychology have suggested it is identical with what they call "bioplasmic" or "biocosmic" energy. Because it underlies and interfuses and directs and controls all things it is in that Being of which Wordsworth speaks in the *Lines Written a Few Miles Above Tintern Abbey*. It is that "presence" which "disturbed" him with the joy

> Of elevated thoughts; a sense sublime
> Of something far more deeply interfused,
> Whose dwelling is the light of setting suns,
> And the round ocean and the living air,
> And the blue sky, and in the mind of man;
> A motion and a spirit, that impels
> All thinking things, all objects of all thought,
> And rolls through all things.

Could it also be that same Power which entered like "rushing wind" and baptized those gathered in the upper room at Pentecost? That it was a physical, as well as a spiritual, power is testified by the fact that Luke says it appeared as "cloven tongues like as of fire." In fact, Luke's statement is reminiscent of John the Baptist's announcement that one would follow him who would baptize "with the Holy Ghost and with fire" (Matthew 3:11). It also calls to mind Jesus' own statement that he came "to send fire on the earth" (Luke 12:49). New Testament scholars have generally assumed both John and Jesus were using "fire" in a figurative sense to mean a rekindling of religious fervor, but the Greek term, pur, means "lightning" and could also suggest an energy form similar to electricity.

This raises a profound question. Could the Holy Spirit manifest itself in a physical, as well as a purely spiritual, form? If it is the ultimate Power which underlies both mind and matter might its "baptism," or uses, not result in physical as well as psychic manifestations? If so, Luke's statement about the sound of "rushing wind" and "tongues of flame" would begin to make more sense.

THE HOLY SPIRIT AND KIRLIAN AURAS

Modern psychics recognize a fourth state of matter in addition to the traditional three. Besides solids, liquids and gases there are plasmas. In ancient Greek philosophy this division was also recognized. The first three states were represented by earth, water and air. The fourth was known as fire!

New Testament scholars believe Greek scientific and philosophical ideas influenced the gospel writers. Did they call the energy manifestations of Spirit baptism "fire" because they were influenced by Greek philosophy? If they did it may be that what Luke described at Pentecost was some kind of plasma phenomenon.

Recent paraphysical research has developed a technique for investigating plasmas that surround many objects. The technique is called Kirlian photography. It is photography which uses high voltage electricity rather than light to expose photographic plates. It shows plasmas surrounding material objects as energy halos. These are particularly active around living objects and are therefore often referred to as "bioplasmic" or "biocosmic."

Principal centers for Kirlian research are in the Soviet

Union and UCLA's Neuropsychiatric Institute, under the supervision of Dr. Thelma Moss. Kirlian photographs of living objects, such as a leaf or a person's hand, show flamelike emissions of light which are reminiscent of the "cloven tongues like as of fire" described by Luke.

Two journalists who recently surveyed Kirlian research in the Soviet Union described a photographed leaf as being surrounded by "turquoise and reddish-yellow patterns of flares coming out of specific channels of the leaf. The pattern of luminescence was different for every item . . . But a living leaf was made up of millions of sparkling lights."[3]

While some scientists have suggested that halos are due to electrical phenomena connected with the process itself, a leading Soviet researcher, Victor Inushin, says, "The bioluminescence visible in the Kirlian pictures is caused by the bioplasma, not the electrical state of the organism . . . This bioplasma is not a chaotic system; it has specific spatial organization."[4]

Kirlian photography suggests, then, that all material objects, including living things, have energy halos which can be enhanced by invasion of outside energy. The halos resemble cloven tongues of fire.

Luke suggests that those gathered at Pentecost also exhibited halos which became visible when they were invaded by the Holy Spirit. These, too, resembled cloven tongues of fire.

Could the phenomena, in both cases, be the same? Psychic researchers are currently investigating sensitives who claim they see energy auras surrounding people. Some of them appear to diagnose diseases and emotional states from the colors and forms of patients' auras.

Dr. Shafica Karagulla, a neuropsychiatrist formerly associated with Wilder Penfield at Montreal University, is one of these researchers. She tells of a sensitive who sees people's auras as a "vital or energy body or field" like a "sparkling web of light beams." From these she diagnosis diseases. Evaluating her diagnoses, Dr. Karagulla says, "She can see the physical organs of the body and any pathology or disturbance of function. She has not studied medicine or physiology, and often her descriptions are those one would expect of a layman. These descriptions are accurate and clear and easily translate into medical terms. Medical diagnosis has proved that the sensitive is correct and accurate in what she sees."[5]

Other psychics seem to heal diseases by touching afflicted areas of the body or even mentally concentrating on the diseased part. Kirlian photographs show that healers' auras diminish after healing and that patients' auras increase. So Dr. Thelma Moss reports on one study at UCLA in which a healer treated twelve patients for three months. "Typically (though not invariably) the healer's corona grew smaller after treatment while the patients' grew larger and brighter."[6] Similar photographs of a nonhealer, used as a control, failed to show such changes.

The gospel writer and physician Luke tells of a similar observation. The healer was Jesus. A woman who had an "issue of blood" for twelve years came to him while he was on his way to heal another patient. As Luke tells it, she "had spent all her living upon physicians, neither could be healed of any." Approaching Jesus, she "came behind him, and touched the border of his garment: and immediately her issue of blood stanched. And Jesus said, Who touched me? When all denied, Peter and they that were with him said, Master, the multitude throng thee and press thee, and sayest thou, Who touched me? And Jesus said, Somebody hath touched me: for I perceive that virtue is gone out of me" (Luke 8:43–46). The word Jesus used for "virtue" here is *dunamis*, which means "miraculous power" or force.

PENTECOST AND THE PARANORMAL

In the light of these various findings and experiences it seems likely, then, that those gathered in the upper room at Pentecost underwent some sort of change of energy state as an effect of their baptism. The result was an outbreak of paranormal phenomena similar to those investigated by modern researchers.

Luke continues the story. As the "cloven tongue like as of fire" sat upon their heads they were all "filled with the Holy Ghost." Luke makes the natural assumption that the settlings of the "tongues" caused the "filling." From our preceeding discussion of energy auras it seems more likely that the "filling" with the Spirit caused the auras to increase. And whether they increased to the point of normal visibility, or whether those filled became psychically sensitive and saw otherwise invisible auras, is not clear. It seems probable that, like Dr. Karagulla's sensitive, they saw auras which "unbaptized" people would not have seen.

"OTHER TONGUES"

In any event, upon being filled they "began to speak with other tongues, as the Spirit gave them utterance" (Acts 2:4).

Some New Testament scholars have assumed the "tongue speaking" at Pentecost was a kind of hysterical dislocation of speech behavior—babbling, or what is technically called "glossolalia." So Morton Smith speaks of post-Pentecostal spirit baptism as involving "incomprehensible cries—a common symptom of schizophrenia."[7]

And while some later instances of "speaking in tongues" in the New Testament do involve glossolalia—the "unknown" or "angelic tongue" of Paul—Luke makes it clear that this was not what occurred at Pentecost. Rather, the phenomenon here was xenoglossy. This is the ability to understand, or use, a foreign human language which the speaker or hearer has never studied.

Writing of this, Luke says, "And there were dwelling at Jerusalem Jews, devout men, out of every nation under heaven. Now when this was noised abroad, the multitude came together, and were confounded, because that every man heard them speak in his own language. And they were all amazed and marvelled, saying one to another, Behold, are not all these which speak Galileans? And how hear we every man in our own tongue, wherein we were born?" (Acts 2:5–8).

At first it might seem that this story of a polyglot group all understanding a single language is just another tall tale. And so it might be dismissed were it not that xenoglossy has occurred in modern times under well-documented conditions—often in connection with baptism of the Spirit. John H. Sherrill, a journalist and staff member of *Guideposts*, tells of an interview he had with Harold Bredesen, an ordained minister of the First Reformed Church, Mount Vernon, New

York. The Reverend Mr. Bredesen had experienced the gift of xenoglossy on several occasions. Sherrill reports one in which Bredesen was praying outside a mountain cabin where he was in retreat. Suddenly there was "the most beautiful outpouring of vowels and consonants and also some strange guttural syllables. I could not recognize any of it. It was as though I were listening to a foreign language, except that it was coming out of my mouth." Dumbfounded, Bredesen rushed down the mountain and encountered an old man sitting in front of his cabin. Still speaking, the minister paused, and the old man answered, talking rapidly in a language Bredesen didn't know. When it became obvious Bredesen could not understand the old man said, "How can you speak Polish but not understand it?" "I was speaking in Polish?" The man laughed, "Of course it was Polish." Bredesen reported that, as far as he knew, he had never before heard the language. On another occasion he stated he spoke old Arabic to the daughter of an Egyptologist who understood him, although he, himself, could not understand what he said.[8]

Controlled and well-documented cases of xenoglossy have also been reported by the British Society for Psychical Research in connection with spiritualistic séances. In his book *The Life Beyond Death*, Arthur Ford tells of one of the best-known of these. Four different mediums, all independently, gave alleged communications from F. W. H. Myers, a classical Greek scholar and the deceased founder of the society. The messages included lengthy quotations from Homer's *Iliad*, in classical Greek, which none of the mediums had studied. Each medium received a separate part of the message, which was afterward coordinated into complete quotations. The "control," Myers, claimed to have devised these "cross correspondences" to prove his survival of bodily death.[9]

Tongue speaking continued to be an important part of apostolic Christianity. The Apostle Paul, speaking of his own involvement, says, "I thank my God I speak with tongues more than ye all." (I Corinthians 14:18) This extraordinary man, who authored nearly a third of the New Testament, has overshadowed all subsequent Christian thinkers. As the most outstanding Christian theologian of his age—and perhaps of all time—his word on tongue speaking carried, and still carries, great weight. He approved of glossolalia but laid down strict rules for its use. He stipulated that when it occurred in public there should be translators present. Otherwise, he stated, he preferred that the unknown, or "angelic" tongue (I Corinthians 13:1) be practiced privately where, he implied, it had value as a mode of prayer or praise to God. So he says, "If any man speak in an unknown tongue, let it be by two, or at the most by three, and that by course; and let one interpret. But if there be no interpreter, let him keep silence in the church; and let him speak to himself, and to God" (I Corinthians 14:27-28).

SPIRITUAL OUTPOURING

The outbreak of xenoglossy at Pentecost did not end the paranormal manifestations, however.

The crowd which it attracted had swollen until over 3,000 were now collected outside the upper room. The eleven gathered in front of them and Peter, as their spokesman, explained their strange behavior to the crowd—many of whom were ridiculing those baptized. He assured his listeners they were "not drunken, as ye suppose" but had undergone the outpouring of God's Spirit which had been prophesied by the Old Testament Prophet Joel. He then went on to announce the resurrection of Jesus and to proclaim him the Christ. He ended his sermon by urging them to repent and accept the baptism of the Spirit themselves. A rugged Galilean fisherman, Peter was not noted for his oratory or brilliance. The little band of followers had turned to him, after Jesus' ascension, as their natural leader primarily because of his generous and loyal nature and his sheer worth as a human being.

His effect on his audience is therefore another paranormal event of that day. For Luke reports that virtually the entire assembly of 3,000 underwent the birth of the Spirit and became loyal members of the first Christian fellowship in Jerusalem (Acts 2:14-42).

HEALING

One more remarkable event marked the day. As with modern healers, the invasion of the Spirit and the aural manifestations signaled an increase in healing ability. As John and Peter left the gathering and walked toward the temple for prayers they were detained by a beggar who had been born a cripple, unable to walk. He was daily carried to and from the temple area, where he begged. Seeing Peter and John, he asked for alms. Luke then dramatically proceeds: "And Peter, fastening his eyes upon him with John, said, Look on us. And he gave heed unto them, expecting to receive something of them. Then Peter said, Silver and gold have I none; but such as I have I give thee: In the name of Jesus Christ of Nazareth rise up and walk. And he took him by the right hand, and lifted him up: and immediately his feet and ankle bones received strength. And he leaping up stood, and walked, and entered with them into the temple, walking, and leaping, and praising God" (Acts 3:1–8).

THE HOLY SPIRIT AND MODERN PHYSICS

What are we to make of Luke's account of Pentecost? The episodes it narrates can be duplicated and topped many times throughout the entire Bible. "Fire" from heaven, auras, "outpourings" of the spirit, psychic healings—even resurrections and levitations—are reported in both the Old and New Testaments. Are they just the superstitions of a bygone age or mythic elaborations of the folk process? If they are, then why do modern psychic researchers—psychologists and physicists and medical doctors—report similar happenings in modern times? Why have some of the same events reported in Jesus' healing ministry and at Pentecost been duplicated, under laboratory conditions, at UCLA's Neuropsychiatric Institute, and Stanford Research Institute and at Duke University? Are the "tongues of fire" at Pentecost really less believable than Thelma Moss' Kirlian auras? Is Peter's healing of the lame man less believable than those of modern psychic healers who have been investigated by teams of medical doctors, recorded on motion-picture film and subjected to Kirlian photography?

Are these modern counterparts superstitions and myths, also? They have been monitored by some of the most sophisticated scientists in the world. And they have been recorded on graph paper and photographic film, which are not subject to the folk process or mythic elaboration.

In taking a space age look at the Bible it is necessary to realize that the space age has brought more than the exploration of space and computer technology. It has also brought a revolution in our world view.

The scientific materialism of the last century has become obsolete. Relativity theory and quantum physics have given us a new world view. In this view we see the world not as a collection of hard, impenetrable atoms organized into mechanical systems. It has rather become a continuous energy field in which the principal actors are events—not objects.

We still perceive the world as consisting of objects, of course—tables, chairs, people, etc. But physics tells us these objects are really energy complexes in continuous flux and inseparable from one another. Speaking of this, Fritjof Capra, a University of California physicist, says: "In modern physics the universe is thus experienced as a dynamic, inseparable whole which always includes the observer in an essential way. In this experience, the traditional concepts of space and time, of isolated objects, and of cause and effect lose their meaning."[10]

In this new world view, energy, not matter, has become the basic reality. Energy events, not objects, are the "things" that make it up. Change, not permanence, is the real state of affairs, and everything is related to and interacts with every other.

Given this new kind of world view, the miracles of the Bible and the paranormal events of modern psychic research are no longer unbelievable.

If our body is just an energy complex, it stands to reason that a disruption of its energy flow may produce illness. And if it does it also stands to reason that a sudden influx of energy may restore its balance and as suddenly heal it.

And if everything is interrelated to everything else, it also stands to reason that a healer's touch may transfer his energy to an ailing patient. In fact, if mind and matter are related, as Firsoff argues, then his merely thinking of the ailing organ, in his patient, may cause a transfer of his energy to that organ, just as the psychic's thinking of moving an instrument needle may cause it to move. Modern physics opens up vistas of interrelatedness in the world which were not suspected before our generation.

So Sir Cyril Burt observes: "Contemporary physics recognizes four types of interactions ('strong,' 'weak,' electromagnetic and gravitational). Each obeys its own laws, and so far at any rate has defeated any attempt to reduce it to another type." Then he goes on to suggest there may be yet another— "a psychic universe consisting of events or entities linked by psychic interactions, obeying laws of their own and interpenetrating the physical universe ..."[11]

THE HOLY SPIRIT AS LOGOS

As the ultimate Creative Power underlying both mind and matter the Holy Spirit has the qualities of both. It is manifest in matter as energy. As mind it manifests itself as organizing tendency and order in the universe.

In this latter aspect it is appropriately called "Spirit"— cosmic intelligence. And as cosmic intelligence it not only thinks the "atoms from which our minds have grown"—it thinks the atoms of the cosmos as well. Every conceivable actuality is preconceived in it as possibility; every thought as concept.

This is why it is possible for tongue speakers to speak languages they have never learned. They may not know them, but the universal *logos* does and, in the baptism of the Spirit, these speakers are inundated with universal mind.

As the "Spirit of truth" it can instruct us in other areas as well. It can heal our bodies because it contains the cosmic blueprints from which they were made. It can heal our minds and characters because they pre-existed in it as thoughts. It can bring wholeness in social relationships because it is cosmic love. And because it embodies the psychic elements of both male and female identity it can lift human love to the heights of mutuality, overcoming sexist bias and exploitation in true psychic union.

Its restoration to the head of the Trinity is a needed

corrective in traditional Judeo-Christianity. As the union of both masculine and feminine principles it is a counterbalance to sexist views of the Deity. As the Spirit of God the Father and God the Son, the Logos or Cosmic Christ lifts the Godhead above the limitations of gender.

THE "GIFTS" OF THE SPIRIT

When we open our lives up to the baptism of the Spirit we can become channels for directing it outward toward others. When we do, Jesus and the apostles taught, we can use it to accomplish supernormal and paranormal feats. These are the "gifts of the Spirit" Paul speaks of when he says, "For to one is given by the Spirit the word of wisdom; to another the word of knowledge . . . To another faith . . . to another the gifts of healing . . . To another the working of miracles; to another prophecy . . . to another divers kinds of tongues . . ." (I Corinthians 12:8–10).

Through these they who are baptized in the Spirit minister to Christ's church and the world around them. So Jesus and Paul taught. And so the mystics of the ages have taught. Speaking of the Spirit's indwelling as "passive energy," Father William Johnson says that this activity of the Spirit is "an activity that transcends all measurable energy. Sometimes it is found in group prayer . . . or it can exist between two persons . . . usually a master and disciple. . . . or . . . between two people who are in love . . . I would guess that passive energy plays a key role in clairvoyance, mind-reading, telepathy and other forms of extrasensory perception . . . the Carmelite monastery, the Carthusian hermitage, the Hindu ashram and the Zen temple . . . are generating large quantities of a very high and precious energy."[12]

And in ministering with these gifts, sons and daughters of God prepare the world for the coming of Christ's kingdom.

THE HOLY SPIRIT AND THE KINGDOM OF GOD

No teaching was more freqently repeated, throughout Jesus' ministry, than the teaching of the coming kingdom of God. Christian theologians have puzzled over its meaning throughout the centuries. The early apostolic church saw it as the earthly, visible kingdom established by Jesus' physical return—the "parousia," or second coming, which Bultmann finds incredible. Recent scholars have tended to give it a more figurative meaning—the kingdom of Christ's invisible church of believers—those baptized of the Spirit.

Our space age interpretation of this central teaching suggests that both views are correct, as we have already pointed out. The Cosmic Christ does rule, in the birth of the Spirit, in his invisible church of those who follow his way—whatever their creed or culture. Saints and mystics of all ages and every nation belong to this church. Men and women of simple faith who "hunger and thirst" after righteousness—as Jesus put it—belong to this church. And through it the world prepares and moves forward toward the heritage that will be brought by the Celestials when they return.

Members of this invisible church are the beachhead of that Celestial civilization which will make God's kingdom visible on earth. Its citizens will be made up of the redeemed of all ages who have helped carry forward this work.

Joining Christ's Church

The rules for membership in this church are much simpler than for any earthly church or faith.

It is not necessary to learn a catechism or ritual. Attendance is perpetual wherever you are. The code of conduct is simple—whatever you choose to do with the Spirit's guidance. There are no elders or deacons. No one judges your qualifications or behavior. There is no creed—or rather there are as many as man has devised; for the Celestials' original teaching has found its way to some degree and in some form in every faith, and the Spirit is everywhere to inform and guide.

There are just two simple rules, and Peter summed them up in his sermon to the 3,000 at Pentecost. "Repent, and be baptized" (Acts 2:38). Translated into modern terms this means simply, (1) reject what is unrighteous in your life and, so far as you can, try to undo any wrong you have done; (2) accept the way of the Cosmic Christ and follow it to the best of your ability. If you do you will receive the baptism and guidance of the Spirit. And in receiving it you will be taught what else you need to know and given the strength to live up to it.

These are the rules for membership in the invisible church and for citizenship in the coming kingdom. The key to their fulfillment is the birth of the Spirit, for as Blake said, "It is the cosmos to those who know the way and chaos to those who lose it. It is Ariadne's thread whose windings create the world and yet enable us to unravel it—or ravel it. I give you the end of the Golden String. Only wind it into a ball. It will lead you in at Heaven's Gate built in Jerusalem's wall."

CHAPTER XIV

THEY'RE COMING BACK!

And there shall be no night there; and they need no candle, neither light of the sun; for the Lord God giveth them light: and they shall reign for ever and ever.

—Revelation 22:5

Not long ago I picked up a magazine at a newsstand with a feature story that attracted my attention. "Electronic money is coming!" it read. "Soon Americans will be able to complete most financial transactions, 24 hours a day, with nothing more than a little plastic card."

Salaries will be paid in the form of electronic credits recorded in the memory bank of a centralized computer. Commercial credit will be extended in the same fashion. Purchases will be made by inserting a personal identity card into a machine. It can scan the buyer's face or handprint and identification number, and transmit the information, via satellite, to the computer. The computer will match the face or handprint against duplicate information in its memory bank. In this way fraud, forgery and theft will be eliminated. Theoretically such a system could be extended to the whole country or even the entire world.

As I discussed the article with Vivianne we both had a vague feeling of familiarity. Then we remembered why. I went to my bookcase and took out the King James Version of the Bible. We turned to the thirteenth chapter of Revelation, and there it was! The very same account, in effect, told in the apocalyptic language of John the Revelator.

He tells how, at the time of the end, the whole world will be brought under the control of a "beast." In this case the word for "beast" is therion—a "wild animal." Many New Testament scholars believe this to be John's metaphor for a ruthless and dangerous world leader.

John then says his "image" will be made to "live" and "speak"—a reasonably good description of television. And everywhere men and women will be compelled to "worship" his image—a worldwide dictatorship exercising control through the mass media!

He goes on to say that under his regime all men "both small and great, rich and poor, free and bond" will receive a "mark" in "their right hand, or in their foreheads . . ." Further, he states that "no man might buy or sell, save he that had the mark, or the name of the beast, or the number of his name" (Revelation 13:15–17). This is the mysterious "mark of the beast" which has loomed large in the imagination of Christians since John's fearful prophecy was first penned.

Tomorrow's News 2,000 Years Ago

As we read John's account we once again marveled at how exactly the prophecies of the Bible anticipate the developments of today. Like pieces in a jigsaw puzzle things we had read or heard began to fall into place. A recent suggestion that the energy crisis and Middle East oil situation might bring about the formation of a worldwide common market, under a director who would have unprecedented powers. An article on future uses of satellites which explained how a wristwatchlike transmitter could connect anyone on earth, via satellites, with a centralized computer that could manage personal schedules and business affairs and give subscribers access to the world's accumulated knowledge. Recent proposals that all personal data—Social Security, IRS, FBI, military, police, motor vehicle, and business and credit—be merged into a single system under computer control.

If these things should be done, John's vision of the future would become actuality. A worldwide common market could, with modern communications technology, control the economic activities of every man, woman and child. No one could buy or sell without a number given him by the "beast." Superimposed over the forehead on a "mug shot," or the right hand on a handprint, it would be an infallible proof of identity. Unable to buy food, shelter, transportation or communications without identification, people could be controlled by economic restriction as they had never been controlled by the cruder techniques of old-fashioned police states. The "mark of the beast" would be the most coercive and frightening method of totalitarian control ever devised!

It would be impossible to buy a hot dog, feed a parking meter, purchase a tank of gas, ride a bus, enter a theater, make a phone call or rent a room without leaving a permanent record of the transaction in the computer's memory bank. And anyone, knowing the access code, could get the time and place of the act, along with your identification and personal history, by simply dialing a number.

PROPHECY AND THE BIBLE

John's vision of a coming world dictatorship is only one of a number of forecasts the Bible makes for the time of the end. Many of these, as we saw in Chapter II, have already been fulfilled, suggesting that the time of the Celestials' return is at hand. Others, like that concerning the "mark of the beast," are already being predicted, by our own scientists, for the near future. How was it possible for Bible writers, twenty to twenty-five centuries ago, to foresee the present with such accuracy? Is it mere coincidence? Or is foretelling the future genuinely possible? Once again recent research in physics and parapsychology seems to provide an answer.

Before looking at this, however, it will be helpful to see why traditional answers given in the heyday of higher criticism are unsatisfactory.

"IT'S JUST COINCIDENCE"

Many critics have insisted that fulfillment of biblical prophecies is an illusion. Certain that foretelling the future is impossible, they have fallen back on two stock explanations for every seemingly valid case of prophecy. One is that the prophecy is so vaguely worded we cannot determine its exact meaning. As a result it can be arbitrarily interpreted to fit events which happen later.

The other is that, though specific, it refers to events which happened before the Bible received its final form. So, it is claimed, the particular prophecy was written into the record, by later copyists or editors, after the facts it is supposed to foretell.

Unfortunately for the critics, neither of these explanations can account for the crucial prophecy which sets the timetable for the Celestials' return. As we saw in Chapter II, both the Prophet Ezekiel and Jesus forecast the return of the Jews to Israel after a dispersion "among the nations." This event, the founding of the State of Israel, is so unlikely, after a 1,900-year dispersion, that coincidence can be ruled out as a possible explanation.

Some critics have suggested the prophecies of Israel's rebirth refer to one, or more, of the Jews' various returns from exile that occurred before the Bible received its final form. While this could apply to Ezekiel's prophecy—though his phrase, "in the latter years" (Ezekiel 38:8), is standard Hebrew phraseology for the time of the end—it can in no way account for Jesus' prophecy. For there has been only one return from dispersion among "the nations" since Jesus' time, and that occurred 1,900 years after the gospels received their final form. Jesus' prophecy of the "fig tree" putting forth "its leaves" once again, just before the time of the end, is an unambiguous reference to the rebirth of Israel (Matthew 24:32). And its occurrence in 1948 makes it impossible that these words could have been put into Jesus' mouth after the event had already taken place.

Clearly, then, we have in this prophecy a genuine forecast, across almost 2,000 years, of an event so specific, dramatic and unlikely there can be little reasonable doubt its occurrence was a fulfillment of prophecy.

PROPHECY IN THE LABORATORY

How can this be? Genuine prophecy seems so contrary to common sense and what has been taken to be "scientific" that most Bible scholars have been inclined to write these prophecies off as vague references whose meaning can no longer be recovered.

Yet, in many cases they are not vague, and their meaning is quite specific. It just happens to be a meaning which is difficult for skeptical scholars to accept.

Once again a space age interpretation of Bible prophecy puts a wholly new light on the matter. If the prophets were just human fortunetellers, acting on their own initiative, then their remarkable accuracy would be incomprehensible. We would no more expect it of them than we would of tea-leaf readers, crystal-ball gazers or palmists.

But if these prophecies come from a civilization that knew, in their time, more than we now know, then their accuracy becomes more understandable.

For our own psychic researchers are beginning to study people who can foretell the future in the laboratory. This skill, called precognition, has been widely investigated under the most stringent controls.

Recently Helmut Schmidt, J. B. Rhine's successor at Duke University and a brilliant research physicist, has had remarkable success with subjects foretelling the occurrence of atomic events that normally defy prediction. His experiments involved guessing the order in which lamps were lighted by the target impact of subatomic particles—a process that is theoretically unpredictable. Summarizing his success, Arthur Koestler points out that " ... the subjects made correct predictive guesses at the outcome of theoretically unpredictable subatomic processes with a probability against chance of ten thousand million against one."[1] In attempting to explain Schmidt's success, Koestler theorizes, in *The Roots of Coincidence*, that the old idea that coming events cast their shadow before them is true even in the field of subatomic physics. He cites quantum physicists, such as University of London's Professor D. Bohm, who believe future events send out "feelers" which foreshadow them in the present.[2] He also cites Cambridge mathematician Adrian Dobbs, who believes future events try out tentatively "all the possible potentialities out of which one actually emerges."[3]

Koestler's point is that psychics, like those Helmut Schmidt tested, seem to be able to detect these "feelers" and use them to predict future events they foreshadow.

THE CELESTIALS AND PROPHECY

If the Celestials have mastered the uses of psychic power, as we earlier suggested, their prediction of present-day developments thousands of years ago may have involved a similar method.

It is also possible, of course, that they can predict complex social phenomena, such as the rebirth of Israel, by ordinary techniques of scientific prediction, much as our own scientists can predict eclipses or the weather. Though these involve the unpredictable elements of human decision and behavior they are no more indeterminate than the subatomic events predicted by Helmut Schmidt's subjects.

With advanced mathematical and data-processing techniques they could doubtless measure and interrelate the more complex causes of historical events as easily as our own scientists can predict the trajectory of a missile or space probe. And this might be possible even for events thousands of years in the future. In the same way our own scientists can predict comets or eclipses thousands of years before they occur. As we will see later in this chapter, they may even have machines, similar to television receivers, which can translate the "feelers" of future events, or the analysis of their causes, into video forecasts. These machines would be similar to "time machines" envisioned by our own science-fantasy writers which could enable us literally to see the future.

PROPHECY AND THE CELESTIALS' RETURN

Of all the prophecies in the Bible, none is more often or emphatically asserted than the promise of the Celestials' return to Earth. And throughout the ages, no problem has preoccupied conservative Christians, who believe in that return, more than the time of its occurrence. Over the centuries they have continued to echo the disciples' query: "Tell us, when shall these things be? and what shall be the sign of thy coming, and of the end of the world?" (Matthew 24:3).

Jesus' answer was unambiguous. "But of that day and hour knoweth no man, no, not the angels of heaven, but my Father only" (Matthew 24:36).

Yet in spite of Jesus' assurance on this matter a favorite pastime, for students of the Bible's apocalyptic books, has been the attempt to deduce a day and an hour. The apostles expected Christ's final return during their own lifetime. Almost every generation of Christians since has produced some who have been convinced they would live to see the ultimate event.

Numerous dates have been set in the past—the last day of
the year 1000; October of 1844; September of 1936. Needless
to say, the fateful event failed to materialize on any of them.

The logic that prompted their selections was various. The
year 1000 seemed destined to some because it ended the first
millennium following the birth of Jesus. Others seized on
the cryptic reference to 2,300 days in the Book of Daniel and
matched it with an equal number of years calculated from
the rebuilding of Solomon's Temple (Daniel 8:14 and 9:25).
Pyramidologists arrived at the 1936 date because the number
of inches in the passageway leading to the King's Chamber
suggested it—if one let an inch equal a year and reckoned
from the birth of Christ. Why God would have left crypto-
grams in which a year is disguised as a day, or an inch, they
did not bother to explain, but the failure of the advent to
follow their timetables was evident to believers and skeptics
alike.

In the end we are driven back to Jesus' declaration that
"of that day and hour knoweth no man . . . " Yet he did not
say that an approximate time could not be determined. In
fact he, himself, gave one very specific clue. And if we assume his Celestial origin—argued in Chapter XII—he, as
the son of Jehovah who alone knows, should be able to pinpoint the approximate time.

"Even at the Doors"

Jesus' clue is given in Matthew shortly after he assures his
disciples that the exact date and hour cannot be known. He
links it to his famous prophecy concerning the restoration of
Israel. Speaking of that event he says: "Now learn a parable
of the fig tree; When his branch is yet tender, and putteth
forth leaves, ye know that summer is nigh: So likewise ye,
when ye shall see all these things, know that it is near, even
at the doors. Verily I say unto you, This generation shall not
pass, till all these things be fulfilled" (Matthew 24:32–34).

We have already pointed out that the fig tree is a historical
emblem of national Israel. It "put forth leaves," for the first
time since Jesus' day, when the new State of Israel was born in
1948. Jesus' clue to the time of his return is given in his
assurance that the "generation" which witnessed this event

should "not pass" until the rest of his prophecy had been fulfilled. And what was the rest of his prophecy? It is given in the verses immediately preceding. So he says, "And then shall appear the sign of the Son of man in heaven: and then shall all the tribes of the earth mourn, and they shall see the Son of man coming in the clouds of heaven with power and great glory" (Matthew 24:30).

Taking Jesus literally, it is evident he means the Celestials' return will occur during the lifetime of those witnessing the founding of the State of Israel. We can also safely assume he had the biblical lifespan of "three score and ten" (seventy years) in mind. Since this event occurred in 1948, the generation "seeing" it would be those who had reached sufficient maturity to understand its significance—those participating in its founding and their contemporaries.

Being already of age, their average remaining lifespan would be not more than fifty years, according to the biblical standard.

According to Jesus' promise, then, the return of the Celestials will take place before the year 2000! And all those earth-shaking events described in the opening chapter are barely twenty years away.

THE APOCALYPTIC PUZZLE

Though Jesus declared that the day and hour of the Celestials' return cannot be known, the temptation to narrow the time as much as possible has always been irresistible to believers. And to those who are tempted, the clues in the Bible are an endless maze. Principally they are found in the prophetic books—Jeremiah, Isaiah, Ezekiel, Zechariah and others. Especially they are found in the two great apocalypses—the books of Daniel and Revelation. An apocalypse is a prophetic writing that predicts an end of things which is near, swift and cataclysmic. Both Daniel and Revelation make such predictions.

Scholars are undecided about the authorship of both books. They generally regard Daniel as a literary hero invented by the unknown author of his apocalypse. The book is usually dated around 165 B.C., though it tells of a time 400 years earlier. Critics therefore feel the fulfillment of many of its prophecies was due to their being written in after the facts.

Revelation was written toward the end of the first century
A.D. by an unknown author who simply called himself John.
He wrote from the Isle of Patmos, in the Sporades, where
he had been exiled—a common fate for stubborn Christians
who held out against the emperor worship reestablished under Domitian.

Both apocalypses were written in times of persecution to
rally the spirits of their author's contemporaries. Both seek to
show that deliverance is near. Daniel prophesies it through a
Messiah who will reestablish Israel's earthly kingdom. John
sees an end of suffering through the return of Christ to set
up a millennial paradise on earth.

In both works these joyful events are preceded by dreadful
upheavals that purge the earth of evil and prepare for the
triumph of righteousness and peace. The books are fraught
with an unending succession of heavenly portents, natural
catastrophes, wars and judgments. The actors in these dramas
are a strange and nightmarish assortment of beasts with
multiple heads, weird zoological hybrids, malevolent anti-
christs, false prophets and dragons.

Through the centuries Jews and Christians have tried to
fit these strange symbols to events and personalities of their
own times.

And though these speculations have all been refuted by
the failure of the world to come to an end, certain beliefs
about the last days have emerged and remained. They are still
taken today, by conservative Christians, as the core meaning
of the Bible's prophetic books.

Now, in our own space age approach, we must ask, once
again, whether anything can be extracted from the Bible's
prophetic and apocalyptic maze. Does it throw any genuine
light on the happenings of today, and can it give any identifiable signs by which we can verify that ours is the time of
the Celestials' return?

"SIGNS OF THE TIMES"

We have already seen that John's vision of a coming world
dictatorship seems to bear on the coming use of electronic
money. And both Ezekiel and Jesus appear to have predicted
the founding of the State of Israel.

Could it not be, then, that amid the tangle of what Bultmann called "apocalyptic myth" the Bible contains a solid core of Celestial revelation? Just as the gospels reveal Bernhard Anderson's "vivid glimpses" and "small tableaux" of Jesus' life, in spite of mythic elaboration, may it not also be that the prophetic writings afford genuine insight into the last days and the end, itself?

In Chapter IX, *The Bible and History*, we pointed out that the time of Daniel's and Revelation's composition was one in which old oral traditions and forgotten writings were being rediscovered. Their incorporation into the apocryphal and canonical books of that period makes it likely these works include much that is genuine Celestial revelation. The problem, however, is to separate the wheat from the chaff.

As we saw, some critics have tried to distinguish the genuine sayings and deeds of Jesus and his disciples from later additions to the gospel record. In the same way our space age interpretation may provide a key for separating what is Celestially inspired—in the prophetic and apocalyptic tradition which has come down to us—from what was contributed by the times and circumstances of its writers.

In looking for the prophetic core which genuinely applies to our own age we should be guided by the logic of the space age interpretation itself. If the conclusions it draws about the Bible's meanings are valid, then those conclusions will imply certain things about the time of the end. Using these we can construct a space-age scenario for the end of the world.

And using this scenario as a guide we can then search for prophetic scriptures which seem to support it. If we find them, their coincidence with our independent conclusions will be evidence that they are genuine prophetic insights. By this method, then, we may be able, as Jesus put it, to "discern the signs of the times" (Matthew 16:3).

A Space Age Apocalypse

Two assumptions stand out, in our space age interpretation of the Bible, which set the stage for an apocalyptic ending of the world. One is the idea that we are soon to be invaded by highly advanced extraterrestrials who will establish a world order of peace and righteousness. The other is that our pres-

ent world is a prison for rebellious Celestials who exist in
force and have duplicated and stored Celestial technology in
undercover bases.

Given these two ideas, a cataclysmic end to our present
world is inevitable. The logic of the situation requires that
the return of the Celestials will be marked by sudden and
worldwide catastrophe. Let us see why this is so.

We earlier quoted Jesus' remark that Satan is the "Prince
of this world." Since he, and the other fallen Celestials, have
been forced to make this planet their home it follows that
they will not give it up easily, particularly if its takeover by
the victorious Celestials means an end to their reign and the
beginning of some final judgment on them.

Since they have short-range spacecraft, and, in all probability, some military hardware, the logic of the situation dictates that they will make a final, all-out effort at retaining
possession of their domain. Even if Satan believes he is
doomed to failure, his pride, and the fact that he has nothing
to lose, would demand some kind of last-ditch stand.

What form will his campaign take? Our premises dictate
certain moves. The first of these would be recruiting whatever help is possible from human allies. Since the rebels are
outnumbered by the victorious Celestials, their only hope
would be in increasing their strength.

Their approach to the problem would probably involve an
undercover strategy. Humans would be used to front for the
fallen Celestials. A puppet leader would probably be chosen,
along with aides, who would be directed by Satan. With
Satan's superior knowledge and skill the puppet's rise to world
power would be assured. Taking advantage of global problems
(such as the energy crisis and inflation), the building of a
world dictatorship would be accomplished through economic,
rather than military or political, means. Nations would
voluntarily enter a common market under the control of
Satan's puppet leader, who would seem to have the solution
to their problems.

Once his power was established this leader would form an
international police force to "keep the peace." He would
probably also establish himself as leader of a state philo-

sophico-religious system to provide sanction for his power and to extend his control over his followers.

Taking advantage of the current revival of interest in religion and the occult, he would use biocosmic energy to perform miracles. He would probably also employ the traditional device of emperor worship to achieve a fanatical following and unquestioning support. Satan's interest in perverting everything basic to the Celestials' civilization makes this course a predictable one.

When the Celestials' return is imminent (and Satan would be as familiar with the "signs of the times" as anyone) the puppet dictator would be directed to launch a "preventive war" against the nations that have refused to join his common market. The politics of energy and the Middle East power alignment makes this area the likely theater of action, and Israel would be the most probable target for attack. With Jerusalem at its center, it would be the headquarters for the returning Celestials. Any successful resistance to their return would make seizure of this site a first military objective.

The actual return of the Celestials would almost certainly be marked by space warfare and nuclear holocaust. The fallen Celestials would put whatever spacecraft they have into the air to disrupt the takeover. The puppet leader and his army would move on the prospective landing site at Jerusalem. Since the returning Celestials have the advantage of superior numbers and technology the result would be inevitable. Satan's army would be destroyed in the field by nuclear weapons or artificially triggered natural disasters. His spacecraft would be destroyed in the air by missiles launched from the Holy City as it lands. Modules would be sent out from it to pursue survivors of the holocaust. These they would methodically destroy. Satan and his followers would probably be imprisoned in their underwater bases. There they would remain until the end of the probationary millennium when a general judgment would be set up to separate those qualified for Celestial citizenship from others who have failed to meet the requirements. At that time a final disposition would be made of the rebellious Celestials, as well.

Knowing what we do of the Celestials—victorious and

fallen—this scenario seems to describe the most probable course of events at the time of the end. Does Bible prophecy support it?

It most assuredly does. Let's examine the prophetic and apocalyptic scriptures which offer support.

"A Time of Trouble"

The stage for the final drama is set in the last chapter of the Book of Daniel. Speaking of the time of the end, its writer says: "... and there shall be a time of trouble, such as never was since there was a nation even to that same time: and at that time thy people shall be delivered, every one that shall be found written in the book. And many of them that sleep in the dust of the earth shall awake, some to everlasting life, and some to shame and everlasting contempt. And they that be wise shall shine as the brightness of the firmament; and they that turn many to righteousness, as the stars for ever and ever" (Daniel 12:1–3).

The events that characterize this "time of trouble" are described in Revelation. John the Revelator tells how a door is "opened in heaven" and he ascends apparently into one of the Celestials' spacecraft. A voice says to him: "Come up hither, and I will shew thee things which must be hereafter" (Revelation 4:1). His preview is apparently seen on a type of video forecaster—a time machine—such as we described earlier in the chapter. He sees a "sea of glass mingled with fire" (Revelation 15:2)—a remarkable first-century description of a television screen—and his vision unfolds. Satan, the dragon, raises up a world leader—the "beast" or "antichrist." "And I stood upon the sand of the sea, and saw a beast rise up out of the sea ..." (the reference here is apparently to a "sea of glass"—a television screen—not a watery ocean as traditional biblical scholarship has supposed). "... and the dragon gave him his power, and his seat, and great authority.... And they worshipped the dragon which gave power unto the beast: and they worshipped the beast, saying, Who is like unto the beast? who is able to make war with him? ... And it was given unto him to make war with the saints, and to overcome them: and power was given him over all kindreds, and tongues, and nations" (Revelation 13:1–2, 4, 7).

John goes on to tell how this beast is represented by a second beast later called the "false prophet." Apparently he is the high priest of the state religion the antichrist will found, for he "doeth great wonders, so that he maketh fire to come down from heaven on the earth in the sight of men, And deceiveth them that dwell on the earth . . ." (Revelation 13:13–14).

He it is who "gives life" to the "image" of the beast and causes it to "speak" (Revelation 13:15). Apparently he functions as minister of propaganda as well, and uses the television medium to maintain and enhance the beast's power. He is also the one who causes "both small and great, rich and poor, free and bond" to receive the "mark" in their hands or foreheads—the fearful "mark of the beast" whose number is "Six hundred threescore and six"—666! Without it people can neither buy nor sell, and by means of it the antichrist is able to maintain a fearful grip on the lives of men and women everywhere. Those who refuse his mark and worship are put to death.

John then goes on to tell how the dragon and false prophet cooperate to raise a huge army. Working through representatives—fallen Celestials or "demons"—they "go forth unto the kings of the earth and of the whole world, to gather them to the battle of the great day of God Almighty" (Revelation 16:14).

They gather near Jerusalem at Armageddon—the Plain of Migeddo. And there are "voices, and thunders, and lightnings," and "a great earthquake, such as was not since men were upon the earth," so that "every island fled away, and the mountains were not found." Finally "a great hail" falls on men "out of heaven" (Revelation 16:18, 20–21). The degree of the carnage is indicated when John tells us an "angel thrust in his sickle into the earth, and gathered the vine of the earth, and cast it into the great winepress of the wrath of God . . . and blood came out of the winepress, even unto the horse bridles, by the space of a thousand and six hundred furlongs" (Revelation 14:19–20).

With this conclusion to the abortive "Battle of Armageddon" the Celestials land. As they touch down, Satan's aerial army is blasted out of the sky like falling stars and the smoke of nuclear holocaust darkens the sun and dims the moon to a reddish hue. John's account rises to a climax of apocalyptic terror: "And I looked, and behold a pale horse: and his name that sat on him was Death, and Hell followed with him. . . . and, lo, there was a great earthquake; and the sun became black as sackcloth of hair, and the moon became as blood; And the stars of heaven fell unto the earth, even as a fig tree casteth her untimely figs, when she is shaken of a mighty wind" (Revelation 6:8, 12–13).

"Fall On Us"

The mopup operation is described in scarcely less dramatic terms. John sees a "white horse" in heaven and "he that sat upon him was called Faithful and True . . . His eyes were as a flame of fire, and on his head were many crowns . . ." (one of the computerized robots with which we are already familiar). The "armies which were in heaven" follow him on "white horses" (Revelation 19:11–12, 14). Like the robot of our opening scenario a "sharp sword" goes "out of his mouth" so that he can "smite the nations" (Revelation 19:15).

As John tells it, "kings of the earth, and the great men, and the rich men, and the chief captains, and the mighty men, and every bondman, and every free man" will hide themselves "in the dens and in the rocks of the mountains." And they will call out to the rocks, "Fall on us, and hide us from the face of him that sitteth on the throne, and from the wrath of the Lamb" (Revelation 6:15–16).

In the end the "beast" and false prophet, along with the survivors of their army, are consumed with "fire" (Revelation 19:20). Satan is "bound" for a "thousand years" (Revelation 20:2), after which he and the then resurrected unrighteous will be judged and consigned to the limbo of cosmic memories forever.

With the destruction of Satan's forces and his own imprisonment, peace descends. John's vision continues, as the "sea of glass" reveals "them that had gotten the victory over the beast, and over his image . . . and over the number of his name . . ." They stood "on the sea of glass" (an appropriate description of video images) "having the harps of God" and singing, "Great and marvellous are thy works, Lord God Almighty; just and true are thy ways, thou King of saints" (Revelation 15:2-3).

And so, with John's vision, we come full circle to our opening scenario.

THE COUNTDOWN BEGINS

If we have read Jesus' timetable correctly, and if John had a genuine preview of the future, these events will take place within the next two decades. Has the countdown for their unfolding already begun? Are diplomats already working out the coalitions that prepare the way for a coming world dictatorship? Is John's fearful antichrist already quietly preparing for the role he is soon to assume, unsuspected by those around him?

Do today's headlines tell us that the countdown has already begun? Certainly we live in an age that fits Daniel's description of the "time of the end"—a time when "many shall run to and fro, and knowledge shall be increased" (Daniel 12:4). Also it is "a time of trouble" (Daniel 12:1) which invites desperate remedies.

The energy crisis looms as a problem without historic parallel. Because of it world tension is beginning to focus in the Middle East. The rebirth of Israel, which Daniel and Jesus prophesied for the time of the end, has made it the key to this explosive situation. Many analysts of world affairs believe a full-scale outbreak of Arab-Israeli hostilities could trigger a worldwide conflict.

In the meantime, international problems of unemployment, inflation and unstable currency are forcing nations to form economic alliances that look toward world government.

Chief among these is the Common Market, sometimes called the European Economic Community. It began as an alliance of Germany, France, Italy, Belgium, the Netherlands and Luxembourg. It now includes almost a dozen nations. Its architects see it as the beginning of a "united states" of Europe. Other analysts of world affairs believe economic and political consolidation will extend even further. So Dr. Saul Mendlovitz, professor of international law at Rutgers University, recently stated: "It is no longer a question of whether or not there will be a world government by the year 2000. My own indication is that we are moving very rapidly toward this state."[4]

YOUR REDEMPTION DRAWETH NIGH

If these events in today's headlines are "signs of the times," then they do strongly suggest that we are living in the days predicted in Daniel and Revelation. And if we are, then the countdown has already begun. It is a countdown which will continue until it has taken us through economic world dictatorship to the brink of World War III. It will end, before this century ends, with the triumphant return of the Celestials!

THE LAUNCH WINDOW IS OPEN

Apart from biblical prophecy and the "signs of the times" there is one other piece of supportive evidence which adds its weight to our conclusion that the return of the Celestials is at hand. This evidence comes from astronomy.

We have already seen that biblical etymology points to a planet of Arcturus as the Celestials' headquarters. We have further seen how space science dictates that space missions are launched according to schedules requiring the closest approach of the launching site and the target.

Since planets move around their suns, and suns, or stars, approach and recede from one another, ideal times for launching missions occur infrequently. When a launch site and its target are in closest approach, a "launch window" is said to be open. It is then that a mission can be completed in a minimum time and with the least cost and effort.

Astronomers agree that the Celestials' sun, Arcturus, is now at its closest approach to the earth in the last 500,000 years. Its present rate of approach, at about 3 miles per second, has brought it to within 38.3 light-years of our own sun. The time for launching a major mission to Earth has never been better in recent geological times. Further, Arcturus will remain virtually at this distance during the next few thousand years, when the establishment of a new colony might require a succession of follow-up missions.

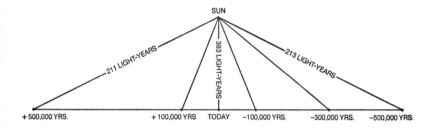

SUN

211 LIGHT-YEARS   383 LIGHT-YEARS   213 LIGHT-YEARS

+500,000 YRS.   +100,000 YRS   TODAY   −100,000 YRS.   −300,000 YRS.   −500,000 YRS.

The launch window is open. Arcturus is now at its closest point of approach to earth.

If Celestials from a planet of Arcturus did visit our earth thousands of years ago, if they continued periodic visits in recent historic times, if they now plan a large-scale migration, and if they will continue to transport large numbers of personnel and equipment over the next few thousand years— then the positioning of Arcturus has, is and will continue to be ideal for their plan of colonization!

The most extraordinary thing about these facts is that we only discovered them after we had deduced, from independent biblical evidence, that Arcturus is the sun of the Celestials' home planet. The remarkableness of this unsuspected coincidence can be better appreciated by examining the accompanying diagram. It shows that the timing and extent of Arcturus' launch window, in relation to our sun, almost ideally fit the requirements for the Celestials' colonization of Earth.

"Heaven at Last!"

And with the establishment of Earth as an actual Celestial colony, humanity's age-old dreams of heaven will come true!

Unlike traditional conceptions of heaven, however, the real heaven will be here and now. It will not exist as some never-never land in the sky—a realm of white-robed spirits playing on harps. Our heaven will be this colony of the Celestials' empire, the planet Earth—our own terra firma. For within hours, after their landing, the incredible technology of the Celestials will have transformed our planet with "new heavens and a new earth" (II Peter 3:13).

An earthly and visible Kingdom of God will replace the invisible church of Christ, whose members will now be its citizens. They will make up "a great multitude, which no man could number, of all nations, and kindreds, and people, and tongues" (Revelation 7:9). And in special roles of leadership, among those redeemed, will be 144,000 of the chosen people, who will be rewarded for the millennia of persecution and suffering they have undergone in carrying out their special mission in the redemption of mankind. These outstandingly faithful and righteous Jews will, at the time of the end, realize the fulfillment of their own hopes for a deliverer and messiah. For Jesus, as the melchisedec of this world, ruling from their holy city, will fulfill their own ancient prophecies for a restoration of the kingdom at the time of the end. So Zechariah prophesied: "And I will pour upon the house of David, and upon the inhabitants of Jerusalem, the spirit of grace and of supplications: and they shall look upon me whom they have pierced, and they shall mourn for him, as one mourneth for his only son . . ." (Zechariah 12:10).

And at last these leaders, and the numberless others of their people who have been faithful to the covenant, will realize Isaiah's great promise: "And the ransomed of the Lord shall return, and come to Zion with songs and everlasting joy upon their heads: they shall obtain joy and gladness, and sorrow and sighing shall flee away" (Isaiah 35:10).

Then, throughout the earth, that "great multitude which no man could number"—both resurrected and living; of "all nations, and kindreds, and people, and tongues"—will begin a utopian life of eternal salvation. As John the Revelator says, "They shall hunger no more, neither thirst any more; neither shall the sun light on them, nor any heat. For the Lamb which is in the midst of the throne shall feed them, and shall lead them unto living fountains of waters; and God shall wipe away all tears from their eyes" (Revelation 7:16–17).

What It Will Be Like

Because it is beyond earthly experience, the idea of heavenly life has always eluded those who try to describe it. Ministers and writers who talk about it usually resort to homely analogies or hackneyed phrases lifted from the Scriptures. The agenda seldom ventures beyond walking streets of gold, playing on harps or singing around the throne of God. Understandably, many people feel this doesn't add up to a very interesting life style.

Now that our own space age has arrived we should be able to do a better job of picturing life in an advanced, extraterrestial civilization. And, with a space age approach to interpretation, we believe the Bible can give sufficient clues to accomplish this.

WHERE IS THY STING?

In breaking away from past notions that are too earthbound or hackneyed we should concentrate on points of difference. And, without doubt, the major point of difference between human and Celestial life is immortality. For eternal life is what most distinguishes gods from humans and heaven from earth.

According to the Bible, the transition from mortality to immortality will be made, here on earth, at the moment of the Celestials' return. It will occur with the mass resurrection of the righteous of all ages. With their restoration to life, humanity's greatest enemy will be wiped out at a stroke.

As the Apostle Paul so eloquently puts it, death will be "swallowed up in victory" (I Corinthians 15:54).

We saw, in Chapter III, that individual resurrection might be accomplished by a mechanical replicator. Mass resurrection, however, would obviously require a different technology.

At first it may seem impossible that any technology could resurrect millions, or billions, of humans in an instant. And even if this were possible, where could the resurrected be accommodated? How could these multitudes of past ages find a place in a world that is already overcrowded with the living?

The answer may be found in new ideas which are coming out of quantum physics and exobiology. In the case of mass resurrection the solution may be in the fact that we live in a two-level universe. As we saw, earlier in this chapter, quantum physicists, such as Professor Bohm, believe the things and events we call actualities are preceded by potentialities which exist as "feelers," or possibilities. In the last chapter this same idea was expressed in a different way when we said the Holy Spirit, or universal mind, contains the ideas of all that becomes actual—including ourselves. As Sir James Jeans put it, it is the "mind" in which atoms, giving rise to our own minds, "exist as thoughts."

But if this is true, then it must also be a record of all that has been, for when actualities cease to be they must return to possibilities in this eternal Logos. And this again must apply to ourselves. Arthur Koestler argues this point forcibly when he says: "We arrive at an overall view of individual consciousness as a kind of fragment of cosmic consciousness—a fragment temporarily attaching itself to a body and eventually returning to and dissolving in the all-prevading mind-stuff."[6]

Ancient religious teachings have also held that such cosmic records exist. Esoteric traditions speak of them as "Akashic records." The Bible speaks of a "Book of Life."

If the Logos, or energy field of the universe, does retain a record of all that has been, including people, then these records would be blueprints from which the dead could be reconstructed. An energizing force applied to the information patterns of the dead would become a resurrection energy. By irradiating the earth with it, as they landed, returning Celestials could bring about mass resurrection, and death could truly be overcome at a stroke! Contemplating such an extraordinary occurrence, the Apostle Paul fittingly exclaimed, "O death, where is thy sting? O grave, where is thy victory?" (I Corinthians 15:55).

RESURRECTION AND QUANTUM PHYSICS

Modern quantum physics views things and events—including ourselves—in a way which supports this explanation of resurrection. For it, "things" are nothing but energy frames (or "information patterns") on which energy events—subatomic particles—are temporarily hung.

In this view a living person is not unlike a television image. A television receiver creates a moving image out of luminescent particles embedded in its screen. In the same way a living person is created by an energy pattern whose form is clothed with subatomic particles.

The blueprint for the television image is an information pattern imposed, by the broadcasting station, on the electromagnetic field that surrounds the earth. The blueprint for a person is an information pattern that is contained in the bio-cosmic energy field that is the universe.

And just as a television image can be recreated again and again, from videotape, so, in theory, could a living person be recreated, or resurrected, from cosmic records of his former existence.

Resurrection, in this sense, would simply be a repetition of the process which brought the person into being in the first place. An information pattern, or energy frame, would simply be clothed, once more, with the particles—or bits of energy—which characterized that person during his, or her, original lifetime.

"I AM NOT YET ASCENDED"

The resurrection of Jesus, as told in the gospels, suggests that a resurrection force was employed for him, for Matthew tells us that "many bodies of the saints which slept" near Jesus' tomb arose, and "came out of the graves after his resurrection . . ." (Matthew 27:52–53). This suggests that a resurrection force was used which was powerful enough to inadvertently resurrect others buried nearby.

Later, when he first appeared to Mary Magdalene on Easter morning, Jesus warned her, "Touch me not; for I am not yet ascended to my Father" (John 20:17). The context makes it clear that Jesus was not referring to his ascension into heaven here, for eight days later he allowed Thomas to touch him freely, although that ascension had not yet occurred. The Greek word *anabaino*, translated as "ascend," means "to grow up from a base." It precisely describes the "clothing" of an energy frame with particles which quantum physics tells us is necessary for the actualization of an object. Jesus was evidently telling Mary he was not yet fully actualized. His state was apparently an intermediate one—something like that of an apparition, which some parapsychologists believe may be a partial materialization of a cosmic record. Had Mary touched him she would probably have been frightened by his shadowy insubstantiality. Yet eight days later he had "ascended," for doubting Thomas probed his wounds freely.

Jesus' appearance, while not yet "ascended," is reminiscent of the "phantom leaf" phenomenon in Kirlian photography. Researchers have found that a leaf cut in half will, under proper conditions, show a Kirlian aura that is intact. Even though half the particles that "clothe" it have been removed, the energy frame, on which they were hung, still remains unaltered and shows on the photographic plate. Like Jesus, the cut portion of the leaf still appears, though it is no longer "ascended."

If our inferences from quantum physics are correct we, too, have "phantoms" which continue even after bodily life has ended. Their occasional partial "ascensions" may be the explanations for apparitions or hauntings—so some parapsychologists believe. Their accidental invasion into the minds and bodies of living persons may also account for seeming instances of reincarnation and for certain types of possession —as well as phenomena of exorcism. As fragments of Koestler's "Cosmic Mind" these "phantoms" are the basis for what theologians call the "soul." And they are the Celestials' blueprint for resurrection.

By tuning a resurrection energy to the "frequency" of the righteous they could accomplish a selective resurrection much as a television receiver can selectively tune in one channel signal from the many around it. And just as the receiver can create images from that signal alone, so the Celestials can apparently resurrect all the righteous of a planet—or the "saints" around Jesus' tomb—as Matthew recounts.

This resurrection force is, in all probability, a concentrated form of biocosmic energy. And just as psychic healers radiate it more strongly while healing, so those who are supercharged with it may be able to bring about resurrection by their mere presence—as Jesus did with Lazarus.

"Many Mansions"

The analogy of television may also explain how the Celestials handle the housing problem on planets where they have accomplished mass resurrection.

A television receiver does not have to be near the broadcasting station to create an image on its screen. The information which it uses for producing the image is broadcast everywhere. In the same way our cosmic records may be broadcast throughout the cosmos. If this is so, we could be resurrected wherever the resurrection force is focused.

The resurrected dead of crowded worlds like our own could simply be resurrected on other worlds that had been specially prepared for them. This may be the meaning of Jesus' statement, to his disciples, that he was preparing "a place" for them among his Father's "many mansions" (John 14:2).

In this way people of past generations, or ages, could be kept together until they had been reoriented to living in a futuristic society. Afterward, new citizens of the Celestials' empire could probably move freely, or even select worlds on which they wished to live.

LIFE EVERLASTING

The second and final phase, in the abolition of death, will be the setting up of a program for maintaining immortality. The Bible leaves no doubt that this is the paramount concern of the Celestials. For without it their other civilizational accomplishments would come to nothing. Without immortality, Celestial administrators could not manage a far-flung empire stretching out over millions of light-years of distance. And without eternal life they could not sustain the continuity of accomplishment that is necessary for a truly advanced civilization.

One of the most far-reaching consequences of our space age approach to Hebrew and Greek etymology has been the discovery that the Bible's images and symbols of immortality have linguistic associations coinciding with today's most advanced theories in rejuvenation and preventive gerontology.

As our research into the Bible's etymological maze has continued, the outlines of a methodology have emerged. We believe it is the Celestials' method for maintaining immortality.

HOW TO LIVE FOREVER

In its essence this method seems to be a perfected version of our own current first steps toward the nucleic-acid therapy of aging. In the first chapter of this book we saw how Hans

Kugler and others are extending the life spans of experimental animals with nucleic-acid therapy. Ingestion of nucleic acids can seemingly rejuvenate aging DNA and prevent imperfect replacement of dying cells which leads to aging and death. Other researchers, such as Dr. Benjamin Frank, have used more elaborate "directed" systems of nucleic acids and metabolites to reverse aging that has already occurred.[7]

In Chapter VIII, *The Experiment Fails*, we showed that the "tree of life," which conferred immortality in the Garden, was probably a chemical model that enabled the Celestials to duplicate individual DNA patterns. With aging DNA completely replaced at intervals, rather than simply repaired, the Celestials are apparently able to halt aging altogether. Regular DNA replacement is accomplished by the ritual of the sabbath.

ETERNAL LIFE AND THE SABBATH

One of the most extraordinary discoveries of our space-age approach to the Bible is the central role the sabbath plays in eternal life.

Traditionally, Jews and Christians have regarded the sabbath as a religious observance which provides some opportunity for rest. Our research shows the Celestials' sabbath additionally, and primarily, is a technique of preventive geriatrics and rejuvenation. The sabbath of Jewish and Christian observance is a mere shadow and type of the more complex ritual practiced by the Celestials.

Fundamentally their sabbath ritual involves three separate ceremonies. The first is a weekly twenty-four-hour period of rest which they have found to be necessary if cell damage is not to outstrip the process of cell repair. For the Celestials it consists of alternate periods of total inactivity and joyous group celebration, much as its human counterpart does in Judeo-Christian observance.

The second is a monthly sabbath, or sabbath "moon," which is more elaborate. Biblical references to it lead, etymologically, to root meanings relating it to the tree of life, in the midst of God's paradise. Chief among these are the ideas of being "coiled," "wrapped," a "matrix" and even a "helix." Such a cluster of meanings inevitably involves the image of

Watson's and Crick's model of the DNA helix—two intertwined strands "coiled" or "wrapped" around a "matrix." In addition to rest and celebration this sabbath seems to involve nucleic-acid therapy combined with elaborate cleansing and detoxification procedures. The Hebrew word used for "moon," *chodesh*, leads directly to the root meanings of "renewing," "repairing," and "rebuilding."

The importance of this monthly sabbath is stressed throughout the Bible. So we read in Isaiah, "And it shall come to pass, that from one new moon to another, and from one sabbath to another, shall all flesh come to worship before me..." (Isaiah 66:23). And John the Revelator tells us that the tree of life, in the Celestials' holy city, yields its fruit "every month." Its "leaves," he says, are for the "healing of the nations" (Revelation 22:2). And again Ezekiel speaks of a holy city with a tree "whose leaf shall not fade." It brings forth "new fruit according to his months" and its leaf is "for medicine" (47:12). These references to a "fruit" (which we have already seen may mean nucleic acids) that heals, restores and renews makes it clear that the new-moon sabbath is a rejuvenation ritual.

The third ritual is the annual convocation, an empire-wide holy day. It is pictured impressively in Revelation 5:8-14, as we have already seen. It seems to be a time of renewal of civic allegiance to the empire and celebration of the values that are basic to the Celestials' civilization.

In its entirety this texture of sabbath rituals defines a life style that programs aging therapy and provides biological, social and spiritual supports for maintaining immortality.

"A CROWN OF LIFE"

One other step is essential to ensuring immortality. This is the prevention of disease, for disease, even more than aging, can lead directly to death. The Bible makes numerous references to a device called the "crown of life." So James assures those who endure temptation that they will receive "the crown of life, which the Lord hath promised to them that love him" (James 1:12). John the Revelator also tells how the "first and the last" says, "be thou faithful unto death, and I will give thee a crown of life" (Revelation 2:8, 10).

Evidently this is more than a figurative reference to eternal life, itself. For its etymology leads, not to the idea of eternality, but to moderation, or balance.

Specialists in preventive medicine are coming increasingly to recognize that disease is not a natural state of affairs in the human body. It gains a foothold only when the body's normal functions and defenses are interrupted. The maintenance of these functions and defenses implies a vital balance—a balance biologists call "homeostasis." As long as perfect homeostasis is maintained, disease processes cannot establish themselves. So one leader in preventive medicine observes: "When all organs are working in harmony, the body machinery is in balance and we have perfect health."[8]

The "crown of life" appears, then, to be a type of biofeedback device which is worn on the head to regulate homeostasis. By monitoring the body at all times, and sending appropriate input to the brain, it constantly maintains a perfect state of homeostasis—a state in which disease can gain no foothold.

"I Don't Want to Live Forever"

To some the idea of everlasting life is a doubtful boon. They remember the nightmare state of advanced aging described by Shakespeare as "sans teeth, sans eyes, sans taste, sans everything" and say, "No thank you!" Some even pretend to prefer the hedonistic philosophy that glorifies mortality. "Live fast, die young, and make a beautiful corpse" is their motto.

Yet, in the deepest recesses of the human mind lurks a yearning for immortality which will not be denied. It expresses itself in our clinging to life; in our cult of youth and in our need to live on through children, achievements and fame.

Early in this century the novelist James Hilton captured people's imagination with his story of Shangri-La, the quiet Asiatic Eden just beyond the Lost Horizon. There priests lived to be hundreds of years old, and princesses remained beautiful young maidens into their nineties.

The Bible tells us a Shangri-La far exceeding the fantasies of James Hilton will come to Earth before the end of this century. It will offer youth and everlasting life to everyone who meets its citizenship requirements. Those who don't want to live forever will not be forced to do so. But to all who relish the prospect of eternal youth and life it extends the invitation with which John the Revelator closes the Bible: "... the Spirit and the bride say, Come. And let him that heareth say, Come. And let him that is athirst come. And whosoever will, let him take the water of life freely" (Revelation 22:17).

And to newly adopted citizens of the Celestials' earthly Shangri-La this invitation will offer limitless vistas of enjoyment, adventure and achievement. For them the passing centuries and millennia will not bring enfeeblement and boredom. They will realize the dreams most of us have had about what we would do if...

Our own dreams may suggest a sampling of the life styles that will be possible. Personally we have looked forward to this most dazzling feature of the Celestials' heritage. Since we first rediscovered the Bible as an outline of that inheritance, we've been making plans. We don't think they are overly ambitious.

We will start by spending a few centuries visiting all the beautiful places on Earth we've never had a chance to see. We will sightsee and shop and play in all the capitals and resorts we've read about and never visited. On the way we'll stop off at unexpected hideaways to explore, or love, or just flake out until we feel like moving on.

If we find some place especially interesting we'll stay awhile. We'll sample the cuisine, add to our wardrobes, participate in their customs and festivals and just generally soak up the atmosphere. Afterward we may visit a few thousand other worlds with exotic cultures, cuisines and facilities.

In between times there are lots of things we will do at home. We'll become proficient in a wide range of sports, learn to play a number of musical instruments, read all the books we've never had time for, take up careers we've always dreamed of and pursue hobbies for which we've never had time.

When we get hungry for social life we will look up our favorite people from the past or cultivate those we've never met who are contemporaries. We can join the Mazzaroth

Opera Guild, or attend the Centennial Andromeda Gala Ball, or have our whole family tree in for Christmas.

And if we tire of all these more ordinary kinds of activities we can change pace by climbing some splendorous peak on one of Jupiter's moons or sailing some quiet sea, on a forgotten planet, in an out-of-the-way corner of the universe.

In fact, as we've continued to dream of our Celestially programmed future, we've concluded we will hardly be able to make a dent in it during the next 10,000 years. But it won't really matter, since we have all the time in eternity. Ten thousand years, more or less, will not be important.

The first 10,000 will be just a sort of warming-up period. As the old fundamentalist hymn of our childhoods so aptly put it: "When we're inside those gates of pearl we'll know a lot of things. We'll have a harp that's made of gold—perhaps a thousand strings! We'll sing and shout and dance about. The Lamb will dry our tears. We'll have a grand homecoming week the first ten thousand years!"

We Go Celestial!

And with the Celestials' homecoming to Earth, the future of this planet will be merged with their own everlasting destiny. An eternal reign of peace, justice and righteousness will begin. Those who have proved themselves "heirs according to the promise" will receive full citizenship in the Celestials' intergalactic federation. As heirs of the gods they will live out their heritage of salvation through endless eons of eternity.

And as they begin that glorious homecoming week they may well lift their voices in another grand old hymn, remembered from pre-Celestial days, to the Redeemer who made it all possible:

And have the bright, immensities
Received our risen Lord,
Where light years frame the Pleiades, and point Orion's sword?
Do flaming suns his footsteps trace, through corridors sublime,
The Lord of interstellar space, and conqueror of time?

EPILOGUE

This is the story of our Celestial heritage as told in the Bible. Its reality is supported by a variety of evidences—evidences from such widely scattered fields as exobiology, etymology, genetics, quantum physics, parapsychology and futurology.

It may be objected that we have not proved our case—that these "evidences" establish only a tissue of possibilities or, at best, probabilities.

To such objections we can only point out that the spiritual "truths" men and women live by have never been a matter of proof. We cannot prove that all men were created equal or endowed, by their Creator, with "certain unalienable rights." We cannot prove that peace is better than war or freedom than slavery. These are matters of moral commitment and living faith.

So it is with our space age interpretation of ancient religious "truths." For some our twentieth-century view of the Bible's challenge and promises may open eyes of faith which other interpretations have left closed. If it does its effort will be vindicated. For living faith needs no proof—it brings with it the substance for which "proof" seeks.

I do not need to prove to myself that I exist if I already do exist. I do not need to prove that the Spirit exists if, with the Apostle Paul, I can say, it "liveth in me." And if it does dwell in me it is not necessary to prove a heritage of eternal life is possible. For, as Jesus pointed out, he that believeth already "hath everlasting life."

Living faith, not proof, then, is the goal of valid interpretation. And if our space age interpretation is to be vindicated it will not be by evidence but by the living faith of those it inspires. Like the writer of Hebrews they will understand the sublime paradox which affirms that ". . . faith is the substance of things hoped for, the evidence of things not seen."

CALCULATIONS FOR "A THOUSAND YEARS IS AS A DAY."

THE EQUATION IS $T_A = \dfrac{T_B}{\sqrt{1 - \dfrac{V^2}{C^2}}}$

T_A Time read on A's clock by A

T_B Time read on B's clock by A

V   Velocity of B's ship as measured by A (A assumes he is standing still).

C   Speed of light (taken as 186,282 miles/second)

At 99.999999999625 % of the speed of light, B's clock only moves 24 hours in 1,000 years of A's time.

That is at 186,281.999999302 miles per second.

Or .000000698 miles per second less than the speed of light.

$$= .0025 \text{ miles/hour}$$
$$= 13. \text{ feet/hour}$$

Velocity of B with Respect to A (Miles/Second by A's Clock)	This is Percent of the Speed of Light (186,282 Miles/Second)	Time Elapsed on B's Clock After 1 Hour Measured by A's Clock	Multiply B's Clock Time by ___ to get A's Clock Time	1 Day on B's Clock Is Equivalent to ___ Years on A's Clock
1000	.536%	59 min, 59.9 sec.	1.00001	1.00001 days .00273
50000	26.84	57' 48"	1.038	.00284
100000	53.68	50' 37"	1.185	1.185 days = .00325 yrs.
120000	64.42	45' 54"	1.307	.00358
140000	75.15	39' 35"	1.516	.00415
160000	85.89	30' 44"	1.952	.00535
170000	91.26	24' 32"	2.446	.00670
180000	96.63	15' 27"	3.883	.01063
185000	99.31	7' 2"	8.538	.02338
186200	99.956	1' 47"	33.71	.09228
186250	99.983	1' 7"	53.95	.1477
186260	99.988	55 sec.	65.07	.1781
186270	99.9936	41 sec.	88.10	.2412
186275	99.9962	31 sec.	115.35	.3158
186280	99.9989	16.7 sec.	215.8	.5908

186281	99.99946	11.8	305.2	.8356
186281.5	99.99973	8.34	431.6	1.182
186281.9	99.999946	3.73	965.1	2.642
186281.99	99.9999946	1.18	3052	8.356
186281.999	99.99999946	.373	9651	26.42
186281.9999	99.999999946	.118	30,519	83.56
186281.99999	5.36×10^{-10} less than 100%	.012	305,190	835.6 years
186281.999999302	3.75×10^{-10} under 100%	.010	365,294	1000.12 years/days
186281.9999999999	5.46×10^{-11} under 100%	.0037	965,096	2642
186281.99999999999	5.36×10^{-12} less than 100%	.0012	3,051,901	8356
186281.999999999999	5.37×10^{-13}	.00037	9,650,959	26422
186281.9999999999999	5.37×10^{-14}	.00012	30,519,010	83556
186281.99999999999999	5.37×10^{-15}	.000037	96,509,585	264,229
186281.999999999999999	5.37×10^{-16}	.000012	305,190,000	835,565 years/days

REFERENCES

CHAPTER I—GENESIS

1 Erich von Däniken, *Chariots of the Gods?* (New York: Bantam, 1970). 1970).
2 Stephen Dole, *Habitable Planets for Man* (New York: Elsevier Publishing Co., 1975).
3 Carl Sagan, *The Cosmic Connection* (Garden City, N.Y.: Doubleday, 1973).
4 Hans Kugler, *Slowing Down the Aging Process* (New York: Pyramid Communications, 1974).
5 *Los Angeles Herald Examiner*, September 17, 1976.

CHAPTER III—HOW TO TAKE OVER THE WORLD

1 Isaac Asimov, *Is Anyone There?* (New York: Ace Books, 1967).
2 Arthur C. Clarke, *Profiles of the Future* (New York: Harper and Row, 1973).
3 Sagan, *Cosmic Connection.*
4 Maya Pines, *The Brain Changers* (New York: Harcourt Brace Jovanovich, 1973).
5 "ERTS Puts the Whole Earth Under the Microscope," *Fortune*, February, 1975.
6 Clarke, *Profiles of the Future.*
7 Clarke, *Profiles of the Future.*
8 Robert W. Prehoda, *Designing the Future* (Philadelphia: Chilton, 1967).
9 Clarke, *Profiles of the Future.*
10 William Smith, *Smith's Bible Dictionary* (Old Tappan, N.J.: Revell, 1967).
11 Clarke, *Profiles of the Future.*

CHAPTER IV—WHO ARE THE CELESTIALS?

1 Clifford Wilson, *Gods in Chariots and Other Fantasies* (San Diego: Creation–Life Publishers, 1975).
2 Wilson, *Gods in Chariots.*
3 Gerrit, L. Verschuur, *The Invisible Universe* (New York: Springer-Verlag, 1974).
4 Sagan, *Cosmic Connection.*
5 Billy Graham, "I Believe There Is Intelligent Life in Outer Space—and That These Beings Probably Look Like Us," *National Inquirer*, November 30, 1976.

6 Sagan, *Cosmic Connection.*
7 Sagan, *Cosmic Connection.*
8 Gerald K. O'Neill, "The Colonization of Space," *Physics Today* Quoted in Adrian Berry, *The Next Ten Thousand Years* (New York: New American Library, 1975).
9 K. A. Ericke, "The Extraterrestrial Imperative," *Bulletin of Atomic Scientists.* Quoted in Berry, *Next Ten Thousand Years.*
10 Asimov, *Is Anyone There?*

CHAPTER V—IN THE BEGINNING

1 Carl Sagan, *Other Worlds* (New York: Bantam, 1975).
2 Sir James Jeans, *The Mysterious Universe* (Cambridge, England: The Macmillan Co., 1937).
3 J. B. Billings, *Your God Is Too Small* (New York: Macmillan).
4 Bertrand Russell, *Mysticism and Logic* (New York: Anchor, 1951).
5 V. A. Firsoff, *Life, Mind and Galaxies* (Edinburgh and London: 1967).
6 Jeans, *Mysterious Universe.*
7 Pierre Tielhard de Chardin, *Hymn of the Universe* (New York: Harper and Row, 1960).

CHAPTER VI—COLONY EARTH

1 H. St. J. B. Philby, *Arabia* (New York: Scribner, 1930).
2 J. B. Rhine and J. G. Pratt, *Parapsychology, Frontier Science of the Mind* (Springfield, Ill.: Charles C Thomas, 1957).

CHAPTER VII—THE EXPERIMENTAL CREATION

1 Bjorn Kurten, *Not from the Apes,* (New York: Pantheon, 1972).
2 Sagan, *Cosmic Connection.*
3 Desmond Morris, *The Naked Ape* (New York: McGraw Hill, 1967).
4 Charles Darwin, *Origin of Species* (Chicago, Toronto, London: The Encyclopedia Britannica Inc., 1952).
5 Kurten, *Not from the Apes.*
6 In Bertrand Russell, *Mysticism and Logic* (New York: Doubleday, 1957).
7 Russell, *Mysticism and Logic.*
8 Joseph Weiner and Bernard Campbell, *Climbing Man's Family Tree,* eds. T. McCown and H. Kennedy (Englewood Cliffs, N.J.: Prentice-Hall, 1972).
9 Theodosius Dobzhansky, *Mankind Evolving* (New York: Bantam, 1969).
10 Kurten, *Not from the Apes.*
11 Dobzhansky, *Mankind Evolving.*
12 C. L. Brace and Ashley Montagu, *Man's Evolution* (New York: Macmillan, 1965).
13 Carleton Coon, *New Findings on the Origin of Race.* Quoted in McCown and Kennedy, eds., *Climbing Man's Famly Tree.*

CHAPTER VIII—THE EXPERIMENT FAILS

1 John Milton, *Paradise Lost,* Book IX, lines 996–1004. (New York: British Book Center, 1974).

[2] Hans Kugler, *Slowing Down the Aging Process* (New York: Pyramid Communications, 1974).

[3] Hal Lindsay, *Satan Is Alive and Well on Earth* (Kentwood, Mich.: Zondervan, 1972).

CHAPTER IX—THE BIBLE AND HISTORY

[1] Soren Kierkegaard, *Purity of Heart* (New York: Harper Torch, 1956).

[2] *The Book of Jubilees or the Little Genesis*, tr. R. H. Charles (London: Adam and Charles Black, 1902).

[3] *The Secrets of Enoch*, in *Lost Books of the Bible and the Forgotten Books of Eden* (Cleveland: Collins and World, 1948).

[4] Edward Murray, *Enoch Restitutus* (London: J. G. and F. Rivington, 1836).

[5] Gerald S. Hawkins, *Stonehenge Decoded* (Garden City, N.Y.: Doubleday, 1965).

[6] I. Shklovskii and Carl Sagan, *Intelligent Life in the Universe* (San Francisco: Holden-Day, 1966).

CHAPTER X—THE PEOPLE AND THE LAW

[1] Joseph Campbell, *The Masks of God Vol. I: Primitive Mythology* (New York: Viking, 1959).

[2] Jacob Katzman, *The Jewish Influence on Civilization* (New York: Block, 1974).

[3] Max Dimont, *Jews, God and History* (New York: Simon and Schuster, 1962).

[4] Lewis M. Terman, *Genetic Studies of Genius* (Stanford: Stanford University Press, 1926).

[5] Bernard J. Bamberger, *The Story of Judaism* (New York: Schocken, 1957).

[6] Sigmund Freud, *Moses and Monotheism* (New York: Vintage, 1939).

[7] J. N. Leonard, J. L. Hofer and N. Pritikin, *Live Longer Now* (New York: Grosset & Dunlap, 1974).

[8] Herman Wouk, *This Is My God* (Garden City, N.Y.: Doubleday, 1961).

CHAPTER XI—CELESTIALS, PROPHETS AND UFOs

[1] Clifford Wilson, *Crash Go the Chariots* (New York: Lancer, 1972).

[2] Josef F. Blumrich, *The Spaceships of Ezekiel* (New York: Bantam, 1974).

[3] Blumrich, *Spaceships of Ezekiel.*

[4] Allen J. Hynek, *The UFO Experience: A Scientific Enquiry* (New York: Ballantine, 1972).

[5] *Journal of Astronautics and Aeronautics*, quoted in Allen J. Hynek, *The UFO Experience.*

[6] Maurice Chatelain, *Our Ancestors Came from Outer Space* (Garden City, N.Y.: Doubleday, 1978).

[7] Hynek, *UFO Experience.*

[8] Ivan Sanderson, *Invisible Residents* (New York: Avon, 1970).

[9] Charles Berlitz, *The Bermuda Triangle* (Garden City, N.Y.: Doubleday, 1974).

10 Berlitz, Bermuda Triangle.
11 Berlitz, Bermuda Triangle.
12 Isabelle Cooper-Oakley, The Count of Saint-Germain (Blauvelt, N.Y.: Steiner, 1970).

CHAPTER XII—THE REDEEMER

1 Milton Cross and David Ewen, Milton Cross' Encyclopedia of the Great Composers and their Music (Garden City, N.Y.: Doubleday, 1962).
2 Rudolf Bultmann, Kerygma and Myth (Guildford and London: Billing and Sons, 1964).
3 Rudolf Bultmann, Jesus and the Word (New York: Scribner, 1958).
4 Bernhard Anderson, Rediscovering the Bible (New York: Association Press, 1951).
5 Morton Smith, Jesus the Magician (New York: Harper and Row, 1977).
6 Albert Schweitzer, The Quest of the Historical Jesus (London: A. C. Black, 1910; first English edition).
7 Mohandas K. Gandhi, Satyagraha (Ahmedabad: Navajwan, 1951).
8 Martin Luther King, Jr., Why We Can't Wait (New York: Harper and Row, 1963).

CHAPTER XIII—PENTESOST AND BIOCOSMIC ENERGY

1 Jeans, Mysterious Universe.
2 Firsoff, Life Mind and Galaxies.
3 Sheila Ostrander and Lynn Schroeder, Psychic Discoveries Behind the Iron Curtain (Englewood Cliffs, N.J.: Prentice-Hall, 1970).
4 On the Biological Essence of the Kirlian Effect: quoted in Thelma Moss, The Probability of the Impossible (New York: J. P. Tarcher, 1975).
5 Shafica Karagulla, Energy Fields and Medical Diagnosis. Quoted in Nicholas M. Ragush, The Human Aura (New York: Berkeley, 1974).
6 Thelma Moss, The Probability of the Impossible.
7 Morton Smith, The Secret Gospel (New York: Harper and Row, 1973).
8 John L. Sherill, They Speak With Other Tongues (New York: McGraw-Hill Inc., 1964).
9 Arthur Ford, The Life Beyond Death (New York: Putnam, 1971).
10 Fritjof Capra, The Tao of Physics (New York: Bantam, 1977).
11 Sir Cyril Burt, quoted from The Country of the Blind, in Arthur Koestler, The Roots of Coincidence (New York: Random House, 1972).
12 William Johnson, Silent Music (New York: Harper and Row, 1974).

CHAPTER XIV—THEY'RE COMING BACK!

1 Arthur Koestler, The Roots of Coincidence (New York: Random House, 1972).
2 D. Bohm, Quantum Theory. Quoted in Koestler, Roots of Coincidence.
3 Adrian Dobbs, The Feasibility of a Physical Thoery of ESP. Quoted in Koestler, Roots of Coincidence.
4 Saul Mendlovitz in the Honolulu Advertiser, quoted in Hal Lindsay, There's

a *New World Coming* (Santa Ana, Calif.: Vision House Publishers, 1973).

5 D. Alter, C. Cleminshaw, J. Phillips, *Pictorial Astronomy* (New York: Thomas Y. Crowell Co., 1974).

6 Arthur Koestler, quoted in *Psychology Today*, April 1977.

7 B. S. Frank, *Nucleic Acid Therapy in Aging and Degenerative Disease:* quoted in Hans Kugler, *Slowing Down the Aging Process.*

8 Melvin Page, *Degeneration, Regeneration, Nutritional Development*, St. Petersburg, Fla., 1949.

INDEX

Bermuda Triangle, 223–26
Bermuda Triangle, The (Berlitz),
  224
Berosus, 183
Bible, the
  apocalyptic books of, 279–84
  apocryphal writings and, 172–
    75, 178
  doubtful deeds and curious
    characterizations in, 176–77
  genealogies, in, 162–64
  as growing and changing, 174–
    75
  higher criticism of, 167
  history and, 162–85. See also
    History and specific topics
  Holy Spirit in different transla-
    tions of, 256–57
  Jerusalem, 67
  New Oxford Annotated, 67
  personal description lacking in,
    171–72
  prehistory and, 177–80
  prophecies in the. See Proph-
    ecies, biblical
  purpose of, 165
  redemptive history and, 164–
    66, 192
  Revised Version of, 67
  right interpretation of, 168–69
  sabbath in, 296–97
  space age interpretation of,
    167–68, 281
  spacecraft in the, 211–16
  See also specific books; Gospels
Bioplasmic (biocosmic) energy,
  106, 107, 259, 283, 294
Birth, giving, 157, 158
Bjorksten, John, 6
Blake, William, 271
Blumrich, Josef F., 210, 211, 215
Bohm, D., 276, 291
Bones (fossil record), human evo-
  lution and, 131–35
"Book of Life" (cosmic records),
  292
Borman, Frank, 221

"Born again" transformation
  (spiritual rebirth), 249–50
  conversion and, 251
  space age view of, 251–52
Brace, C. L., 135–36, 193
Brain, 121–24
  human, 158, 159
  moral responsibility and, 146–
    47
Braincase, human, 132, 133
Bredesen, Reverend Harold, 263–
    64
Browning, Elizabeth Barrett, 85
Buddhism, 242
Bultmann, Rudolf, 234–37, 281
Burt, Sir Cyril, 268

Cain, 56, 113, 135–36, 162, 170,
    176, 177
  wife of, 74–76
California Institute of Technol-
    ogy, 36
Campbell, Joseph, 191
Canaan, 187
Canary Islands, 179
Capra, Fritjof, 267
Carmel, Mount, 134–38
Carnae, 181, 182
Catholicism, 174
Catholics, 251
Cave of Treasures, 135, 176
Celestials
  advanced civilization of, 57–59,
    283
  Bible as history of, 165, 166
  citizenship requirements of, 59,
    106, 107, 241, 252
  colonization of Earth by, 103–
    7, 221–22, 289
  communication system of, 97–
    99
  covert activities of, 216–17, 282
  creation of artificial planets by,
    68–70
  fallen. See Fallen celestials
  home base of, 63–67, 288, 289
  mankind made in image of, 52–
    57

Moral freedom, 149
Moral responsibility, 143–48, 154
Moriah, Mount (Mount Zion),
  88, 90
Morris, Desmond, 120
Mosaic law, 168, 196–204
  as "schoolmaster," 202–4
Moses, 54, 56, 73, 92, 171, 187–
  89, 191, 192, 222
  the law given to, 196–97. See
  also Mosaic law
Moss, Thelma, 261, 262, 266
Mu, 179–80
Music, 61, 170
  Handel's Messiah, 228
Myers, F. W. H., 264
Myth
  Biblical story of the Hebrew
  patriarchs and Moses and,
  189–91
  as redemptive history, 191–92
Mythology, 234
  the gospels and, 234–36

Napoleon Bonaparte, 228–29
National Aeronautic and Space
  Administration (NASA),
  208, 210
Natural selection
  overendowment of human be-
  ings and, 124, 125
  See also Evolution of man
Nazarites, 64–66, 121
Neanderthal people, 132–37, 139
Neuropsychiatric Institute, 261,
  266
New birth. See "Born again"
  transformation
"New Jerusalem," 88, 89, 112,
  213
New Testament. See Gospels
Nicodemus, 249
Nietzsche, F. W., 247
Noah, 138, 170, 177
Nobel prizes, 194
Nonviolence, 247–48
Not from the Apes (Kurten),
  110

Nucleic acids, 147, 155, 295–96.
  See also DNA
Numbers, 121, 197
Numbers (Book of the Bible),
  64, 92
Nutrition, 200–1

Oannes, 183
Old Testament. See Bible; Torah
O'Neill, Gerald K., 69
"Original sin," 140–41
  "forbidden fruit" and, 141,
  143–48
*Our Ancestors Came from Outer
  Space* (Chatelain), 220
Overendowment of human be-
  ings, 124–26
Ozias, 164

Paleoanthropology, 131
Paraclete, 257
Paranormal phenomena, Pente-
  cost and, 262–66
Paraphysical research, 260–62
Parapsychology, 98
Paul (apostle), 22, 31, 33, 37–40,
  48, 57, 70–71, 75, 81, 118,
  121, 141, 202, 229, 258,
  264–65, 291, 292
Penal codes, 248
Penfield, Wilder, 34, 261
Pentecost, 107, 250, 262–63
  paranormal phenomena at,
  262–66
Peter (apostle), 27, 30, 253, 262,
  265, 266
II Peter (Book of the Bible),
  289–90
Philby, H. St. J. B., 92
Philippians, 230
Phillips, J. B., 83–84
Philosophy (philosophical reflec-
  tion), 61, 118–20
  as unearthly capacity, 126–27
Physics
  Holy Spirit and, 266–68